YESTERDAY, TODAY AND TOMORROW

By

DAISAKU IKEDA

A Collection of Essays
translated by Robert Epp

Published by WORLD TRIBUNE PRESS

International Standard Book Number: 0-915678-05-5
Library of Congress Catalog Card Number: 75-458-43
The World Tribune Press, Santa Monica, CA. 90406
©1976 by The World Tribune. All rights reserved
First edition published 1973.
Printed in the United States of America

INTRODUCTION

Entering Soka University in Hachioji City, the visitor is struck by the words inscribed on a bronze statue which stands before the administration building:

"Never forget why you cultivate your minds."

Hoping to encourage the students to see beyond their immediate studies and aim at living a life full of meaning, President Daisaku Ikeda, founder of the university, has given this motto to the school. The same motto also serves as an underlying principle for this book.

These essays first appeared during 1971 and 1972 in the *Yomiuri Weekly* as a series entitled "Essays on Civilization." They were well received by the general public and among intellectual circles throughout Japan. However, their scope extends far beyond Japan, and so we have felt the need to translate them into English, allowing their message to reach many more people.

Civilization arises from the people and it should be returned to the people—this is the basic theme of these essays. The author himself is never apart from the general public and knows their daily problems and joys. He is continually trying to share with the public his own love of humanity and passion for life.

He is himself a great representative of the public. As a philosopher talking about the everyday problems of the common people, he sees himself as the subject. With this approach, he elaborates his ideas with the well-being of humanity at heart.

Too often today, we find that civilization, itself a product of past generations of people, has become something quite separate from the people. Our culture has become too complicated, too gigantic or too microscopic for the ordinary man to comprehend. There is nowhere for people to turn and find release from their problems; their routine of competitive struggle must then come only to a dead end. And ever-present are the major concerns of poverty, disease, pollution, racial strife and war.

President Ikeda's essays deal with these problems in a clear and engaging manner, treating each one in a highly individual way. He begins with topics of everyday interest, like the rising price of food, and gradually expands his discussion to issues of global significance. His range of thought is broad, touching on news media, archeology, literature, science, economics and ecology. In some essays, he expands on Buddhist theory, while in others he compares the civilizations of the East and the West.

Yet his is not merely an academic approach, for while showing a responsible grasp of the problem at hand, he is warmly encouraging the reader to find hope and give meaning to life on this "global desert." His wisdom is pointing mankind toward a life-philosophy which places the highest value on the dignity of life.

I am sure that readers will be deeply moved and challenged to reconsider their thoughts on modern civilization. They will come to realize that within man is an immeasurable potential for a higher way of life.

On behalf of President Ikeda, I would especially like to extend my deep appreciation to Dr. Robert Epp and his staff for their work in preparing this translation, thereby making these essays available to the English-speaking public.

GEORGE M. WILLIAMS
General Director
Nichiren Shoshu Academy

CONTENTS

FOREWORD

I do not think I'll ever forget the following passage which I came across in some Chinese classic. An aged advisor remonstrates with his young prince, anxious to go to war:

All who intend to wage war are under the impression that the course of history will be determined by a single engagement. When I was young I believed the same thing and risked my life in battle. But looking back to those days, I have even utterly forgotten the name of the battle.

The flow of history appears charged with permanence despite its radical change. For the single leaf floating on the waves, the surge of each and every moment is enough to affect the leaf's entire existence. Nevertheless, from the vantage point of the ocean currents, raging waves are little more than handfuls of noise. They eventually disappear into the endless flow beyond, leaving not the slightest trace.

A daily increasing mass of information is constantly spewn out at us by this contemporary monster, the mass media. In a twinkle it all fades into the past. The flow of events we read about in the morning paper or hear about on the evening newscast alternately moves us to joy or sadness. Yet a month later these stories are no longer even mentioned in the papers and we no longer remember what had moved us.

Conversely, looking from the macroscopic viewpoint of history, even slight and unnoticed trends may often effect tremendous changes. The industrial revolution, for example, was accompanied by such discordant incidents as the Luddite movement, though on the whole it was such a quiet, long-range accumulation of changes in industry that it is not worth calling a revolution in the usual sense of the term. Viewed from our day, however, it was certainly a major revolution, significant for how it brought about changes in the way men live.

Our day has been termed a time of trial for civilization, an important turning point in history. To be sure, it goes without saying that this is a time when the ideal form of civilization, the very way man lives, is being systematically reexamined. For that very reason, however, if we would gain a clear insight into the fundamental factors that affect history, we need to

utilize the vast amount of information and the countless incidents which impinge on us each day of our
lives. A true insight into these factors is, after all, the
basis of the correct perspective needed to avoid mistak-
ing the trend of the times.

Pesticides are a case in point. These have been laud-
ed as the "darlings" which would bring about a revolution in agriculture. Certainly they have changed farming from an industry that had no choice but to rely
on the luck of nature to one in which human management could largely affect the results of the harvest.
But these chemicals have already begun to threaten the
existence of man himself. Immediate gain may merely
lead to disaster.

It is quite possible that, taken up with the foam of
the wavecaps, a person could miss discovering that the
ocean current had unexpectedly shifted toward a new
direction. But we must take care to foster the sort of
perspective which discerns the larger trends.

Still and all, I am neither historian nor social critic.
I am only a plain citizen. Or, stretching it a bit, I am a
religious man. That means I possess neither the critical
eye of the professional historian nor a sensitive vision
of the future. I merely continue to imagine that I must
search out within the eternal flux of time and space
the path which will throw the brightest light on man,
and that I must make this search as an average citizen
who agonizes through and eagerly lives out his day-
to-day life.

Thus I was nonplussed when representatives of the *Yomiuri Weekly* editorial department asked whether I might not write something along the line of "impressions on the state of civilization." I thought at the time that the theme was too broad. Although I do not regard myself as an essayist, for some reason or other I frequently get requests for manuscripts. Each time I feel uncomfortably inadequate, and yet end up writing them. But the *Yomiuri* request, I felt, was somewhat beyond my powers and I thought I could be firm in resisting.

But I let them talk me into doing it, giving in to their urgent pleading and thinking shamelessly that it might not be a bad idea to present the proposals of a common citizen to the readership of the *Yomiuri Weekly*. Writing an essay a week has been quite a burden, but as I labored through the task I used news items from time to time as basic material and stuck my neck out by writing about a wide variety of topics. Of course I do not pretend to be a specialist in any of these areas, and no doubt informed people will find that my smattering of knowledge has spawned many frivolous conclusions. But I know no greater joy than if my inexpert statements lead some to take even a moment for reflection on the way man should live, on the path which civilization should take.

Finally, I should like to offer heartfelt thanks to those who worked so hard to see this book published.

August 3, 1972

DAISAKU IKEDA

YESTERDAY, TODAY

For the first time in some years I had a chance to visit Europe this spring. I spent about ten days in Paris and a week in London. My schedule was rushed because I had to stop off in the United States on my way home, but it was a fruitful trip.

Whether in Paris or London, I always have the feeling that European cities in general truly value things that are old. The past remains alive. Walking through the streets of Paris, one comes across cornerstones on which have been chiseled the year the building was made. Structures a hundred or even a hundred fifty years old are not in the least rare. And among the slightly more elegant buildings are those which boast a "pedigree" of two or three hundred years.

Yesterday, Today

What I admire about these structures is the way they always function as active areas in the Parisian's life. On the ground floor facing the street are tidy shops that quietly carry on their business; the second floor and above is devoted to apartments. Even on main thoroughfares throughout the central portion of the city, one rarely finds buildings reserved wholly for business. The places where people live and the places where they conduct their business coincide. It seems to me that this accounts for the dynamic characteristic of the streets of Paris.

In Japan, too, at such places as Nara and Kyoto there are structures which reach far back into history. Most are special buildings like temples, however, and they do not therefore function as arenas where people carry out their daily activities. Indeed, these buildings no longer even fill their original roles as temples but serve at the moment as nothing more than objects of tourism or as important cultural properties. This means, then, that they have already "expired" as buildings.

There are a number of old structures within the London city limits, but I was particularly deeply impressed by a building I saw on the way to visit Oxford and Cambridge. On our way to Oxford we stopped to rest in a place that appeared to be a farmhouse. They told me it had been constructed in the 14th century. Its pitch-black pillars and beams formed clean contours which merged solidly and communicated an indescribable sense of tranquility.

Yesterday, Today

The cities of Oxford and Cambridge boast colleges that were founded in the 12th and 13th centuries. Even now these tradition-packed seats of learning train young men to meet the 21st century. They showed me some student rooms in which even the furniture remained a part of the distant past. I understand a student feels proud to study at the same desk and in the same room as some alumnus who made a glorious name for himself in history.

Treasuring old things—no, more than that, actually putting them to use—cannot be dismissed as simple miserliness. The furniture or the old buildings, the town itself or even the natural surroundings, are material things which could be converted into economic value. But when such material things are intimately involved in the human activities of life itself, when history has become etched on them, they are no longer mere pieces of matter. They become objects which can no longer be regarded merely in terms of economic value.

What is it that sustains this attitude of the French and the English to continue to use things of the past with such respect? Is it not a single-minded concern to keep the past from melting away? It seems, too, that one might say this attitude is infused with a reverent anticipation toward the activities of men of the past, activities which have become part and parcel of these historical objects. This attitude obviously manifests itself in the form of powerful restraints on the way moderns in France and England conduct themselves.

YESTERDAY, TODAY

There is a sense in which history has acquired excessive weight in modern-day England. As a result perhaps it constricts behavior. If that is the case, then of course we must not say the more weight the better but rather urge that some balance be struck between the past and progress.

At least for contemporary Japanese, I doubt it would be possible to overstress the need for balance. In Japan, precious legacies with multiple cultural and historical values are ruined or destroyed one after the other without even the slightest hesitation. But we do not stop at our man-made cultural heritage. We heartlessly ravage the forests, lakes, and the seas—parts of our natural heritage which have been millennia in the making.

Apparently even we Japanese once had the custom of regarding old things with a sense of reverence and of trying to preserve them. Our forebears believed that the spirits of those associated with cultural treasures continued to reside in them. And it was said that the mountain god in the virgin forests and the water god in the lakes would curse any who despoiled their domain. From our contemporary vantage point, I wonder if this does not show the shrewd wisdom of our ancestors!

In the modern era we have come to regard vengeful ghosts and the curses of the gods as "superstitions" cooked up by our cowardly forefathers. By now we have arrived at a point where we ruthlessly lay waste to nature for the sake of immediate profit. We clear away virgin forests and plant profitable cryptomeria and Japanese cypress. Thanks to industrial progress, we turn lakes into contaminated ponds.

The result? Somehow or another the legendary curses which our ancestors predicted seem on the verge of being realized in a most vivid way—fearful proof of ancient fears. Having contaminated lakes and streams and the seas, we afflict those who live near these waters with new pollution-caused maladies. And cutting down the forests has brought on landslides and floods.

Moreover, as we destroy cultural assets inherited from ancient times we further expand the desert of alienation and the mutual mistrust (the generation gap, for example) which afflict our society. Would it be too much to say that, by evaluating everything in materialistic or economic terms and by distilling from them their spiritual and human essence, we curse the future generation with the price of our conceptions? Or that we will suffer grave consequences for our behavior?

Our forefathers passed down an attitude of awe toward spirits and gods. In contemporary terms we might describe this attitude as respect for the spiritual, for the human aspects which underlie material things. Or perhaps we can think of it as the will to be in harmony with the forces and rhythms of the natural world. What has happened is that we become aware of this truth only after we have been cursed severely by our behavior. But if we were willing to cherish old legends about "spirits" and "gods," and if we would humbly give thought to the meaning of these legends, contemporary man might be able to rejuvenate what they stand for.

After the middle of the 19th century, the Japanese adopted elements of European science and technology to build a truly modern technological society. But they took from the West only the by-products of its culture —the techniques and material aspects of European civilization—and apparently ignored the morality and the humane attitudes, the prime movers of that culture. Too anxious to pursue and overtake the West, Japanese engaged a superb engine but overlooked providing it with brakes.

This has intimate connection with each individual. For after all, if a new attitude is to come, it must arise from within. It might therefore be prudent to keep in mind that Japan still has a great deal to learn from Europe.

EAST AND WEST

One notices the nights getting progressively longer. Autumn is upon us. It is the season when Japanese lose themselves in reverie the moment they are free from the pressures of daily routine. In the fall, we almost instinctively look up at the moon and find it beautiful but sad.

Autumn might be called the season for reverie and sadness. At least this is true in Japan where mere mention of the word "autumn" fills most people with loneliness and sadness for what is about to pass. These feelings have produced an incredible amount of poetry which reflects man's sensitivity to the transient. Poets throughout Japanese history have time and again produced masterpieces while unburdening their hearts to

11

the harvest moon, exchanging pleasantries with fall leaves, or feeling deeply touched by the lovely yet lonely songs of autumn insects.

The typical Japanese reaction to autumn is captured in the following *waka* composed by Oe no Chisato around 900 A.D.:

Gazing at the harvest moon,
I am moved by the sadness in all things,
Knowing that autumn is not for me alone.

Similar sentiments have been expressed in China. The following poem, still a favorite in Japan, was written in the eighth century by Li Po, who often sang of autumn's brilliantly clear moonlit nights.

Bright moonlight before my cot:
I wonder, could it be frost?
I look up at the bright moon;
I look down and think of home.

Perhaps these tender sentiments toward nature originate in a spiritual tradition which encourages men to intuit a mind or a spirit—and to see life pulsating— even in the hills and streams, in the grasses and foliage, of nature. Because man exists in nature, the Oriental tradition assumes that he of necessity partakes of nature's cyclical rhythms and duplicates their constant change and decay. Indeed, Eastern man believes that one can fully grasp reality only if he participates in it. And man can participate in reality only if he is in harmony with nature. Thus, the lyrical expressions of the Oriental mind are always rooted in harmonious relationship with, rather than objective observation of, nature. That is the source of the Orient's refreshing landscape paintings and her profound poetry of quiet but elegant beauty.

In the West, by contrast, we find a considerably different relationship with nature, despite the fact that human feelings are everywhere the same. Needless to say, when spring comes, men in the West also feel the throbbing beauty of life. In winter they, too, shiver from unrelenting icy blasts. In East or West, man lives in nature and instinctively responds to natural phenomena.

But there are notable differences in the nature of his response. In the Occident one rarely hears of people becoming involved with natural objects or revelling in sentiments about the nobility and inaccessible "mind of nature." More often than not, Western man treats natural forms and seasonal changes as though they were nothing more than objects for use in a painting or a poem. Man is regarded as the center of the universe and he uses nature to express his feelings. A man in the West acts, one might say, as though nature were antagonistic to and stood entirely outside of him.

Professor Zuien Hara, an authority on Western art now retired from Kyoto University, has commented on the Occident's objective approach to nature. He once discussed the distinctions East and West make between "heart and object" while analyzing the painting techniques of that genius of the Renaissance, Leonardo da Vinci:

"When Leonardo was about to sketch people, he considered in great detail how he would depict them: the aged or children, those who were angry or those who despaired. He wanted to register reality; it was as though he were trying to charm his subjects into the painting. Of course Leonardo thought painters must adapt themselves to those they intended to paint, and he tried to represent objects in consonance with the seasons. He also paid close attention to light and color and shadow. Although his was a very scientific and analytical method, Leonardo's paintings do not tell us much about what a man feels deep in his heart, nor do they suggest what a man ought to feel."

Professor Hara concluded that, "Generally speaking, painters in the East and painters in the West have different emphases. It seems to me that the latter emphasizes precise calculations about reality while the former emphasizes going straight to the essence of reality."

I certainly agree. East and West are obviously more than geographical regions that can be spatially differentiated. They are distinct cultural spheres with substantially dissimilar orientations rooted in centuries of historical development. In a word, the issue seems to go much deeper than disparate esthetic sensibilities.

Recent developments in the world of medicine illustrate what I have in mind. Specialists have become

interested in certain fundamental ways in which Eastern and Western medical practices diverge. Note, for example, the indigenous Chinese practices of acupuncture and moxa anesthesia. The new interest in China has produced growing amazement over Chinese medical practices; we are now being urged, in fact, to reevaluate our thinking about these practices.

The truth is, the Chinese can produce a general anesthesia in which the patient is entirely conscious simply by introducing a number of needles into nerve points, something Western medical science has yet to accomplish. It is also possible to treat stomach cramps by inserting a needle at an appropriate point in the thigh (which seems totally unrelated to the affected area), thus immediately ending both the spasms and the intense pain which accompany them. It should be clear from either of these examples that Chinese medicine does not seem to fit into the customary orientations of Western medical science.

Objectives of medical practice also differ. The practitioner in China does not deal directly with his patient's sickness or injury, nor does he treat only the affected area; he tries rather to deal with the whole individual. Because the aim is to consider the entire body (not to mention the entire environment), we can say that Chinese medicine presents a revolutionary challenge to certain long-accepted and unquestioned assumptions of Western medical practice.

16

There can be little doubt that this creative Chinese approach to healing has sprouted from the soil of Oriental philosophy, and that the orientations of this philosophy differ from those of the West. This seems particularly true with regard to the Eastern view that "heart and object" are complementary rather than antagonistic. This viewpoint manifests itself in poetry. But once again it may be even more strikingly apparent in attitudes toward medicine.

Recently I talked with a young doctor about the traditional Chinese orientation to medicine I have been describing. He substantiated much of what I had already heard. Treatment, he said, is based on two fundamental ideas. First, practitioners consider the health of the patient in terms of his relation to the continuous movement of the seasons and to the phenomena of the entire universe. Second, at the same time practitioners never deal with the human body without carefully considering the fine balance between what goes on inside and what happens outside the body.

By contrast, Western medicine has historically conceived of the human body in an objective manner. Western doctors see the body as a combination of various systems and organs, and they view their patients as analytically as possible, the way Leonardo regarded the subjects of his paintings. In the East, on the other hand, the patient is considered in relation to the universe and natural phenomena. Furthermore, the body resonates with the rhythms of the seasons. It functions properly, therefore, only when all its systems and organs are in a delicate and complex balance—internally and also externally with nature.

When we consider these contrasts in the way Chinese and Western medicine approach the patient and his well being, we have little choice but to agree. The two approaches represent divergent cultural orientations. Implicit in them are comprehensive philosophies of life which understandably differ, particularly with regard to the way each sees the relation between subject and object.

In the West, the fact that "heart and object" are considered antagonistic opposites has resulted in the rise of objective rationality, the awakening of a tenacious individuality, and attempts to bring society and nature under man's control. In the East, the fact that subject and object have traditionally been considered complementary parts of a whole has resulted in a stress on man's natural relationship with his environment; this, in turn, has encouraged the Oriental to live quietly with the unlimited universe and to ponder the magnificence and eternal beauty of nature.

One dominant pattern of the past century, which historians describe as both the glory and the shame of our age, has been Western encroachment into the East. The fact that East and West have not met each other with a give-and-take attitude has increased the tensions of modern civilization, which is sorely troubled in this latter half of the twentieth century. At such times I hardly imagine I am alone in thinking that one solution to this cultural malady lies in our facing up to the problem of "heart and object."

September 21, 1971

WHAT IT MEANS TO BE HUMAN

André Malraux, the celebrated French intellectual, is back in the political arena. This time he has forsaken his study for the cause of Bangladesh.

He has not participated in political battles since 1969, when he left the government with his old friend Charles de Gaulle in the aftermath of turmoil precipitated by the May Revolution in 1968. And now Malraux is ready for action again. A man in his seventies would normally be expected, after having achieved such fame and distinction, to spend his days in quiet retirement. Not André Malraux. This great author is determined to fight for his convictions right down to the last second of his life. That, more than anything else, is what I admire in him.

Malraux the thinker has ever been Malraux the man of action. Witness his activities during the tragic wars and revolutions which characterize our century. His zeal for action has compelled involvement in that turbulence. Particularly well-known are his activities during the Spanish Civil War in the late 1930s, the first storm of the fascist hurricane that swept over Europe. Malraux, who supported the Republicans against Franco's reactionary forces, eventually became wing commander of an air group composed of international volunteers.

His exploits during World War II are equally renowned. Malraux was captured by the Germans as he engaged in guerrilla activity at the height of the Nazi occupation of France. He subsequently made a dramatic and much publicized escape to rejoin the Resistance.

Since 1945 he has been an indefatigable activist. He and Charles de Gaulle provided leadership for the creation of the Fifth Republic in 1958. The next year he used his talents as Minister of State for Cultural Affairs to carry out reforms.

Political activities notwithstanding, Malraux has somehow found time to write fiction. He published *La Condition Humaine* (Man's Fate) in 1933, a novel based on an eyewitness account of China's internal disorders in the late 1920s. In 1938 he published

What It Means To Be Human

L'Espoir (Man's Hope), a moving social novel based on personal experience in the Spanish Civil War. In these and other works, Malraux again and again returns to the image of a man whose energetic political activities push him to the verge of annihilation, where he stands with his back to the wall.

Actively involved, yet writing. Writing, yet preparing for his next involvement. Malraux is the sort of intellectual who literally glows with a fierce compulsion to put thought into action. Small wonder, then, that such a man would—even in his seventies—choose to emerge from his study to support the Bengali cause. He said he volunteered to serve with the Bengali Liberation Army because, "The only intellectual who can make a convincing case for Bangladesh independence is one prepared to fight for it."

At this very moment, East Pakistan is in the throes of utter misery. Government use of military power to suppress the Bengalis has already resulted in the massacre of a million people and driven more than nine million refugees into India. Malraux's willingness to fight for Bengali independence is tantamount to a protest against Pakistani brutality. His act implies, it seems to me, that he regards it utterly disgraceful for a man to stand on the sidelines watching such merciless and inhuman acts against mankind without protesting them.

"As a writer," Malraux says, "it has been the cause of mankind that has most inspired me over the past

23

decade." At every step along the way, the cause of man has elicited his sharpest insights. But whenever he talks of mankind and what it means to be human, be assured that Monsieur Malraux does not have in mind a person sitting quietly in his study or in front of a warm fireplace. He is thinking of a person reduced to the barest essentials, a person with nothing but his humanity to protect him from the torrents of social change which threaten to overcome him.

Malraux himself has embarked on an endless quest to discover what it means to be a vibrant and active human being in the context of seething change. His search may take him beyond the horizon, but he is no wild visionary. He knows better than to think he'll find a pot of golden hope and happiness at journey's end. He is realistic. He knows the likelihood that frustration and failure may await him. He acts nevertheless as though his proper function as an activist author is to transcend the limited schemes of human wisdom, to take the road of commitment, and to trust in mankind. That is his personal testimony to humanity.

I cannot help being impressed by such an attitude. We may have differences in creed, but there can be no doubt that he has set an example worthy of imitation: he expends every ounce of energy to teach us what it means to have ideals and what it means to put them into practice.

In looking at Malraux's career I have been moved to wonder, as I am sure others have wondered, whether

Bertrand Russell

Jean-Paul Sarte

André Malraux

he may not harbinger a new kind of intellectual. A man like Malraux makes me think of intellectuals and other cultured people who do little more than criticize, for its own sake, or manipulate concepts and empty theories.

Apparently there exists in the West a tradition which supports intellectuals who dare to be activists or who try to translate the ideas of a thinker like Malraux into action.

This tradition has produced the thirty-six year old poet revolutionary Byron, whose youthful ardor evaporated in a single flash as he fought far from home for Greek Independence. This tradition has produced Bertrand Russell, who though over eighty thought nothing of leading a demonstration against nuclear weapons down the streets of London, his snow-white hair tossed in the wind. The same tradition has also produced Jean Paul Sartre, who is the symbol of French youth in their struggle against the Establishment. And it is this tradition which presumably nurtures the steadily increasing number of Western intellectuals who participate directly in politics.

I certainly do not mean to suggest that every intellectual and every educated person imitate Malraux or Russell. I recognize the value of the lone researcher in his lab, absolutely absorbed in his project; I also think it important that society produce people who, in the quiet of their studies, reflect deeply on the meaning of life.

What It Means To Be Human

The question I mean to ask is, What is the purpose for acquiring knowledge and wisdom? It is the purpose of research and reflection that I wish to challenge. I feel certain that learning and knowledge were never meant to be divorced from reality; basically, they are to help reduce mankind's gasps of anguish and his tears of distress.

If you agree, you may also share my belief that the intellectual's central task is to be a true human being. He must take a stand as a man when a stand must be taken, and his decision to stand must transcend petty differences in viewpoint and belief.

Intellectuals have been led to commit themselves to causes by a tradition encouraging activism. But activism is also supported when statesmen show tolerance for opposing views. I have in mind the noted episode demonstrating the late General Charles de Gaulle's breadth of insight and clarity of vision. When police were about to seize Sartre for his anti-government activities, de Gaulle steadfastly prevented the arrest. His reason for intervening was magnificent: "I cannot arrest Voltaire!"

Consider this: Sartre was, so to speak, the regime's political enemy, having provided theoretical underpinning for students who led the May Revolution. Sartre had therefore helped create the movement that eventually toppled de Gaulle's government and forced the general to retire from politics. Despite the threat, President de Gaulle believed that France could ill afford to jail Sartre, even if his political activities were illegal. Crisis or not, France needed the integrity and honesty of its "20th-century Voltaire," hence reference to the 18th-century philosopher.

When I heard this story I couldn't help thinking, now isn't that just like the great Charles de Gaulle! It occurred to me then that perhaps a Malraux or a Sartre can appear only when there are statesmen able to transcend trifling differences in viewpoint and able to feel deep within their hearts the value of men with ideas.

We are approaching the 21st century. In the violent flux of the 1970's, both statesmen and intellectuals seem to have arrived at a time when they have come to think and act humbly, transcending petty antagonisms and rivalries, and to ask first of all *as men* what it means to be human. I wonder whether there is not the need for men of action as well as men of thought to join together and seek counsel from all the people as to how we might best navigate the Japanese ship of state, floating as it is on the edge of the Pacific, through the years ahead? But I do not know whether we have among our statesmen and intellectuals the kind of leadership we need: men with courage and resolution, men who have the long-term perspective to perceive the tenor of the times.

October 5, 1971

A GLOBAL DESERT

Mackerel pike have traditionally been the favorite autumn fish in Japan. As its name—"autumn swordfish"—suggests, this long, silver pike resembles a sword. Despite its appearance, however, we somehow find a droll attraction in the fish. It could be that its waggish look strikes a responsive chord in the common man. In any event, it is safe to say that the mackerel pike has long been our favorite fish during the autumn months.

The moment they hear the sound of oil sizzling on the grate, the moment they see black smoke billowing from the kitchen in the fall, many Japanese experience an immediate urge to eat pike. These sounds and sights give the full savor of an autumn evening. Aside from filling our fall season with rich aromas, the pike has always provided the limited diet of the common man with a high number of calories in the cool fall months.

Recently, however, the price of the mackerel pike has risen considerably. The poor can therefore no longer afford this fish, as recent cartoons have indicated.

One cartoon brilliantly satirizes the situation. Over several frames the cartoonist shows how the wife of a white-collar worker impresses on her husband how expensive the pike has become. He cannot sit down to supper unless he is dressed properly, as one would be attired in a high class restaurant when eating a very expensive meal. Though he had already peeled off his uncomfortable suit and tie, the man dutifully dresses up and sits down to supper, able to face the pike with the solemnity the occasion demands.

Satire or not, it is true that the savor of the pike has recently become a delicacy which the common man can only rarely afford.

One reason for the inflated prices is predictable: lack of effective government. On the whole, the catch is said to be shrinking, and yet I hear that pike still sells for reasonable prices in fishing villages. The problem is what happens after the fish pass through the labyrinth of the distribution system. By the time they surface the next morning at urban markets, their prices more often than not have taken a terrific leap. That's why we need at the earliest date a government geared to running the economy for the people instead of for the businessman.

A GLOBAL DESERT

Indiscriminate fishing is another reason why pike is so expensive. This is a terribly complex matter which cannot be understood apart from consideration of various related problems that crop up throughout our modern civilization.

One persistent issue underlying all these problems is the nature of man himself. He is a creature who feels compelled to master and control anything that appeals to his palate, anything that will suit his fancy. He ignores the various ramifications of his obsession to control and seeks merely to pamper his egoistic cravings. He accordingly pays no attention to the balance of nature and ends up polluting and destroying his environment. Nature in turn visits on him her fearful retribution.

A concrete example appeared in the newspaper only the other day. An article reported the fate of a flock of snowy herons. The herons had died one after the other in a part of Tokyo Bay once noted as a sanctuary for wild birds. They were apparently killed by large amounts of a poison contained in chemicals used by farmers in the area.

Birds, as is well known, respond more sensitively than any other living thing to the slightest change in their environment. For that very reason, it was shocking to discover that the environment we shared with these birds became unfit for them. This augurs poorly for our own future.

A Global Desert

If the deterioration of our environment continues at this rate, the human species may be left to itself on the edge of the universe in its foolish revolt against nature. On second thought, however, if man is allowed to continue being made a fool of by his imprudent obsessions, he will end up destroying the environment that supports him.

Several years ago I recall experiencing how that is possible. I was flying over the Great Plains of the United States of America, amazed at the endless prairie. It was truly vast. But it was also absolutely desolate, though it in no way resembled the sandy and rocky wastes of the Gobi and Sahara deserts.

Most impressive was its vastness—that remains vividly stamped on my memory. No matter how far we traveled, I could see the copper-colored wilderness stretching beyond the distant horizon.

Amazed by an expansiveness unknown in Japan, I had the feeling that I was viewing the geography of an unspoiled virgin area. It was a dazzling and spectacular sight. I was astonished to learn that I was wrong. The seemingly endless red soil was once a fertile plain covered densely with grass and shrubs. I could not help shuddering when I was told how man had turned such a lush plain into the nude wilderness I had seen stretching below my window on the plane.

Long, long ago the Great Plains were a green sanctuary for the American bison, squirrels, wolves, and prairie dogs. Bison and squirrels fed on the vegetation

and were hunted by the wolves, who fed on their flesh. The prairie dogs, experts at burrowing, unintentionally cultivated the grassland; the Plains Indians hunted buffalo and led relatively peaceful lives.

But then in modern times the white man appeared. Bringing with him the tools of civilization and his gun, he changed the Great Plains completely. Settlers slaughtered the bison and drove the prairie dog out to make room for herds of cattle and sheep. Others tried farming, but were not successful until the invention of the steel plow allowed them to cut through the thick mat of prairie grass.

Insects and domesticated animals had no natural enemies, so they were free to multiply. They certainly must have rejoiced over their good fortune. At the same time, turning parts of the plain into planted fields deprived the land of its natural cover; the limited rain could thus run off quickly. Eventually man turned large sections of the Great Plains into dust bowls, creating the vast wilderness I had viewed from my high-flying jet.

The great prairie, which once sheltered an abundance of throbbing wild life and verdure, ultimately but reluctantly succumbed to man's foolishness. I cannot help thinking in retrospect that the steps which men took to create an endless wasteland on America's Great Plains were steps into the darkness, steps on the path to a slowly-dying natural environment.

Who would choose that path once aware of where

it leads? If man knows where it leads, will he never consider the prudence of maintaining the balance of nature? Or must he be like an insect which eats even the roots of the plant that provides its food, blindly indulging his appetites as he digs up the earth's resources? Will his insatiable desires eventually turn our entire globe into a boundless expanse of desert?

If from the outset man had been deprived of his energetic ambitions, he likely would have turned into a creature which was merely at the mercy of nature. Looking at the history of man, moreover, we see that he has probably not been the sort of creature who has laid nature and his environment waste by rashly following where his instincts led him. There is not the slightest room to doubt that he has caused this waste because he was at his wits' end in order to escape hunger and thirst. It is also an indisputable fact that the progress and development we enjoy today are the results of man's ambition.

If man's ambitions are not responsible for the destruction of man's natural environment, what is? Lack of perspective is. Ambitions have gotten out of hand. People are so anxious to achieve their aims and fulfill their desires that they forget to see things in perspective. Ambitious desires have created prosperity. But it is a lopsided and imperfect—a "crippled"—prosperity that has lost its equilibrium.

If man wishes to regain a proper balance with nature he must begin by rooting out his arrogance. He can no longer imagine that simply because he is a human being he stands at the apex of the pyramid of all living things. Man must see that flora and fauna throughout the globe are interrelated, and that his destiny is related to theirs. All are parts of the same delicate, but grand and magnificent chain of interdependence in which man is no more than a single link.

For that reason it is certainly no exaggeration to claim that the species which has depleted the mackerel pike and destroyed the prairie has now arrived at a point in time where he must take stock once again of the fundamental reasons for his existence and learn to get along with nature.

October 11, 1971

CURRENCY PROBLEMS

Several months have passed since President Nixon's monetary policies caused the furor in Japan called "Dollar Shock."

The tales which we understand were told in economic circles during those days chill one's spine. Most of the talk was gloomy. It dealt with bankruptcies, rising prices, recession. The crisis was particularly severe in midget enterprises which constitute such a large part of the economic picture in Japan; small businessmen fired a large number of their employees. Many observers offered the icy prediction that this trend would continue for some time.

Dollar Shock struck like a thunderstorm. Immediately in its wake a considerably exaggerated rumor flitted around the country. People were saying that Japan had been outfoxed. The foreign exchange she had accumulated with such great care seemed at the moment little more than a pile of leaves. The situation was in reality much less drastic than rumors had it. Nevertheless, waves of bankruptcy lapped even against medium-sized enterprises, usually considered comparatively stable. That suggests how powerful the shock really was.

As an involved citizen, I cannot help being concerned. How might we hold to a minimum the damage caused by these waves?

One theory tries to explain Japan's severe reaction in terms of the way Dollar Shock affected public opinion. The currency crisis directly caused the economic slump, this view urges, and also adversely affected public confidence. Indirectly this intensified the slump. The news, in excessively stressing the fact that currency revaluation would produce a recession, outstripped the flow of events. Shaken by rumors, the financial experts lost their usual sense of perspective and inadvertently contributed to the slump. How typical of a country which suffers from "news pollution"!

If the theorists are correct, however, what a sorry situation faces us now. Is human wisdom so frail that it cannot stand firm in the face of a severe test, or that it cannot remain dispassionate enough to probe the essence of the crisis? And is our government so irresponsible as to allow its high officials to make unwarranted connections between high prices—or other results of accumulated maladministrative practices—and Dollar Shock? I would like to see these officials refrain at least from shifting blame for their practices to Nixon's monetary policies.

As far as economics is concerned, I admit that I am no specialist. Nor do I claim to have either minute knowledge about currency problems or the qualifications to comment on them. I merely wish to report the way I feel about the situation.

The Dollar Shock crisis has very graphically illustrated to me how easily our economy is influenced by that sacred cow, national interests. It is as though engaging in worldwide economic activity has become tantamount in our day to engaging in an endless series of bitter battles with other countries. When America can force a substantial change in the value of the yen, it is clear that America's national interests take precedence over Japan's.

Nevertheless, the problem as I see it is not whose national interests have priority. The problem is that the international economic scene during the 20th century continues to be swayed by concern for *national* interests.

The truth is, however, that we no longer live in a day when a state can be economically self-sufficient. Irrespective of the country involved, no economy can grow independently—it can grow only as one element in international society. It is thus inevitable that if the commodity in question (in this case currency) does not flow freely, the economy will collapse.

The International Monetary Fund has been established to deal with economic activity and to handle currency problems arising in the international dimension. There are also movements, such as the European Common Market, which seek to apply the concept of co-prosperity to vast regions and thereby transcend national interests.

As far as plans and organizations are concerned, doors have already been opened internationally. But economic activity itself is another matter. Here we find that controls uniformly remain in the hands of the individual states. That is of course how it has always been. This is particularly true of economic activities, which are relatively so important to a modern society. Such activities must always be controlled by the nations involved.

At the dawn of the modern age, economic activity was literally the act of accumulating national wealth. Those countries which are now well developed launched into the modern world by breaking out of the gloomy medieval period. They scrambled to build industries and accumulate wealth; with their new power they attempted to control the high seas.

Ever since those days, there has apparently been little change in the basic principle: a country engages in economic activity in order to increase its national wealth. The principle has become entrenched over the

centuries. In the interim, capitalism in its classical form was laid to rest and socialism saw the light of day; fixed notions of how the economy should function have thus been subjected to scrutiny a number of times. One conclusion was that the equal distribution of wealth advocated by socialism would probably do away with the nationalistic principle once and for all.

The fact is, however, that economic activity continues to be pursued for the same old purposes: the euphemistic idea of "prosperity for the state." It is immaterial whether the state is socialistic or capitalistic. Rather does it seem that the socialistic state frequently bases its economic activity on the premise of the "people's will," whereas the capitalistic state continues to give free scope to individual activity.

Of course wherever national interests have been an issue in modern times, they have in principle related directly to the benefit of the people. There is ample historical justification for this. Even today there is some truth to the generalization. But it seems to me that the time has come to take a detached view of the results which this principle has produced.

We must realize that we now face a new situation. On the one hand, one-third of the peoples of the world suffer from chronic starvation. On the other, many people in an advanced country like America suffer from heart trouble caused by cholesterol build-up resulting from excessive consumption of animal fat. This startling contrast presents us with a gigantic contradiction. Some people think this contradiction is reason enough to demand that the richer nations extend aid to the developing nations.

Even if aid to underdeveloped countries seems the best way to solve this particular problem, what about the other crises that confront humanity in our time? What about overpopulation and the depletion of natural resources, for example?

The tasks facing modern civilization no longer affect merely a single nation. They affect all mankind and thus raise the most fundamental question of all: survival of the human race. Unless we make a keen analysis of every condition which has contributed to the current crisis, how can we as intelligent people continue to give credence to the idea that economic activity consists in the pursuit of narrow national interests, i.e., in the prosperity of each isolated nation?

As we move into the 21st century, it seems to me that our basic perspective should change. We must see economic activities in a new light and speak not in terms of national but of human interests. We should cease talking of the prosperity of a single nation and talk instead of the prosperity of the entire globe.

In reality, rather than a problem for economics this may be a task for government, which plays the necessary role of ordering economic activity for the benefit of the people. The economy is a task for government, whose role is to order it for the benefit of the entire polity. Governmental action is the issue here because the economy of a given nation has by now developed to a point where leaders must consider the international scene even when they talk of national prosperity. Institutions which further such considerations have already been established.

If this view is correct, it seems safe to say that any conscious attempt to restrict these new economic institutions to the framework of national interests betrays the extent to which government leaders continue to be unaware of the changing times.

Compared to the infinite universe, our earth is no more than a speck of phosphorescence, a mere poppy seed on which more than three-and-one-half-billion people exist. This is a cold fact. If we think about it for a while knowing what we know now, how can we refuse to move beyond the artificial and short-lived barriers of nations and institutions? How can we refuse to move ahead, guided by the principle that human happiness and the future prosperity of the entire world come first?

In any case, I cannot help thinking that problems brought to the surface by Dollar Shock will never be solved merely by debating the technical aspects of re-valuation of the yen.

October 15, 1971

THOUGHTS ON LIFE AND DEATH

The film *To Die for Love* (Mourir d'aimer) is extremely popular. Or at least that's what I hear from my younger friends, for I rarely get to the movies these days.

Set against the 1968 May Revolution in France, this movie is supposedly based on a love affair between a thirty-two-year-old teacher and one of her seventeen-year-old male students. The affair developed until charges were eventually filed against the teacher in court. Disgraced, she committed suicide.

We associate France with Paris and Paris with love and gaiety. The truth is, Paris has a dark side, too, namely the old and extremely rigid social order depicted in *To Die for Love*. Apparently the movie was filmed with the intention of creating an intense disdain for that order.

One plausible reason for the film's popularity among youth in Japan is the tremendous impression made by the heroine's readiness to die for love. At first glance, contemporary young adults seem indifferent to such things, readily scoffing at sentimentality. But they cannot lightly dismiss as "sentimental nonsense" a woman who is willing to sacrifice her life for love. Deep down, the heartstrings of Japanese youth were plucked, even by the somewhat quaint notion of sacrificial love.

I wonder whether the younger generation's outright adoration of this film may not betray both a deep yearning for so pure an experience and a poignant search for genuine love. Such a search concerns all who are human.

But what does "love" mean? Miss Ayako Sono, author of a currently best-selling novel, defines it as readiness "to die for one you love." Needless to say, people since ancient times have sought fulfillment through love and have described their search in prose, poetry and plays, thus creating a considerable number of literary works that deal with love or disappointment in love.

An excellent example of this genre in Japanese literature is Chikamatsu's *The Love Suicides at Amijima* (1721). This play depicts two hapless lovers caught in the web of social convention and unable to marry because they were not social equals. Unfortunately, they lived in an era when normal human feelings were sub-

ordinated to social obligations, to duty and the pres-
ervation of class lines. In that milieu they could live
together as man and wife only in the world beyond
death.

Why does Chikamatsu's drama continue to move
the modern viewer? I think one reason is that the
more the lovers were oppressed by social conventions,
the more they tried to fulfill their lives and the more
their love transcended the fear of death. Their resultant
"short happy life" was like a bolt of lightning. Another
reason we are moved could be that something in the
play appeals to people who live in a parched and
mechanized society geared to sexual pleasure; something awakens them to an awareness of what life really
means, making them bold enough to spit death in the
face.

By no means do I wish to imply that I especially
applaud those who go about gambling with death.
But I would suggest that such people can teach us a
lesson. It is certainly true that being ready to give one's
life is to be catapulted into a trenchant awareness of
what fulfillment means.

I was very deeply moved when I heard a famous
Japanese author speak about his personal awareness
of the meaning of life. Growing into manhood during
the Pacific War, he had been conditioned to look forward to the battlefield. He was never in terror of dying.
In fact, he couldn't avoid thinking about it whenever
the possibility flit like a shadow across his mind. Nor

could he help being intensely aware of the moments of life that remained. How irreplaceable they were! Primarily as a result of this experience, he decided after the war to become a writer, hoping to plumb the depths and the awe of life through literature.

Before 1945 many youths burned with the awareness of what it means to be alive. Unfortunately, they became aware of that positive value only by having experienced the consequences of war, its wretched tragedies, its unbelievable waste of human life.

After 1945, however, virtually everyone who had experienced the war understandably rejected its senseless expenditure of life. A loathing of meaningless sacrifice caused people to conclude that risking their lives for *anything* was a big mistake. Today even those with no memory of the war feel a similar loathing of sacrifice, even as they grope frantically and uneasily to find the meaning of life in the midst of an empty existence.

The uneasy feelings that plague the young manifest themselves in various ways, driving some to become passive hippies whose life style constitutes a rejection of the entire Establishment and its values. The same uneasiness drives others to become active radicals whose activities aim at destroying the Establishment.

The way an awareness of death generates a positive awareness of life was recently brought home to me in a newspaper article I read about prison inmates. The article described how men on death row usually demonstrate a finely-honed sensitivity to life; the condemned,

48

in fact, are abnormally responsive to extremes of feeling—to joy and anger, to sorrow and elation. By contrast, the "lifer" is barely sensitive to anything and displays few extremes in feeling. Prisoners under life sentence seem oblivious to their emotions; they become so servile that they lose their individuality.

The writer of the article concluded by comparing the psychological malaise of the lifer with the malaise of those "sentenced for life" to our present-day "managed" society. The "free citizen" is, like a prisoner, seldom lucky enough to feel that his existence is fulfilled and meaningful. His environment is polluted with noise and terribly congested. Most of what he does is prescribed. He has few options and feels harassed by the trivial nature of his daily routine.

Now and again some individual decides that he can no longer allow his life to be prescribed. On November 25, 1970, we were shocked to learn about the grizzly suicide of Yukio Mishima, the internationally acclaimed author and playwright. Here was a man who had refused to be managed, who had chosen to die for his principles. When the mass media showed Mishima as he pled—several minutes before death—with members of the Japanese Self-Defense Forces, charging them to act like true soldiers instead of salaried employees, I suppose many of us realized that, though his demands may have sounded irrational, Mishima's pleas constituted a challenge to an age incapable of honestly facing up to either life or death.

THOUGHTS ON LIFE AND DEATH

Of course no one can deny that to stand before the jaws of death is to be intensely aware of life. In facing death it is as natural to be abnormally aware that one's moments are numbered as it is normal to be deeply affected by that awareness. An excellent example is the experience of the famous novelist Ryunosuke Akutagawa, who wrote the story on which the movie *Rashomon* was based. Before he committed suicide in 1927 at the age of thirty-five, Akutagawa commented how remarkably beautiful nature seemed to him. But he was hypersensitive to beauty only because he viewed it through eyes about to close forever.

To tell the truth, I personally feel certain reservations about making people aware of life by reminding them of death. I wonder if one can become intensely aware of beauty and of life only when death is imminent? Such an outlook is too limiting, it seems to me, because it views life and death in simplistic polarized terms.

Not long ago I was struck by an observation which drove home to me the fact that there are alternate ways to view life and death. In the course of conversations with Count R. E. Coudenhove-Kalergi, a proponent of European unity, we touched on this problem. The Count pointed out that people in the East tend to think of life and death as a single page in a book. By contrast, people in the West tend to think of life as the first page and death as the last page of a book. I think this metaphor superbly illustrates contrasting ways to look at life and death.

Thoughts on Life and Death

Life is an eternal continuity that constantly repeats birth and death—this is the Asian view. But a person stakes his own life, he seeks personal goals and a mission, in a dimension which lies beyond life and death. I wonder whether an inexhaustible sense of fulfillment in life does not issue from that sort of commitment. What I mean to say is that this is how one breaks away from the mere struggle to live, this is how one achieves the frame of mind concerned with the purpose for which he spends his life.

Each and every person ought to make the effort to discover that which will constitute a characteristic motif for his life. An earnest attitude of commitment to living at this moment in time, the readiness to face death without regrets, will determine a person's entire life.

We saw examples of such commitment in this morning's paper, which reported the way thousands of young Japanese celebrated International Anti-War Day. Articles described how youthful energies were once again dissipated, how youthful hopes were once again frustrated and dashed against the pavement. These tragic young men and women on the streets of Tokyo in 1971 somehow merged in my mind's eye with pictures I had seen of French youths carrying anti-Establishment banners on the streets of Paris in 1968. The faces of those who fell wounded during those demonstrations continue to haunt me.

October 22, 1971

IMITATION AND CREATIVITY

November 3 is a national holiday in Japan. Since 1947, we have called it "Culture Day" in commemoration of the promulgation of our new Constitution. Before 1947, this holiday marked the birthday of the Emperor Meiji (1852-1912).

Thanks, perhaps, to the vagueness of the word "culture," the purpose of the holiday is not very clear. What does it mean to "promote culture"? Regardless of the meaning of the phrase, at least we can say that November 3 gives us an excuse to reconsider the significance of our culture.

Whenever talk turns to Japanese culture, people usually mention the term *imitative*. As the poet Kitamura Tokoku (1869-94) complained, "Imitation, slavish imitation—that's the most deplorable characteristic of our people." Many years have passed since he wrote these words. By now imitation is no longer considered merely a characteristic of the Japanese, it is used to denigrate the whole culture.

Certainly the poet made no mistake in pointing to imitation as one characteristic of the Meiji Japanese. During the Russo-Japanese War the Tsar himself reportedly called the Japanese "monkeys." Presumably he did not mean that we look like but that we acted like monkeys because we imitated everything. Hostile feelings toward an enemy may have influenced his choice of words. Still, it seems impossible to deny the truth of the accusation if we take a glance at our own cultural history.

The fact of the matter is that for centuries after the dawn of our recorded history, we looked to China as our cultural model. When we learned of the system of laws and administration that contributed to the greatness of the T'ang Dynasty, we immediately adopted the Chinese system. The moment the Chinese built a new capital on the grid pattern, imitations at Nara and Kyoto appeared like peas in a pod.

Following the 1868 Meiji "revolution," the model became Europe. Rather than decreasing her avid intake of foreign cultural elements, Japan actually increased it during the Meiji period (1868-1912). Indeed, it seems that the intake reached new heights of grasping imitativeness during these years. Thus one suspects that the Tsar's evaluation only reflected what was actually occurring at the time.

After the Pacific War the model changed again, this time to the United States of America. Since 1945, we have been living in a period when Japanese virtually worship everything made in the U.S.A.

This attitude has even surprised Americans. A Japanese writer tells how extremely amazed a certain American was to discover that the same people who had produced a Kamikaze Corps, the same people who had vowed to fight to the last man, could be so docile. Far from frustrating the Occupation, the Japanese relished imitating American ways.

Japanese statesmen also made an abrupt about-face. The moment Japan lost the war, the very same men who had been condemning the Anglo-Saxons as "foreign devils" began to take a patently pro-American stance. In a trice these leaders had switched from one extreme to the other. Fickleness is of course not particularly praiseworthy. But is imitation really as bad as some would have us believe? I think not.

Needless to say, no one would support the undesirable sort of imitativeness that indiscriminately worships foreign cultures. But I would like to think that skill at imitation indicates certain positive virtues such as flexibility in response to alien cultures and the fertile spirit of enterprise.

The most serious bottleneck faced by the developing nations in our day may be their inability to absorb the experience and expertise of the developed nations. From this perspective, we can see how vital it has been to have the mature ability to assimilate the lessons of history. An aptitude to learn from advanced civilizations has enabled Japan to achieve its present-day level of civilization.

Suppose that the Japanese had been deficient in the ability to imitate. Could they possibly have achieved such a miraculous rate of modernization during the last half of the 19th century, especially amid fierce imperialistic rivalry with the Powers? The same question can be asked regarding our reconstruction following the Pacific War.

I dare say that the Japanese propensity to imitate is hardly a source of shame. Rather does it seem one of our people's outstanding talents.

A close scrutiny of our history will show, moreover, that imitation is not the primary characteristic of the Japanese people. Far from it. We have never taken over lock, stock and barrel, the cultural objects and ideas of countries more developed than our own. We have always skillfully Japanized them and made them a part of our cultural genius.

In this respect, Japanese culture very likely occupies a unique position in the world. I suspect its uniqueness derives from its marvelous ability to digest the elements of any foreign culture it admires.

Look at the *Manyoshu,* that collection of indigenous lyrical poetry compiled in the 8th century during

the Nara period when our culture was dominated by influences from the continent. Our ancestors were also clever enough to use Chinese characters to write Japanese and, subsequently, to devise an indigenous syllabary—itself a work of art. And then, from the Kamakura period through the Muromachi and Edo eras, from medieval to modern times, Japanese originated in their own inimitable manner a number of richly original creations in architecture, painting, literature and the like.

There are also down-to-earth examples of indigenization. The Japanese devised soybean buns (*anpan*) when they learned how to make bread dough. And they invented sukiyaki as soon as they learned to eat beef. Whenever I see foreigners fumble with chopsticks as they enjoy this typical Japanese treat, I see the basic nature of Japanese culture in a different light. It seems at such times a good deal more than a matter of mere imitation.

Voltaire said that creativity is nothing more than prudent imitation. Perhaps that is the key to understanding Japanese culture. In a book on creative writing, a noted Japanese intellectual advises people to imitate the sentences of outstanding authors. At first glance imitation and creativity appear to be located at opposite ends of a continuum. The fact is, they are two sides of the same coin, as Voltaire suggests.

Needless to say, a number of people will object to this view. Small matter, for I myself do not for a moment imagine that mine is the most accurate interpretation of Japanese culture. Arguing for this or that viewpoint, seeing our culture in terms of creativity or imitation, is little more than a result of the basic premises on which one's argument rests. The facts themselves do not change.

That's the point I would like to make. These are the simple facts of history: imitation of a foreign culture has always stimulated the digestive juices of the indigenous culture. As non-indigenous aspects become completely digested, Japanese absorb elements of the new culture in the same way our bodies absorb nutrients. The ability to generate new forms of cultural expression certainly constitutes a kind of wisdom—a wisdom charged with the potential of making great contributions to the development of human culture as it moves into the 21st century.

But of course at the moment we can talk only of potential. Despite the strong points of the cultures of the East and the West, the former stressing the development of the spiritual and the latter emphasizing material aspects, the one is weak at precisely the places where the other is strong. As a result, neither cultural pattern has brought its people complete happiness. The culture the West encourages men to pursue their ambitions; the culture of the East encourages men to spin aimless webs of ideas.

Some point out that Western culture has reached an impasse and that a fresh start may be possible by studying the cultures of the East. No matter what means is used to end the impasse, the ideal culture of the future must be focused on human values; it will be a mirror of man.

How is it possible to fuse into a universal culture the fragments that now exist in each separate tradition? Perhaps the special nature of Japanese culture might make a significant contribution at this point by functioning as the point where East and West converge.

This is not to suggest that I imagine Japanese culture perfect in every aspect. Each strength has its own particular "Achilles' heel," just as the best medicine becomes poison through misuse. I am aware of that. The problem is how to bring to the fore the positive strengths of our own culture, strengths which have been centuries in developing. We shall need a good deal of wisdom to accomplish that.

Japanese have recently begun to reconsider their hasty rejection of tradition. They are taking a second look at the positive aspects of "old Japan." And at the moment we are in a period of transition with regard to our absolute devotion to American ways of doing things. It is time therefore to ask what our culture should look like in the future. In a word, we are at the stage when the attitude we adopt toward this vague term "culture" will have important and far-reaching effects on our lives.

October 30, 1971

THE MEANING OF AFFLUENCE

Begun in Hachioji City, Tokyo, "Ban the Car" move-ments are now being carried on in 16 localities through-out the country. The people heartily applaud this experiment, which will not only rid certain roads of the glut of automobiles but contribute to the reduction of carbon monoxide emissions.

It is quite touching to note man's resistance to the day-by-day dehumanization of society brought on by the automobile. People have been attempting for about a year to recover their humanity, if but for a moment, either by banning cars from or by creating a tem-porary "Pedestrian Paradise" on major thoroughfares in congested areas.

THE MEANING OF AFFLUENCE

At first glance some may think this resistance to the automobile will develop into resistance to progress itself. The fact is, however, that any movements which gain widespread public favor should be taken seriously, for they give us a good glimpse into the ironies of our age.

I understand there were similar reactions in the wake of the Industrial Revolution. During the second decade of the 19th century, for example, the Luddites in England went about smashing machines in the new factories. They were furious over being deprived of their livelihood and took their rage out on the machinery which had displaced them. Observers in those days tended on the whole to assess this anti-machine movement negatively; they said the Luddites engaged in pointless opposition that ran counter to the march of historical progress.

In our day, by contrast, it seems that resistance to the automobile—could we call it a Second Luddite Movement?—should be interpreted positively. I mean that people in developed countries find there has been too much progress. Their environment is now so clogged with things that they cannot even move about freely.

One critic of our contemporary civilization points out its similarity to a very skinny person wearing baggy clothing. This is an odd way to put it, but the view has merit. One who cannot gain sufficient weight to keep his ribs from showing might demonstrate better wisdom and more honesty by wearing well-tailored clothes than by trying to camouflage his condition.

The Meaning of Affluence

We cannot determine to what extent contemporary man has become skin and bones, or to what extent his material civilization has become obese. However, it is obvious from the limited amount of land available for human use in Japan, at least (less than 20 percent of the total area), that we have more automobiles than necessary. While it is, of course, impossible to determine how many cars are necessary, we know this much: We need perspective on the problem, and we must see the tremendous significance in banning cars from certain thoroughfares. But if through movements to "Ban the Car" we can once again bring into sharp focus certain values we have allowed to slide into oblivion, then these movements will have an extremely deep significance.

The fact of the matter is that we do need such movements. They can help us recover, if only for an instant, something quite precious, something we once took for granted—something as simple as the right to walk safely down the street. Over the past several years people living in large metropolitan areas have enjoyed less and less opportunity to plumb the joys of stretching out their arms and striding down a boulevard in broad daylight.

Some time ago I saw the documentary, *The Chinese People*. I noticed in this record of events in China before the Great Proletarian Cultural Revolution got underway in 1966 that automobiles were conspicuous by their absence. Even on the broad avenues in Peking there were mainly pedestrians and bicycles. Of course this suggests the extent to which China lags in developing its transportation; no one could contest that. Still in all, as I watched the documentary I felt an indescribably tranquil serenity in the calm expressions of those who strolled so leisurely along the avenues.

Progress has robbed us of the knowledge of what it means to savor such serenity. If we think about it carefully—no, there is no special need to *think* about it at all—we might conclude that there is nothing more natural than the experience of serenity. It is the most fundamental, the most obvious birthright of man. But we have come to think that our birthright is unnatural, that it is difficult for us to appropriate. Why do we think so pessimistically about what is actually ours?

One reason may be our contemporary life style. We now put the greatest value on having things "convenient." Contemporary man has the extremely simple-minded outlook that if only he has enough conveniences he will be "affluent." Conveniences have no doubt contributed much. They make life easier, they rationalize our daily activities, they allow us more leisure. It is hard therefore to contest the fact that they have a positive value for mankind.

But conveniences are by no means the measure of the true affluence which men desire. The affluence we long for lies in a dimension far removed from the utilitarian concerns of mere conveniences and gadgets. There are, for example, the joys of fulfillment, the feelings experienced when at long last we see our struggles

and years of effort bear fruit. At such moments a man feels true affluence as a human being.

Actually, one's richest blessings are those moments during which he has toiled hardest and perspired the most. They are not the immediate physical conveniences that money can buy.

This is not to suggest that I oppose time-saving and labor-saving conveniences. Surely we ought to make every use of them. But as we use them we must realize what can happen to us the moment we get caught up in enjoying them: We can get so used to short cuts that we shy away from those arduous roads through toil and sweat which lead to real harvests. When we become too comfortable in our nests of handy gadgets, we all too easily strike that dreary pose of the poverty-stricken "affluent" man who has an empty heart and an empty mind.

There are men who have forgotten what it means to hold a hammer. There are men who slosh through the flood of the mass media unmindful of the very first principles of humanity: the use of their minds. Will men in the future deteriorate into wretched ghosts with empty minds and feeble limbs?

The convenience of transportation suggests that they might. We can get from Tokyo to Osaka in three hours now using the Tokaido "bullet train," the acme of "convenience" in transportation. During the Tokugawa period these cities were joined by a highway with fifty-three post stations. From our frantic contemporary standpoint, perhaps the hours consumed on the road were an utter waste of time.

For premodern men, however, time spent traveling did not seem a waste. A large number of travelers put their feelings into poetry as they enjoyed the scenery—even as they were being jostled around in their sedan chairs or on their saddles, even as they leaned on their walking sticks. How many of those who ride the bullet train between Tokyo and Osaka—rushing to get their "business" done—compose poetry?

One way to view the problem is to realize the unalterable fact that each day has no more than twenty-four hours. You cannot change the fact no matter what type of transportation you use. In these terms, the really important thing is not where you are going or how you get there. It is what happens to you personally as a human being. The question is how you fulfill yourself so that each day in life becomes a fulfillment. That is the key to achieving real affluence, for that is to put the affluent life and the affluent society under your control.

Being surrounded by conveniences does not in itself make life affluent. I think true affluence much rather consists of creating the kind of wisdom which seeks to understand how we might utilize conveniences to fulfill and enrich our inner lives.

Despite working at the same place and having similar kinds of families, the affluence of each of the many people around me is different. Even those who

67

wear fairly plain clothing can exude the "fragrance" of true affluence because true affluence is not external. It lies at the depth of each individual's inner world.

In the 16th century the Portuguese brought firearms into the country; Japanese were astonished. In the mid-19th century Admiral Matthew Perry's black ships appeared; Japanese were awakened from two-and-one-half centuries of national isolation. In both cases, Japanese seemed to imagine that Western culture with its advanced science was the true kind of affluence. Unfortunately, these people were deluded into thinking that affluence consisted solely of acquiring things. One inevitable result of that delusion may be to degenerate into non-thinking animals who seek nothing but material prosperity.

I prefer to think that affluence cannot be quantified or measured. It exists in more than the material dimension. Perhaps these movements to ban automobiles teach us that we now live in an age when we must conceive of affluence in terms of its multiple dimensions, spiritual as well as material.

November 6, 1971

STRONGHOLDS OF PEACE

The other day I read *The Battle of Okinawa,* one volume in a series on the history of the Ryuku Islands. The book describes the bombardment and invasion of Okinawa in 1945, a battle in which more than 200,-000 people lost their lives.

This book is a record of interviews with a thousand anonymous civilians who experienced that gruesome battle. A shocking document that covers more than a thousand pages, this volume tells the stories of these civilians without any particular bias. The book is neither blatantly antiwar nor does it denounce the war makers.

The Battle of Okinawa is merely a record of facts, presented objectively and unemotionally. Nothing else.

Simply because these are ungarnished reports of actual experiences, however, they make the more vivid impression. And they have all the more power to move the reader to tears. Reading the book, I found that I could not repress my anger and indignation.

The record of a peasant woman who was thirty-nine at the time of the battle is especially pathetic. She and her family were fleeing for cover to a nearby trench when the U.S. bombardment commenced. Theirs turned out to be an endless flight dogged by disaster.

Members of the woman's family were hit one after the other. First her eighteen-year-old daughter, on her way to help nurse the wounded, took some shrapnel in her back as she washed her face by a stream. She died three days later. The woman's thirty-four-year-old sister was also hit in the back; she died in two hours.

"It happened so quickly," the woman reported. "There wasn't time to notice the others. My five-year-old daughter was hit in the wrist and a piece of shrapnel ripped open her belly, killing her instantly. My mother set up such a ruckus that I became hysterical. I found myself screaming, 'Gramma's stomping on my daughter's stomach. She's squeezing out my girl's guts!' Mother said she wasn't doing anything of the sort."

The bombardment drove the woman further from her home. She continued:

"We had taken refuge in an empty house in Shin'ei-pei. We were hit there by shrapnel, maybe from a naval shell. At the time I was holding my eighteen-

month-old baby who was gashed on the arm, forehead and chest. And Tsutomu, my second son, knocked flat by the shell, suffered abrasions on his head. After I came to my senses I found that the explosion had instantly killed my mother-in-law.

"My aunt died at Shingaki. The shelling was just as fierce there, let me tell you. Chunks of flesh came flying out of nowhere. Bodies were strewn all over the place."

The woman's baby died of malnutrition soon afterwards. All told, she lost ten members of her family. What fearful carnage!

Still, her experiences were in no way exceptional. Every one of the thousand people in this book tells essentially the same story.

It is quite possible that some Okinawans had been even more cruelly manhandled by Fate than those whose experiences are recorded in this volume. There is, for example, the story of a woman who refused to be interviewed by those gathering material for this book. She told them, "If you get me talking about the war, I'm afraid I'll fly off the handle and end up hitting one of you."

What cruel, what pathetic scars war leaves on people! War is so stupid, so brutal, so destructive. And it is always the anonymous masses who suffer and groan and mourn the most because of it.

I would like to suggest that the agonies of these unchampioned masses deserve more consideration than they usually get. I for one believe that in the groanings of the people—and there alone—will we find reactions to war that ring true, that are far more effective than grandiloquent theories about peace. Any antiwar movement, any talk of peace, must assuredly begin from the agonies suffered by the people.

We have, unfortunately, utterly ignored the people's sufferings. Perhaps we do not see them as the obvious cornerstone of a peace policy because they are simply too commonplace. However, it is because we have paid no attention to the common people and their agonies that the stench from that cataclysmic battle for Okinawa continues to oppress the island.

Human history over the past quarter of a century lists any number of man's crimes and follies, including Auschwitz, Hiroshima, Nagasaki, the Korean War, the war in Vietnam, East Pakistan. . . . Such crimes against humanity have been scathingly denounced in the 1959 publication, *Listen: Voices from the Deep!* One passage from this collection of notes scribbled by young students who died in battle reads as follows:

"Deep inside I feel that something evil, something like callousness, is ingrained in the human race. Ever since he devised society, man has failed to make progress. There is no longer any question of such things as justice in war. War is nothing but a matter of nation detesting nation. Countries which are antagonistic to each other will not likely cease fighting until they annihilate each other. Ah you descendants of the ape, you human beings—how horrid, how inhuman your acts!"

73

Such sincere humanism, such concern about love and justice for all, is however absolutely impotent and inadequate to stem the trends of international politics. Notice, for example, how it failed to stop the nuclear test on Amchitka in the Aleutians. The bomb was exploded despite the clamor of protests and world opinion opposed to it.

How can leaders continue to be so callous? I suspect that they turn a deaf ear to justice because they are imbued with the nationalistic ideology which justifies such acts.

If we are to survive, a stronghold for peace must be fashioned within the mind of every single man, woman and child on the earth. This stronghold must resolutely hold out against the invasion of any idea to make war. It makes no difference how feeble a fortress others may say the mind is. We have no choice. There is no other way to change man's pathetic potential for evil.

An appeal of this nature may well be ridiculed as sentimentality. Some will point out that the appeal shows no discernment of complicated political realities. Well, if it is sentimental to call people's attention to the obvious direction in which they should obviously move, then it doesn't bother me in the least to be called sentimental. How could I let that bother me in view of the magnitude of the problem that faces man?

I believe that the most vital task confronting us at this moment is to make something of our indignation. We must discover how to congeal the outrage, how to intensify the pain felt by all who read *The Battle of Okinawa*. Only then will private reactions become the collective cry of an entire people.

The term "nuclear allergy" has been in vogue in Japan for a generation. It suggests how extremely sensitive we Japanese are to the question of nuclear weapons.

If we do not make our minds equally sensitive to the very idea of war, and if we do not reject the tendency to become immune to our "nuclear allergy," we shall most certainly face a serious crisis. We shall know that the crisis is near when we see the long shadows of increased nuclear tests creeping up on us.

I have visited Okinawa several times. Dark blue skies, beautiful coral waters, dazzling sunshine—everything one expects to find in the romantic South Seas. Okinawa is truly beautiful. At least its natural setting is.

Though set in the beauties of nature, how gloomy and lacking in beauty has man's world become! It is as though the various ploys and artifices carried out by those holding power in our modern world have obscured the human element in society. It seems to me that the beast, which has already transformed the beautiful island of Okinawa into a hellish landscape, continues its reign over men; it is more ominous than ever.

November 13, 1971

CITIES—ANCIENT AND MODERN

An interesting article about ancient Egypt recently appeared in the newspapers. It reported that Nile valley dwellings, which existed even before the pyramids, had tile floors, stucco walls and other features which made them more advanced than some homes in the West.

This data was revealed by an Austrian archaeologist who had carefully studied some shards excavated near the pyramids; he says they date from about 3000 B.C.

Five thousand years ago! That means these shards antedate the pyramids, not to mention hieroglyphics. It is surprising to learn that people in antiquity lived in dwellings that would put many fashionable homes of modern times to shame.

Considering conditions in Tokyo, where you can find a family of five crammed into a room that measures only nine by twelve feet, I suspect that we are somewhat worse off—as far as housing is concerned—than many Egyptians who lived five millennia ago. It's really ironical that we have apparently made so little progress in this area. It chills me to think of it.

Egypt wasn't the only ancient culture whose cities give one the impression of an advanced civilization. One of many such sites is Mohenjo-Daro, assumed to have been built 4,500 years ago near the Indus River in what is now the southern part of West Pakistan.

Mohenjo-Daro presumably means "The Tombs." But close examination reveals that the city seems to have been much too well planned to merit that unpromising name.

To begin with, Mohenjo-Daro was provided with a superb sewerage system. This made it possible for waste water to run from the second floor through vertical clay pipes directly into the home's baked-brick drainage system. From there it flowed into sewers on the side street which, in turn, were tied in with the primary drainage system under the main thoroughfares. These primary sewers, scholars say, were spacious enough to accommodate a grown man standing upright.

The city fathers of this ancient Indian city furthermore gave careful attention to trash disposal. I understand that every house was equipped with a trash chute that sloped down to the street. Researchers wonder

whether or not the city had men comparable to "sanitary engineers" who might have made regular rounds to collect trash from these chutes.

Of course Mohenjo-Daro had none of the splendid rows of high-rise buildings seen in our modern metropolitan areas. In actuality, however, this city had been carefully designed to make life more convenient for human beings. Such care gives the impression that ancient planners had a gem-like wisdom.

By contrast, look at our modern cities. Have we really concentrated all our wisdom into designing them so that men can live more comfortably?

As far as large cities like Tokyo and Osaka are concerned, unfortunately I cannot help feeling that the human element has been entirely forgotten. Such cities have ballooned far beyond the point where any fundamental considerations of human comfort are taken into account.

Some time has passed since informed people talked of the gloomy warning that our cities would soon be unfit environments for the human species. Choose any problem you please—auto emissions, skyrocketing prices, the struggle to get through traffic, our urban housing shortage—and you will find it difficult to conclude that modern cities provide man with a pleasant environment.

The difficulty of living in a contemporary metropolis is aptly illustrated by the problem Tokyo is having with trash disposal.

Until quite recently, two-thirds of Tokyo's trash had been used to fill in and reclaim parts of Tokyo Bay. In the fall of 1971, however, the ward under whose jurisdiction these reclaimed areas fall announced that it would oppose further dumping. At one stroke, Tokyo's trash disposal problem faced a crisis.

Residents in other wards have also been generating opposition to trash disposal. Those who live near the city's huge incinerators in Nerima, for example, have initiated a move to shut down the plants. These citizens claim they can no longer bear being plagued by the odors. And I hear that residents in Suginami Ward have succeeded for more than five years in opposing the city's attempts to construct a new incinerator in their district.

We cannot shrug off the problem just because it's "only a matter of trash." The fact is that Tokyo daily produces 12,500 tons of refuse, enough to fill up the thirty-six-floor Kasumigaseki Building in only thirteen days! Every imaginable item is discarded, from plain garbage to furniture and junk cars, including even plastic materials which emit poisonous fumes when incinerated. It is a foregone conclusion that residents would oppose construction of such a plant near their homes.

On the level of a man's day-to-day urban existence, the trash disposal problem clearly illustrates the pathology of the modern metropolis. It seems to me that trash disposal itself somehow becomes a metaphor of the city dweller's existence.

CITIES — ANCIENT AND MODERN

There can be no doubt about it. The solution to this problem will not be easy, as the mere fact of the increased volume of refuse suggests. Over the past decade it has increased nearly 250 percent while the population during the same period increased a mere 1.4 percent. What clearer indication that ours is an era of mass-production and mass-consumption? We now live in what might be called a "throw-away age."

There is little doubt that the "throw-away" mentality is a primary source of our present trash disposal headaches. Once upon a time we reclaimed and recycled paper refuse and reused it. Human waste products were previously returned to nature in one form or another. But modern plastic products, which have facilitated our "throw-away" age, are another matter. They are man made and do not break down into components that readily return to nature. This obviously gives rise to serious problems of disposal.

Whether or not these are the essential sources of the problem, I must say that it certainly depresses me to have to refer to trash disposal in discussing contemporary cities. Nevertheless it seems true that the whole problem of refuse symbolizes what we have done to the face of the earth. We are making it into a vast soot-polluted region that daily chokes out the green.

Is it not true that our modern cities are divesting human life of every trace of civilization, that they mercilessly convert the environment into lifeless dens unfit for man?

Cities — Ancient and Modern

Look at the way high-rise buildings vie for new height records. Look at the way subways and elevated toll roads spread their networks over and under the surfaces of our cities. If a cultured man from ancient times could see what is happening to us, if he could observe the way we so skillfully utilize space in creating multi-level crossovers, wouldn't he be absolutely startled?

But how would this man evaluate the plight of the city dweller? How would he view our agonizing battle with trash disposal, a problem that is intimately connected to our daily lives? I doubt that our cities are any longer fit for human beings. They have gotten out of hand, becoming nondescript monsters which serve one master: the profit motive.

Article 25 of our postwar Constitution guarantees that "All people shall have the right to maintain the minimum standards of wholesome and cultured living." Does "wholesome and cultured living" mean to be squeezed into the little space left over in a teeny rented room that bursts with electric gadgets?

Whenever I think of the problems posed by our cities, I wonder whether man has not once again arrived at the stage where he must reconsider the meaning of "wholesome and cultured living."

November 20, 1971

ANALYSIS AND SYNTHESIS

My chilly yard:
Strings from the moon
Accompany the insects' song

(Matsuo Basho)

This is the season when the moon and the stars sparkle beautifully in the crisp and chilly sky. Orion, the chief constellation of midwinter, appears in the south during the dead of night. This constellation is composed of four stars that form a square. Two kitty-cornered stars are of the first magnitude, the other two are second magnitude stars. Three others line up on a splendid slant across the middle of the square; they are familiar sights in Japan and in the West.

Analysis and Synthesis

Lady Sei Shonagon exclaimed enthusiastically in her *Pillow Book,* written near the end of the 10th century, that of all the stars the Pleiades were most exquisite. This cluster in the constellation Taurus continues to twinkle mysteriously.

Recently, however, the smoky haze from gigantic industries near our urban areas has obscured the eternal natural beauty of the stars. Smog spreads across the sky like a curtain, heartlessly intercepting the bundles of light sent to us from hundreds of thousands, from millions of light years away. Though this is certainly deplorable, I nevertheless get a fresh perspective on the complications of our tiny world whenever I gaze at those distant but dimmed stars.

Stars and man. An endless number of romantic tales have dealt with this subject. This is particularly true of ancient man who, when he viewed the brilliance of the constellations, discovered the themes which later informed his myths. Perhaps these men of old, in conceiving of themselves as nestled in the bosom of the cosmos, sought with their myths to resolve the endless vicissitudes that confronted them in their daily lives.

Talking of the cosmos reminds me that the planet Mars was closer to the earth several months ago than it had been for fifteen years. Glowing with an intense redness that seemed almost ominous, Mars was suddenly on everyone's lips. The small "star" which men dispatched to capitalize on this rare opportunity completed its long journey and now orbits the planet, photographing its features. Naturally we cannot see the satellite but we can be sure it is snapping pictures from the skies above Mars.

Someone has said that it is as difficult to send a satellite to study a planet millions of miles away as it is to toss a dime into the coin slot of a vending machine from thirty feet. I humbly tip my hat to the brilliant accomplishment of the Mars probe; it is proof of the accumulation of knowledge and the accuracy of scientific analysis.

But ironically, irrespective of the accuracy with which computers can guide a satellite to some distant planet, the fact is that we cannot even estimate where a single piece of paper will land if we drop it from a mere three feet above ground.

A computer programmer told me recently that it is quite erroneous to imagine that computers have the answers to everything. A computer can answer only those questions it has been programmed for. The programmer said, "Computers cannot foresee earthquakes or the path a typhoon will take, nor can they predict landslides; how much less then can they know the human heart . . .?" He certainly spoke with great perception.

Human beings in their wisdom have been able to increase the yield of agricultural products through insecticides and chemical fertilizers. They were not able to perceive in what ways and to what extent these artificial products would produce a backlash that plagues their environment by upsetting the delicate balance of nature.

Undoubtedly the glory of science glitters everywhere like a finely polished blade. But we soon discover how all that glitters is not gold when we ask about the overall, long-range results of scientific progress. We see then what seem to be distortions in the blade, and we realize that the glorious glitter of science pales in the face of the uncomplicated beauty of the lights nature has provided.

This is to say that in the area of *analysis* science has made tremendous strides. But what has happened in the dimension of *synthesis?* Science can take things apart easier than it can create new unities. Obviously, when we deal with synthesis, we find problems that cannot be solved by science alone. But we have no right to expect the harmonious development of human society if we refuse to come to grips with problems that science was never meant to solve.

I recall having heard a scholar perceptively lay his finger on the problem. He said, "From the viewpoint of traditional scientific technique, perhaps the achievements of microbiology amount to extraordinary progress. If we look at this progress from the viewpoint of the human being, from the standpoint of a living organism unable to avoid death, however, I wonder whether we can really talk of progress?"

They say microbiology is one of the most advanced fields in modern science. This discipline seeks to un-

derstand the structure of living things by microscopic analysis. No doubt we should keep close tab on the discoveries in this field and make the greatest possible practical use of them. At the same time, I think that we also face the unavoidable task of trying to gain deeper insight into man and living things on a more macroscopic scale.

In this respect, it seems to me that ancient man took a much more open-minded view of the world than we do. He thought the cosmos was composed of four elements, earth, water, fire and air. He also apparently thought that man himself was composed of identical elements. Ancients in both the East and the West shared this insight. The only difference is that sages in the East added a fifth element, flux *(ku)*.

From the standpoint of modern science and the more than 100 elements it has acknowledged, ancient man's ideas about the building blocks of the cosmos certainly seem primitive. Nevertheless there is something in his insight that we dare not overlook. The ancients attempted to view man from the perspective of the cosmos, thinking that both were composed of the same basic substances; they took a penetratingly long-range, macro-view of everything. The basic correspondence of such views in both East and West may derive from the fact that classical Greek civilization had contacts with Eastern culture. But whatever the reason, there can be no doubt that this correspondence is amazing.

It is doubtful that ancient man regarded what he considered the basic elements in a materialistic way;

that is, he probably did not see them as we see chemical elements. He simply thought that man and the cosmos were harmonious. Thus he had the notion that sickness arose from an imbalance in these elements and that at death these substances returned to the cosmos.

If we stretch the point a bit, we might say this viewpoint assumes that every cosmic rhythm has its counterpart in man's body. His heartbeat quickens and his blood pressure rises in the daytime. His heartbeat slackens and his blood pressure drops at night. This seems an inexplicable correspondence with the rhythms of the universe. Some have thought that the elements in man respond to the elements in the cosmos, creating an exquisite flux. With that in mind, my teacher used to tell me to get to bed before midnight; his wise advice hit the mark.

The rhythms and the timepiece of the body resemble those of the universe. This principle is called biorhythm, a new field of research which seeks to understand man as a single harmonious entity interrelated with the universe.

Ancient man in the West created myths based on the constellations. Perhaps he did so not so much because he regarded the stars as awesome but because he believed that they reflected his own essential "stuff." The ancient Chinese thought that movements of the stars were directly related to man's fate. The idea itself may be unscientific. Its imaginativeness is magnificent.

ANALYSIS AND SYNTHESIS

The universe is complex. It is vast. Yet it throbs like a marvelous living body. Man, who cannot escape from the cosmos, is himself a small-scale universe. That is why he must direct his wisdom toward that criterion which is also the central force of the universe, I mean, toward mankind and questions which concern him: How we can gain a more profound insight into man's essential nature and how we might help him live in perfect harmony.

November 28, 1971

ASSESSING THE PAST CENTURY

Bustling December winds announce the expiration of another year. Each time we begin year-end preparations, it seems we hear a crescendo of people assessing the events of the preceding twelve months as they voice expectations for greater happiness in the new year.

We have long thought that ten years constitute a rather long period of time. Things that happened a decade ago seem to belong to "the distant past." Nowadays we live amid a technological revolution, however, which constantly assails us with enormous amounts of information. Each day becomes a bewildering whirl of events. In a time when there is no end to turmoil, incidents that occurred only a year ago may seem part of "the distant past."

Accumulating these daily events into decades or even centuries allows us to mark off periods of time, each with its own history. In many cases, these histories demonstrate how values have become reversed or how the evaluation of men and events has been totally revised.

This brings to mind a thinker and a writer born just about a century ago. The thinker is Shusui Kotoku, born in 1871. The writer is the principal woman novelist of the Meiji Period (1868-1912), Ichiyo Higuchi, born in 1872. Although born at approximately the same time, the thought and accomplishments of each differ radically on several essential points, and not merely because they are of different sexes. There is one point, however, which they seem to have in common: the basic focus of their thinking and activities was always the people, the common people.

Man is of course fated to live in the crucible of history. Looking back on the way a given person thought and acted in the flux of that crucible, we can readily discover contradictions or limitations and, at times, mistakes as well.

In Ichiyo Higuchi we find a woman who was terribly hedged in by feudal constraints. We know that she did not express her criticisms of society assertively but quite gingerly, due perhaps to the fact that her instinct as a writer was to express herself through feelings rather than through logical analysis.

As can be seen in her short story "Growing Up" *(1896),* Ichiyo does point out a number of contradic-

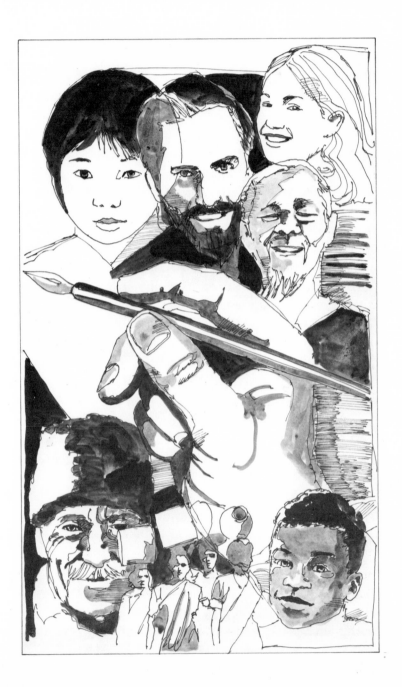

tions in a society which retained strong traces of pre-modern human values. This story also clearly reflects a writer with a fresh awareness of self.

It seems important that we note this piece not in terms of how it reveals her limitations as a novelist but how it indicates that Ichiyo was a conspicuous harbinger of the modern concern for human values. Though born into a family that once belonged to the elite samurai class, Ichiyo's work crystallized the anguish that gushed from the depths of her womanhood, from her humanity, as she coped with the bitter lot of common people in the lower classes. I cannot help but feel a certain dead seriousness in the short life of this novelist (she died of tuberculosis at twenty-four), the kind of seriousness one can discover only in those who run their short span of life at full throttle.

Shusui's criticisms of his society were far more severe, far more sweeping, than Ichiyo's. Confronting the entire social system head-on, he collided with the very cornerstone of the Meiji state: the imperial institution. Accused of having taken part in a plot against the life of the Emperor, Kotoku was convicted of high treason and hanged in 1911. Scholars now believe that he had been framed by the authorities and that he actually had had little to do with the plot.

Though I am not conversant with every detail of the incident, it seems apparent that Shusui was inclined to approve of radical and anarchistic acts. But throughout his life—in which he experienced a succession of storms and struggles—he consistently confronted the injustices and contradictions of his society with a passion that clamored for the truth about the human situation.

This passion manifested itself with particular clarity in Kotoku's famous stand on pacifism, developed primarily on the pages of the *Commoner's News,* a paper he helped found in 1903. In the face of the boiling torrent of public opinion bellowing for war with Russia, Shusui wrote, "I know it would be easier for me to hold the entire Yellow River in my palm than to prevent the outbreak of war single-handedly. Nevertheless, I have no choice but to say what I believe in accord with the dictates of truth and justice."

When war broke out in 1904, Kotoku did not hesitate to advocate the unpopular view: "Though war has come, I shall not cease opposing it from this day on as long as I have a voice, a pen and a piece of paper." Though the government closed down the *Commoner's News,* indicting and imprisoning Kotoku, he refused to be silent.

Reading his words of commitment to truth and justice from the vantage point of six decades does not diminish their force. They pierce one to the very quick. Kotoku's indomitable, uncompromising struggle against authority eventually cost him his life. Even as he stood on the gallows, they say his heart was at peace, his mind composed. He was only forty.

No doubt there is a good deal of room for debate on how to evaluate Kotoku's thought and action. My personal feeling is that the basic principle that governed the life of this revolutionary—this rebel with such a distinctively Asian aura about him—is more important than such debate. I believe that the most vital fact about Shusui Kotoku was the passionately righteous indignation which he expressed for the common people, for those gasping under the weight of the entire society.

In the struggle to live their principles, both Shusui Kotoku and Ichiyo Higuchi suffered as they collided with barriers set up by their society and their government. Stymied, they must have felt frustrated. But during the century since their birth there have been great changes. What was once only a minority struggling for the people has now become a majority.

Of course, many problems remain to be solved. It is also true, moreover, that the very progress of movements to give the people a voice develops fresh problems. Single individuals may think they have insufficient power to influence the course of events or solve these problems. I would like to believe differently. I would like to think that the individual's struggles will now begin to etch out a new path that will alter the flow of history, and that the individual will actually become the motive force in ushering us into a new future.

One thing is vital for us at this moment. We must fix our sights firmly on the people, the common people, as the new force in history. It was the people who dominated the concerns both of the revolutionary Shusui

Kotoku and the woman novelist Ichiyo Higuchi. If we are to make this the century of the people, the century of *mankind,* should we not continue to develop and maintain our persistent and unyielding struggles for the people?

Tsunesaburo Makiguchi, founder and first president of the Nichiren Shoshu laymen's organization, was also born just a century ago. The year 1971 marks the hundredth anniversary of his birth, recently celebrated with a modest ceremony. We also conducted a memorial service this fall in remembrance of his passing. Many people are taking considerable note of his life and achievements these days, particularly his accomplishments in education. These include his *Theory of Descriptive Geography,* published at thirty-two, the *Philosophy of Value,* his life work, and many research papers on related topics.

Makiguchi's life as educator and scholar falls into two periods. First, the period of preparation and study. Second, beginning in 1930, the period in which he established the Soka Kyoiku Gakkai (Educational Society for the Creation of Value), dedicated himself to producing true educators, and agitated for a religion concerned with practice rather than theory.

It seems to me that a common thread runs through both periods: Makiguchi's love for human beings, particularly for the impoverished masses. That love never diminished, even when the militarists imprisoned him in 1944. He died in jail at the age of seventy-three.

When I assess the last century, I think of several fated thinkers martyred for their dedication to justice, for their profound love of the people. Though born 150 years ago, Dostoyevsky also comes to mind as a thinker and writer concerned with justice and the people. I hear that although his works were for some time in disfavor, they have recently been making a 'comeback' on the literary scene in the U.S.S.R. That in itself allows one to suggest that in our own time we are witnessing fulfillment of a long-cherished expectation: concern for human values.

In any event, while only modest progress has been made during the last hundred years toward realizing this expectation, I should like here to stress the positive. I want to celebrate the fact that we have at last begun to make progress in getting people concerned about mankind.

December 31, 1971

PEOPLE AND NEW YEAR'S DAY

A new year. I haven't the slightest idea when festivities celebrating the beginning of another year began. But I feel certain that people must have celebrated the first day of the year ever since ancients first discovered that the globe—our speck on the edge of the cosmos—completes its cycle around the sun every 365 days.

In Japan, it appears that New Year's festivities have been deeply influenced by the traditions of an agricultural society from which most of our people come. Consider the customary trappings of the day: Round, pure-white rice cakes made from freshly harvested grain. Dried persimmons. Mandarin oranges. Pine branches. The sacred rope. All reek nostalgically of the countryside.

The fact that the earth needs 365 days to complete its trek around the sun is an inescapable fact to any who observe the stars or seasonal changes. But no doubt there were countless debates over when to begin counting the 365 days. For example, I understand that the ancient Greeks actually celebrated New Year's on the first day of summer, while the old Hebrew calendar listed it as the first day of spring.

Until Japan began using the Gregorian calendar in 1873, our ancestors celebrated New Year's Day on what is now January 15. Today we call this "Little New Year." Apparently people in rural areas continue to prefer seeing their new year in on the 15th rather than the 1st. Perhaps "Little New Year" may be a more suitable time for farmers to look ahead with hope for a year of rich harvests because by mid-January they have completed all the work related to the autumn harvest and can approach the festivities in a relaxed mood.

Several generations of my own ancestors sprang from the area that is now Tokyo, where I, too, was born. They regarded themselves as typical city people despite the fact that the ancestral home in Omori (toward Yokohama), where I spent my boyhood, was surrounded by fields and rice paddies. Indeed it seems to me that before 1945 there was much less of a gulf between city and country than one finds in present-day Japan. No matter where you went, the place had a strong pastoral air about it.

The Ikeda household was not connected with farming. Nevertheless as I remember it, we naturally tended

at New Year's to feel grateful for having gotten safely through the old year, and we faced the new with prayers for health and prosperity. At least we definitely had the feeling that with the dawning of another year everything would be renewed.

In those days people were less conscious of their personal birthdays than of the fact that on January 1 they began another year of life. The custom was to count the number of years during which one lived, so there was deep meaning in confronting another New Year's Day. This may be one reason for the strong sentiments which were experienced at that time of the year, and why these sentiments seemed to motivate people to turn over a new leaf.

One might even say that people in former times met the new year with immeasurable feelings of relief as well as with a lively sense of excitement. They felt, after all, that man identified and was in harmony with rhythms generated by the cosmos. They believed that everything—nature and society and man himself—moved together into the new year.

Unfortunately, in the wake of rapid industrial development during the postwar period, Japanese seem to have lost the sense of being in harmony with the rhythms of the universe. The fruits of agriculture, pitifully neglected and overshadowed by modern industry, are no longer regarded as gifts of nature. We imagine they have been made possible by pesticides, chemical fertilizers, and plastic sheeting that allows new hothouse growing methods.

People and New Year's Day

Thanks to such artificial means, we can obtain our favorite foods irrespective of the season. With these conveniences, however, we have become utterly deaf to the natural throbbing of the fields and oblivious to the invigorating sense of seasonal changes brought home to us in the past by varied produce which characterized each quarter of the year.

We have even become strangely indifferent to the traditional New Year decorations. We mechanically display the circular white rice cakes, the pine branches, the sacred rope. But rather than symbolize a wealth of natural blessings, they are used to parade the buying power of our wealth. The year annually renews itself, but somehow its renewal no longer seems to affect *us*. It has little relation to people. I get the impression that New Year's has become little more than an occasion allowing companies and government offices to wind up their annual schedules.

Despite these criticisms, I haven't the slightest intention of urging return to an archaic agricultural society. Nor do I for a moment think it advisable to go back to the old way of counting one's age by the number of New Year's Days he has greeted. I merely wish to ask whether there may not at this time exist the necessity for a greater openness to certain ideas of the past. In particular do I think of the need to keep in mind the pulse of nature and to adopt a way of life that responds to that pulse.

It is obvious that maturation is a natural process which creates its own specific rhythm. Just as farmers plant and harvest crops with respect to the appropriateness of the season, the weather and soil conditions, people should decide how to live by asking themselves how they might best cultivate their lives, how they might tend them and bring them to fruition.

The rhythm of growth, the very pulse of life itself, varies with the individual and differs from day to day, month to month, year to year. But it seems to me that the ring of an extra year of growth will be most vividly and most deeply impressed on a person's mind if the maturation of his life from one year to another is clearly noted each January 1.

The ancients made it clear that the standards by which they lived changed with age. Confucius, for example, presents us with the following standards in the *Analects* (II:4): "At fifteen I set my heart upon learning. At thirty, I had planted my feet firm upon the ground. At forty, I no longer suffered from perplexities. At fifty, I knew what were the biddings of Heaven. At sixty, I heard them with docile ear. At seventy, I could follow the dictates of my own heart; for what I desired no longer overstepped the boundaries of right." Many intellectuals have since used these words as a model for their lives.

I do not find these standards particularly ideal for modern men. But I have great respect for the cool and lucid will power which permeates the sage's approach. He took a step back to observe his life and asked how to perfect himself.

This contrasts with the way so many people live today. They dash ahead with their eyes on the immediate, conquering new worlds, taking in everything, living each moment to the hilt. This certainly seems a vibrant and promising way to live. Still, I cannot resist wondering whether being driven somehow like a horse pulling a wagon can really be to live the way man was meant to live.

In my opinion the ultimate misfortunes befalling modern man stem from several sources. For one thing, he has utterly lost the freedom to observe himself dispassionately in order to discern how his life, a product of his making, is a function of his autonomous free choice.

For another, modern man labors under the illusion that he is what he is not by dint of individual ability and brains but by influences exerted on him from without: by society, by his job, by his teachers. In fact, in our day this is far more than a mere *illusion*. Apparently the problem is that modern man has sold to various powers and organizations the most precious and irreplaceable right to shape his own personal life style.

Statistics tell us that life expectancy has increased slightly. But a small increase does not make life all that long. Nor can we know whether the end will come before our time. This uncertainty may be why man so nonchalantly surrenders control over his life to strangers. It seems to me, however, both essential and fundamental to human dignity to preserve the frame of mind that seeks to create, improve, and perfect our life styles, each in his own way.

In any event, as we face another new year I suspect it is meaningful to concentrate on the problem of how each of us might live as a human being who is true to his own potential.

December 10, 1971

THE TRUE AND THE TRUTH

Nothing moves people more effectively than facts. This is particularly true in a society plagued by distrust and discontinuities. People in such a society are more readily convinced by one solid fact than by one hundred vague assertions.

I heard the following story when pollution was just being recognized as a tremendous threat to our society.

An incident occurred involving chemical wastes discharged into the ocean by an enterprise in an industrial area. The wastes contaminated fish along the shore, giving them a foul taste and making them inedible. Naturally the local fishermen's union demanded long-term compensation. Although officials from the offending enterprise agreed for a time to the union's demand, they subsequently desired to terminate payments, asserting that the problem had been disposed of. But the union, whose members had been deprived of their livelihood, was not convinced.

Company officials racked their brains trying to come up with a way to get by without paying out enormous sums of money. Finally hitting on a plan, they filled a pond on the company grounds with the treated wastes and stocked it with fish. They then planted grass around the pond and opened the site to local citizens as a place to relax on Sundays. The intention was to demonstrate that the wastes were not polluted, thus creating public support for their bid to terminate compensation payments.

The scheme had precisely the result the company intended. The sight of fish swimming in the waste chemicals gave people the impression that the liquid was not polluted. Public opinion favored the company against the union's demands for compensation.

If the word applies, this was indeed an ingenious solution to the company's problem. The incident illustrates—as in the adage that a picture is worth a thousand words—how much more effective it is to present people with one clear fact, even if it amounts to a deliberate deception, than to spend a thousand words making vague assertions. In the end, the company cut off the payments. If only the union had had the wisdom to demonstrate its case as effectively, the fishermen

might not have been forced to give in to the company.

In any event, when I heard this story I could not help being impressed by the force, by the almost magical power, of a single "picture."

I have no doubt that the pond had been filled with waste chemicals. It was also true that fish were swimming in these chemicals, though even that fact offers no clear answer to the doubts that remain. Was the liquid in the pond identical to what the company had been discharging into the ocean? In the long run, would that same waste continue to remain *un*polluted?

Reality is undeniably reality, a fact a fact. These facts were neither false nor imagined. I do not mean to imply that the enterprise concealed the truth, but as a general statement one cannot unconditionally claim that a single true fact represents the whole truth. Though each fact may be true, instances arise when, viewed as a whole, the facts suggest a conclusion quite contrary to the truth. As a matter of fact, the more effectively facts prevent refutation, the more likely that they may be taken as the absolute authority.

Undoubtedly one cannot arrive at truth without a grasp of the facts. At the same time it is not always possible to grasp the truth through a few facts. We have the expression that though a man be heartbroken he must wear a smile on his face. No one contests the reality of his smile. But what we see on his face in no way reveals the truth about how the man really feels.

THE TRUE AND THE TRUTH

Television newscasting demonstrates the same thing. During the past several years clashes between university students and riot police have frequently appeared on our screens. The students tear up city streets, throw homemade bombs and Molotov cocktails. The riot police counter with tear gas and billy clubs. Live scenes of people injuring and killing one another are piped right into our living room. It's enough to make a person ill.

Television cameramen seem intent on capturing the spectacle: now the agonized expressions of students, now the fury of the police assault. I'm sure cameramen burn with the conviction that their mission is to show viewers precisely what is happening. But the average citizen who watches TV in his living room can be shown no more than a specific scene or two in the limited time of the program. It is totally impossible to record the clash in its entirety even if many more cameras were used.

This amounts to a tremendous limitation in television newscasting. Unfortunately the average viewer does not watch the tube with this limitation in mind. Much rather is he inclined to regard the partial scenes he sees as the total picture. Most people have no choice but to construct the whole from the fragments they see.

Thus, if on the one hand the TV shows an impressive scene of riot police dispersing students with fire hoses, the viewer may sympathize with the students and resent police brutality. If on the other hand the TV shows students tearing up the streets and beating

113

up policemen, the result—regardless of the newsmen's intentions—is that viewers may shift their criticism to student violence.

There can be no doubt that every picture constitutes a fact, that each fact represents stark reality. If we then ask whether such facts, true as they may be, systematically reveal the truth, we realize how extremely knotty the problem is.

I intend to respect the facts, for if we do not properly grasp details our judgment is bound to be distorted. At the same time, I think we must avoid the stupidity of regarding truths arrived at through partial descriptions of reality as though they constituted the whole truth.

Certainly there are times when a single fact does tell the whole truth about something. If a fact captures the essence of an issue, even a fragment can give an insight into the whole. But in order to get such an insight, it is necessary to determine whether that single fact really leads to an understanding of the whole.

It seems to me that we need to make special efforts, particularly in these troubled times, to arrive at a synthesis of the facts, painstakingly tying them together before making up our minds about the truth—and doing it without making premature conclusions on the basis of limited data.

My opinion is based on the belief that the antagonisms, conflicts and malice that plague contemporary society arise in the final analysis from the way in which people so readily regard a single fact as the whole truth. I think it no exaggeration to say that hostility in the family, antagonism at work, and even disputes between nations stem from failure to grasp the total picture.

The mere fact that it seems so very plausible to regard one fact as the entire truth makes it easy for those in power to pull the wool over our eyes. Presenting the part as the whole is a hackneyed trick that the common people must have the good sense to see through.

That's precisely why it is necessary for us to take the time to think of possibilities or of facts beyond—and even contradictory to—those presented to us. Particularly with respect to evaluating human beings should we realize that nobody is absolutely good or absolutely bad. Interpersonal relationships require, it seems to me, an attitude of tolerance and a readiness to understand what lies at the bottom of how people act.

I suspect it will take a good deal of wisdom to develop such an attitude and to drive us to seek out the truth implicit in the isolated facts.

December 16, 1971

HISTORICAL RESEARCH AND THE CRITICAL SPIRIT

The other day I read Takehiko Furuta's *Yamatai Never Was,* a book which has recently caused a stir in Japan. The title is quite a shocker, yet Furuta's argument is solid and persuasive. As I read along I became very involved, as though I had been reading a genuine detective story. It is easy to see why the book is so popular.

Over the last several years we have seen the development of a boom in the study of Japan's ancient history. Many fascinating questions are being asked, such as: When did our ancestors come to these islands? What sort of political organization existed in ancient

Japan? How was the country unified? Where was the kingdom the Chinese called "Yamatai"? And now Mr. Furuta calls the very existence of Yamatai into question.

One section of the *Account of the Three Kingdoms* (*San-Kuo chih*), compiled before the end of the third century A.D., states that Yamatai was ruled by Queen Himiko. For some decades there has been a spirited debate over the location of her realm. Two influential theories have developed. One holds that Yamatai was in the Kinki or Yamato region, around present-day Nara and Kyoto. The other holds that it was in Kyushu.

The basic assumption of the author of *Yamatai Never Was* is that the Chinese character used for the *tai* of Yamatai is in error. He further avers that the Kinki and the Kyushu theorists who claim that the Chinese chroniclers meant Yamato when they wrote Yamatai are equally in error. The former theorists maintain that Yamato refers to the Kinki region; the latter, that it refers to a place in Kyushu. Furuta's challenge actually begins at this point. He writes, "Can scholars presume to correct the original text so nonchalantly without offering evidence? I'm naive enough to regard that as suspicious."

Furuta's suspicions extend to the two dominant theories held by historians, particularly to interpretations assuming that certain characters in the original text are copyists' errors or mistakes of some kind or another. He marshals data in great detail to substantiate his novel interpretations.

According to the author, the motive for revising the original text was rooted in the preconception—held by those advocating either the Kinki or the Kyushu theory —that Yamatai must stand for Yamato. This preconception, Furuta argues, has moved scholars to modify any number of places in the original to agree with their interpretation.

By contrast, Furuta starts with the question, What happens if we assume that the Chinese characters used for Yamatai in the original text are correct? He then offers his own conclusions as to the location of Queen Himiko's realm.

Needless to say, I am not qualified to debate the academic merits of Furuta's case, nor can I tell whether his deductions are correct. But at the very least I can say, after having read the book, that his proofs seemed quite convincing in the main. It remains to be seen how specialists in ancient Japanese history will evaluate Furuta's theory.

In any event, as an avid reader I have often had reservations about what scholars have said regarding the location of Yamatai. I have wondered naively why only modern historians seem to debate the issue. According to Furuta, not one first-rate 18th or early 19th century Japanese scholar who looked into the Yamatai question decided that the original text meant to register *Yamato*. That interpretation did not appear until very modern times.

Because I am not well acquainted with Academe and the world of scholarship, it is prudent to refrain from making rash judgments. Nevertheless, it seems certain that the antagonisms between factions of historians at Tokyo and Kyoto Universities—long Japan's leading seats of higher learning—underlie the antagonistic theories on the location of Yamatai. Most scholars trained at or influenced by Tokyo University support the Kyushu theory, while those related to Kyoto University tend to be exponents of the Kinki theory. I do not feel, therefore, that the near polarization of views on this question is based purely on academic grounds.

Until recently Furuta was a high school teacher. That makes him somewhat of an outsider, a "loner" in academic circles. It was probably because he was a loner untainted by preconceptions and loyalties that he was able to carry out the daring research that produced this book.

We cannot know whether Furuta's conclusions will one day be proved, the way the theories of Heinrich Schliemann (1822-90) were substantiated by later scholars. The dauntless Schliemann believed that Homer's descriptions in the *Iliad* and the *Odyssey* were correct. This belief ultimately led to his discovery and excavation of the site of ancient Troy. At the very least, it seems to me *Yamatai Never Was* reveals a similar attitude, one which pursues the path of independent historical research with a passion as extraordinarily tenacious as Schliemann's.

Furuta's book also illustrates the importance of textual criticism. One can ascertain historical truth only through a critical study of ancient texts of significant historical value.

As one who is quite concerned in gaining a proper perspective on history, I think methods of critical inquiry should be applied consistently to all historical research. Actually, that's only proper in view of the fact that history is an academic discipline.

As a matter of fact, the development of modern historical studies owes a great deal to the technique of textual criticism. Nineteenth century historians who studied ancient Greece, the wellspring of Western civilization, gained vital new insights when they critically examined the original sources. The same is true of the history of ancient India, long shrouded in mystery. Scientific elucidation of ancient Sanskrit texts stripped away the shrouds.

In view of these two breakthroughs, it would seem that the scientific analysis of ancient texts has indeed been a vital factor in developing modern historical methodology.

What is important to note here is the meaning of the word *criticism* in the term "textual criticism." We are apt to think it means no more than criticism of whatever runs counter to the modern spirit of rationalism. In our day, the "critical spirit" is a typical manifestation of rationalism; in fact, it is only another way of describing modern man's rational mind-set.

This is not to suggest that such a mind-set is in itself undesirable. Rationality is, however, all too often substituted for common sense so that a person may well be criticized as lacking it if he does something that appears "irrational."

But how can we pretend that such an attitude fits a rational mind-set, in the strict sense of the term? It seems to me that the great trust we moderns put in knowledge is excessively rooted in an uncritical attitude. Note, for example, modern man's astonishingly arbitrary assumption that ancient and medieval times were exceedingly simple and primitive; or note our post-Enlightenment view that the knowledge of premodern men was extremely crude.

Certainly there is a vast difference in the quantity of data available in our times. But facts aren't everything. When we come to the qualitative side, to wisdom and the ability to perceive phenomena and human affairs "in the round," to see them in their relation to the whole—well, it is difficult for me to imagine that we are more advanced than the ancients.

Rather is it not true that, at least in some cases, these "crude" premodern men cherished the kind of wisdom which transcends time itself, and which presents our own age with many profound insights? Is it not possible to have encyclopedic but shallow knowledge and at the same time to be simple-minded and genuine as a human being?

It is necessary to be scrupulously critical in the study

of history. But it is also essential that the critical spirit eliminate as far as possible biases and preconceptions. Then we must address ourselves dispassionately and with a precise focus to the topic of inquiry. If we fail to do so, if our critical eye remains warped, the object of our inquiry will obviously reflect our biases.

December 23, 1971

BETWEEN MACROCOSM AND MICROCOSM

According to a recent news report, a Soviet scientist said, "It now seems possible that some form of life exists on Mars." He made this conjecture on the basis of information received from Mariner III, which has been making a photographic survey of the planet.

H. G. Wells (1866-1946) wrote in his *The War of the Worlds* (1898) about Martians invading Earth. The fact that there might be living creatures on Mars, as Wells imagined, has been suggested by various scholars. Whether or not such creatures do exist, however, has till now been wholly a matter of conjecture, based on data acquired exclusively by viewing the red planet from Earth. But now we shall be able to talk about the results of observations made from Mariner III in orbit around Mars, and so the probe has great significance.

Sending probes deep into space, exploring the moon, observing Mars from close quarters—who could have imagined that man would be doing such things in our day?

Nevertheless, the Mars probe has only barely touched the surface of one planet in our solar system. Will we ever be able to stroll leisurely through the gardens of the infinite macrocosm? At the other end of the scale, in the microcosm, I understand that the unknown increases faster than we can keep up with it. While man spends his life between the macrocosm and the microcosm, what power does he have over either extreme?

It was Blaise Pascal (1623-1662) who said that man was a creature standing between extremes. He wrote in Section 72 of the *Pensées:* "What is man in nature? A Nothing in comparison with the Infinite, an All in comparison with the Nothing, a mean between nothing and everything."

On the grand scale of the macrocosm, which transcends the categories of human imagination, man is smaller than a poppy seed. At the same time, to borrow an expression from Pascal, compared to the minuteness of a drop of blood man is indeed preposterously huge. In short, man floats like a reed in a world between extremes.

BETWEEN MACROCOSM AND MICROCOSM

To what extent has science probed the regions of these extremes?

To begin with the macrocosm, we have the planet Earth and its moon. Beyond them is our solar system, which is part of the Milky Way galaxy, a spiral nebula. This galactic nebula combines with the great spiral in Andromeda and the Megallanic Clouds to form a scattering of galaxies known as the Local Group. Groups of similar galaxies form the macrocosm—this seems as far as our knowledge takes us.

In the microscopic dimension, on the other hand, we find first of all that molecules combine to make up a human being. Of course, molecules consist of atoms, each of which can be split into a nucleus and its electrons. The nucleus can further be split into hundreds of elementary particles. That's as far as we have probed the microcosm, a region which lies beyond the ordinary imagination.

I am quite impressed by the way modern science has so resolutely been pushing into the world of extremes, which Pascal says that man "is infinitely removed from comprehending. . . ."

The ancients apparently understood something of these extremes. They gazed at the heavens and called the handful of stars visible to them the *universe*. They also believed that man, not to mention everything animate and inanimate, was composed of basic particles they called *atoms*. In actuality, however, the microcosm and the macrocosm as we know them are more complex than that. They are composed of several divisions, each of which forms a separate, well-ordered world; in aggregate, these become part of an even greater entity.

When Japanese look into the heavens in July we think of the legend of the Cowherd Star and the Weaver Princess Star—Altair and Veda—who annually cross the Milky Way to meet on the seventh day of the month. It sounds very romantic. By contrast, the scientist sees the Milky Way as a spiral nebula which looks like a saucer in cross section because from Earth it can only be seen edge on. Nevertheless I find it refreshing to have scientists assure us that the universe is not a chaotic conglomeration of matter.

In the human dimension, in society, appropriate laws hold sway. In the dimension of heavenly bodies and atoms we find laws that differ from those ruling the human realm. Because man forgets the laws of the realm immediately beyond himself, of the earth on which he lives, and thinks only of his own self-centered interests, because man puts the pursuit of profit and productivity before everything else, he has created a grave crisis: pollution.

Both the microcosm and the infinite macrocosm operate according to determined regularities and rhythms. Man must have a clear insight into these rhythms and regularities if he is ever to realize that he dare not ignore them.

The vast cosmos and the world of elementary par-

ticles exist in dimensions so remote from man's that we find their laws beyond our imagination. One such law is Einstein's theory of relativity. Albert Einstein, a genius of German-Jewish extraction, based his theory —the pinnacle of modern science—on two simple principles: (a) all movement is relative, and (b) the constant velocity of light is exceeded by no other wave. The conclusions Einstein drew from these principles continue to stagger the imagination.

For example, a person in a rocket departing Earth at near the speed of light finds that time telescopes, material contracts and weight increases. Nor do simple mathematical computations suffice to deal with the relative speed of the rocket. It is quite upsetting to find this theory assert that those on the rocketship will return to Earth like modern-day Rip Van Winkles who failed to age as much as those who remained behind. In a word, Einstein's bold theory obliterates our common sense notions of time and space with its concept of closed four-dimensional areas modeled on the universe itself.

Our imagination is also strained by the microcosm, particularly the unsolved riddles of the elementary particle. In the fourth century B.C. Democritus hypothesized that the smallest unit of matter was the atom. He almost hit the bull's eye, but today we realize that reality is far more complex than that.

Scientists in pursuit of the smallest unit of matter have been forced to conclude that what they have discovered is, ironically, not simple matter. The so-called elementary particle behaves both like a particle and like a wave. On the basis of this hard fact, scientists are in the process of adjusting their understandings of the basic nature of matter.

At first glance, the laws of the macrocosm and the laws of the microcosm seem unrelated. Actually, once we look beyond the surface we find they are closely related.

Einstein's theory of relativity—which laid bare the grand laws of the macrocosm—was later substantiated, I understand, by scientists probing the microcosm of the elementary particle. For one thing, researchers observed that the life of these particles increased as they neared the speed of light. Having encountered the riddles of the elementary particle, modern scientists now attempt to describe the furthest limits of matter using concepts like "energy," "field," or "motion." Presumably the most universal equation of all is based on the quantum field theory, one which describes the elementary particle and which has been modeled on the macrocosm.

It is interesting to note that as both the microcosm and the macrocosm continue to be probed, scientists more and more express their findings in extremely philosophical terms. Is man, that "mean between nothing and everything," destined to struggle zealously to keep from being dominated by materialism?

How shall human energies and the sphere of human

life—existing within a macrocosm unified by orderly laws which are multidimensional and multi-layered— be developed? I cannot help thinking that an answer to this question will force us toward a life philosophy which sees man as part of the universe.

December 28, 1971

THE ROOTS OF
CONCEPTUALIZATION

I spent the first several days of January on the outskirts of Fujinomiya, a town in the foothills of Mt. Fuji. The mountain seemed close enough to touch. Though quite familiar with the scene, I was struck with what seemed a greater than usual crispness.

Without a single cloud in the lucid sky, the morning sun dazzled the snow on the pure-white peak. A second glance revealed how the mountain's gentle slope seemed to melt into Suruga Bay, not far off, beyond which the Izu Peninsula stood out with surprising clarity.

Once again I was deeply moved by the simple but vigorous beauty of nature. The clearness of the air may have been a momentary phenomenon resulting from the temporary shutdown of factories over the New Year holidays. When they start up again, I suppose man-made smog will soon blanket the area, and Suruga Bay, hidden by the haze, will no longer be visible. But the crispness of that scene made me aware that the simple beauty of nature retains its essence despite our smog.

Things that strike us as beautiful fall into two classes: those which are simple and those which are complex. It isn't necessarily true everything in nature is simple and everything man made is complex. Generally speaking, however, even what seems to be a complicated pattern in nature is fundamentally quite simple, while the beauty of man-made things may at first glance seem simple and yet, on closer examination, turn out to be quite elaborate. Apparently, our sense of beauty is perfectly capable of responding to either the simple or the complex type.

The temperament of each individual probably determines which type takes greater priority. Nevertheless it does seem that modern man's sensitivity to beauty has come to favor the complex and the subtle. And there certainly is a tendency for simplicity to shade off into flatness. Perhaps it is natural that people dissatisfied with that sort of thing would turn to something more delicate, more elaborate.

I sometimes wonder whether we have not made too many things too delicate and too elaborate. Isn't it true that at times these attempts at studied and well-wrought delicacy ironically end up producing dimensionless stereotypes?

I don't mean to generalize from my personal taste. Nor is it my intention to make the radical plea that we should, for example, reject everything that is man made. All I wish to say is that I wonder if our civilization does not need at this time to return once again to uncomplicated basic principles if we ever hope to escape getting lost in what seems a maze of things that are too extremely complicated.

We are often made aware of the complexities of modern life. For example, in a society where people's stakes and interests are so intricately intermeshed, we certainly need the organs of bureaucracy. Nor do we have a choice but to create systems of law that cover extremely minute particulars. For the very reason that they have become so necessary, however, what happens is that these institutions and laws soon come to exist for their own sake, and they begin to weigh heavily on our autonomy. Ironically, liberties are then restricted and the original purpose of these human institutions readily becomes forgotten and betrayed.

Complexity also seems to characterize the essence of the human mind. The more we analyze it, the more dispassionately we study it with the unjaundiced eye of reason, the more we find elements that are unfathomable. In our efforts to come to grips with these elements, we discover that we must further refine our analytical methods. We can see how this occurs in the attempt to search out the depths of the human mind, to probe beyond superficial behavior to the deep layers of the psyche and to the subconscious. I wonder, however, whether we can perfectly grasp and express the truths that lie at the extremities of these probes in terms of analytical logic alone.

The attempt to do so is, needless to say, never totally meaningless. If one forgets that it is a human being he is dealing with, however, it makes little difference how repeatedly he applies a certain concept to the facts, for it is unlikely that his understanding of man will be deepened. Unless we are cautious, it may be that such attempts will do no more than lead us deeper into an interminable maze.

This is not meant to imply that I think I'm the only one who has had second thoughts about scientific approaches to understanding human beings. Far from it. But it bears repeating to call attention to the fact that whenever a person becomes involved in the forest of words that surrounds subtle speculations and gets more lost in the maze, he has no choice but to return once again to the starting point, to simple basic principles.

It is interesting to note that whenever Western philosophy tended to become ingrown, when it began to practice philosophy for the sake of philosophy and became clad in all sorts of complicated terminology, there were always those who invariably went back to basics. They stressed the teachings of Socrates, Descartes and Rousseau, thinkers who needless to say had the wisdom to deal with fundamental principles. Socrates stressed "Know thyself," Descartes verified his

existence by thinking, Rousseau urged man to "Return to nature."

A moment's reflection suggests that the concepts lying behind these statements are not at all complicated. Rather, I feel convinced that in each case they reveal exceedingly simple and unsophisticated basic principles.

Of course the process of thought these sages went through to discover these truths was far from simple. In most cases, these discoveries resulted from the accumulation of insights into a single phenomenon as these thinkers came face to face with some heroic challenge to their work.

I merely wish to emphasize two facts: first, that the discoveries and truths which have influenced history are certainly not complex, and second, that the antecedents of truths which ultimately affected history lie in clear and simple first principles.

Once Columbus had discovered the New World, his feat seemed very ordinary. Indeed, once any great undertaking or discovery has been accomplished it no longer seems beyond the capability of ordinary men. To the contrary, it appears quite commonplace, quite unextraordinary. It is nevertheless nearly impossible for the average person to generate the courage and the resolution to probe areas of his daily life that are usually taken for granted and thus overlooked: areas which, we might say, are too ordinary for us to concern ourselves about. It takes great courage, not only to cast light on these areas but to carve out of them universal truths.

Behind the activities and probes of the philosopher and the mastermind, I am sure there lies an epoch-making conception, a latent discovery which at first glance average people would find hardly worth paying attention to. It is primarily because these men have paid attention to such "ordinary" ideas that their names occupy a place in history.

In our day, it seems we are being flooded with a surge of knowledge. In the wake of this flood we tend to overlook the concepts and the discoveries which have in the past created the sort of sparkling values stressed by these great philosophers.

In order to determine whether one particular philosophy is superior to another, I think it vital to extricate ourselves from trying to decide its complexity or simplicity. We must ask instead to what extent the philosophy is capable of producing truly creative concepts.

At the basis of any superior system of thought one will assuredly find concepts so common to experience that anyone can grasp them, that anybody can understand and respond sympathetically to them. A philosophy unrelated to the people's everyday life and feelings amounts to little more than empty words, even though it boasts a splendid system.

I am inclined to believe that the sources of concepts which plumb the very depths of life itself cannot be uprooted no matter how deep you dig, and that the concepts themselves are to be found only in the sweat and the heat of human life itself.

January 10, 1972

GOODNESS, BADNESS

In the third essay of this series I recall having discussed André Malraux's intention to join the Bengali Liberation Army. In the wave of excitement over whether the French writer would actually join, India liberated Bangladesh. At this date there is no way of ascertaining what Malraux had in mind in offering to fight for that independence.

It is quite clear, however, that the Bengali independence movement created a new nation from East Pakistan. The passing of the years has in fact witnessed an increase in the number of nations in the world, as illustrated by the division of Germany into East and West and of Korea into North and South. The chance for a world federation—the hope of so many people across the globe—seems to be fading.

The countless East Pakistani refugees who fled to India presented a wretched spectacle. No less wretched, no less repelling, were scenes of retaliation meted out to traitors by those in the liberated areas. Bengalis showed no mercy in taking stern measures against the Bihari, who cried desperately to be spared.

People apparently find it necessary to take revenge when a rebellion is over. Recall the guillotine made famous by the French Revolution or the purges that followed the Russian Revolution. Oppressed people perpetrate outrageous acts of violence to vent their wrath. In expiating the crimes committed against them, they commit even more heinous crimes. Alas, man remains incapable of extricating himself from this chain reaction of malevolence.

Only when an animal is confronted with starvation, a radical crisis, will he kill and eat one of his own species. Human beings, by contrast, kill one another on impulse, to gain personal advantage, for ideological reasons, for sport. Either side in a feud is convinced that it is absolutely in the right and its enemy absolutely in the wrong. Thus does each justify coercion or retaliation against coercion. It grieves me to see a "justice" which sanctions taking human life.

If we regard wars in the light of this pattern, we find that either nation in a dispute inevitably asserts that justice is on its side, that it alone is right, that its

opponent is the personification of evil. A classic example of this attitude is our own government which, during World War II, cursed the "Anglo-American devils." But I wonder whether it is ever possible to discriminate so sharply between goodness and badness.

This brings to mind a short story which describes how good men banded together to foment a revolution. Asserting that the depraved always seem to hold power and the upright always seem oppressed, these men thought that peace would come only if the genuinely virtuous seized power, only if the wicked were liquidated. Based on the belief that revolutionaries alone are "pure," the rebels refused to acknowledge that they were capable of the slightest evil. Their thinking persistently revealed the "just cause" mind-set, one which asserts that a society of virtuous men cannot possibly be realized until after the wicked are eradicated. The story was charged with bitter irony, however, for in the end the reader suspects that it may have been the "virtuous" conspirators who were, as a group, inadvertently transformed into the most depraved of wicked men.

In *The Heart (Kokoro),* published in 1914, the novelist Natsume Soseki (1867-1916) touched on the possibility of differentiating between those who are virtuous and those who are wicked. We find the following passage in the last will and testament of the man whom the "hero" of *Kokoro* regarded as his mentor:

"You probably remember my having told you that there is no such thing in our world as people who are innately evil, and that you should be on guard because a virtuous man will frequently turn into a scoundrel without warning if the occasion demands." In this passage Soseki pungently probes a strange riddle of the human heart: nobody so readily becomes a scoundrel as a virtuous man.

Buddhist life philosophy expounds the "Ten Realms," a concept which divides man's existence into ten states. The lowest state is hell, the highest is enlightenment or the realm of the Buddhas. The most typically human state, man's realm, stands midway between these extremes. Most men exist, so to speak, between the best and the worst possible states. This philosophy maintains, moreover, that man's inherent tendency is to be influenced—internally and externally—toward either extreme. It seems to me that this is a profound insight into the essence of the human condition.

Good and evil, heaven and hell, the pure and the impure. Many people in the West have been concerned with such polarities and think in terms of mutually antagonistic principles. The concepts of spirit and flesh most aptly illustrate this polarity. Spirit is regarded as the never-failing path to God; flesh is seen as leading to destruction and darkness. What this implies is that one will be saved only if he rejects the flesh and earnestly turns to things of the spirit.

This polarity suggests the simple conclusion that spirit is good and flesh is evil. Those who see good and evil as antagonistic either-or's and the spirit and the body as polarities will constantly be forced into choosing one or the other alternative.

People may say flesh is evil. But the stark reality of man's existence is that he is bound to his flesh. Even if he rejects it and seeks to identify with the spirit, the fact is that as long as he is alive he cannot avoid struggling between the two dimensions. In the final analysis, this polarity drives a person to the conclusion that he cannot experience the Good in this life and must look forward to life after death: in short, to Heaven. Moreover, from the viewpoint of men who do not believe in Heaven, life on earth is nothing more than hell itself, hence their nihilistic expressions.

Even to this day, many Westerners not only practice extreme forms of asceticism and austerities as means of seeking perfection, they persist in hedonistic and nihilistic attitudes which likely stem from the polarization of good and evil.

But good and evil are not in the least an either-or polarity. Man is rather a coherent being who harbors tendencies toward good and toward evil. Men must discern this truth in the unclouded mirrors of their innate wisdom. Once they do, those who are virtuous will no longer suddenly become scoundrels, nor will they continue to force people to become hypocrites in their pursuit of goodness.

It seems to me it is the same with the ego, which in modern times has been regarded as the source of so much evil in man. Though capable of goodness or

146

wickedness, the ego is not of itself evil. If we assume that it is, then (as with the flesh) as long as man lives he will be the embodiment of evil, and he will never solve the problems posed by his ego. In a word, the issue is to discover how to capitalize on and guide man's ego by means of a value orientation that will lead him away from evil.

In order to do that, we have no choice but to perceive the ego realistically as something with the potential to be influenced one way or the other. Since man can plumb the depths of knowledge about human life, he is capable of such a perception. It is for this reason that I think we have made a major step forward in shifting the focus of concern from the impasses of contemporary civilization to the depths of the inner man, to the ego.

Beyond that, much seems to depend on the extent to which man can overcome his perennial tendency toward arrogance, and on whether he can then humbly and accurately begin imitating his true self, the self latent with possibilities for good. I have the feeling that this will be our task for the turbulent year ahead.

January 17, 1972

THE DAY OF OPPORTUNITY

The Japan National Railways (JNR) will at last begin construction of an experimental super-express scheduled to negotiate the distance between Tokyo and Osaka in one hour. If the JNR succeeds in making this express operational, Japan will have a train that travels at better than 310 miles an hour.

Transportation in our country will take another step forward when a section of the new Sanyo Line opens in March, 1972. This line further shrinks our islands, making western Honshu more accessible to travelers. Visitors to the area will certainly increase, thus bringing people in that section of Japan into direct contact with many from other parts of the country. Truly, our world is shrinking.

Ironically, however, the distance between men's minds is not shrinking. In fact, people have never been more alienated from one another than in our age. How many in their teens and twenties identify with the way people in their forties and fifties live and think? How many youth model themselves on adult life and thought? I would guess that perhaps ninety percent of the young are repelled by, and look critically on, the life style and ideas of the older generation.

A clear indication of the rejection of adult values can be seen in the sad plight of our traditional arts and entertainments. These historical possessions, handed down from our ancestors, are in danger of dying out because young people are unwilling to carry on the tradition. The chasm between college teachers and their students may also indicate the seriousness of our contemporary generation gap.

It is unnecessary to get philosophical in order to illustrate the rejection of old values. Take the example of the woman who shouts for help when her purse is snatched. We are no longer surprised to read in the newspaper that not a finger was raised to help her. In fact, we live in a time when it would be front page news if a passerby cooperated to apprehend the purse snatcher.

In typical modern cities like Washington, D.C. and New York, people have for some time been unable to walk about safely at night. Despite the fact that the politics and economics of the free world depend on

what happens during the daytime in these metropolitan areas, at night they turn into anarchistic jungles. One truly takes his life in his hands merely to walk a block without a bodyguard through certain sections of these cities.

Even at the apex of contemporary civilization we find areas clouded by distrust and mutual suspicion. This brings to mind an era in human history which bears striking resemblance to the situation in modern urban centers. I refer to the last days of the Roman Empire, a technological civilization characterized by great architectural skill and exulting in unprecedented prosperity.

The Colosseum symbolized that prosperity. There were also aqueducts spanning the valleys and crossing the fields of the Empire; their ruins can be seen in Gaul (central France) and Spain. The largest aqueduct rose to a height of 160 feet, rivalling high-rise apartment buildings in modern cities.

In contrast to the architectural splendor of the Empire was the plight of the masses in Rome, holding body and soul together on daily handouts of food. As the poet Juvenal wrote, the people longed for "bread and circus games." It was by games in the Colosseum —brutal contests between man and beast—that the rulers tried to keep the plebeians from becoming melancholy and bored. Handouts and gory entertainment dampened political discontent and provided an outlet for frustrations.

THE DAY OF OPPORTUNITY

The methods used by the administrators of ancient Rome to placate the populace seem to resemble the stress in our milieu on leisure activities. There also seems a similarity between the interest our society shows in pornography and the chaotic sexual morality of the Roman aristocracy.

Whether in literature or the arts, might we not say that toward the end of the Empire the Romans had lost the vibrant creativity that characterized their early period and had become culturally static? And do we not find ourselves in a similar position today?

In the summer of 1971, President Nixon pointed out the close affinity between the last days of the Roman Empire and our present age. He sounded a warning against the direction which the United States was taking, citing the resemblance between American life and the declining society of the later Romans. His warning has relevance for Japanese society, too.

Even the potent Roman Empire, which not only held the lands bordering the Mediterranean in the palm of its hand but had also conquered distant Gaul and Britannia, was eventually destroyed by invading Germanic tribes. Some scholars say the primary reason for Rome's fall was not external but internal. At the height of glory, the Romans sought instant pleasure and thus their society rapidly disintegrated.

Rome fell like a gigantic tree that toppled over after having been honeycombed by termites. What were the reasons for its internal disintegration?

In its later days, the Empire suffered from moral confusion. Various ideas and religions had been imported, but none was capable of becoming a spiritual asset, none could shore up Rome's mammoth civilization. Eschatological teachings alone were able to make headway through the confusion.

The following passage, taken from a letter by a martyred Christian leader, illustrates: "In winter, we haven't enough rain for seeds to sprout; in summer, we haven't enough sunlight for grain to grow. . . . Impartiality has disappeared from the Forum, justice from our courts, harmony from friendships. . . . A nation walking the path of decadence and approaching its demise cannot prevent its people from decline. This is God's judgment on the world; it is His justice."

The sparks of a vibrant and hopeful life, the necessary driving force behind creation of a new culture, cannot be sensed in these words. Whenever a society becomes dominated by eschatological thought, by the hope that happiness lies beyond this life, that society can expect but one end: death.

We find a parallel case in Japanese history following the late ninth century. In those days, the last years of the Heian Era, there was wide circulation of the idea that the period of *Mappo* had begun, that degenerate times marked the end of Buddha's law. People in the late Heian accordingly no longer sought to be spared from the trials of their world. They looked instead for salvation in the world to come, hoping avidly for a paradise after death. This attitude has been vividly, albeit grotesquely, described by the novelist Ryunosuke Akutagawa in his story *Rashomon* (1915).

What does history teach us about how a dying culture comes back to life, how a new culture might be fashioned on the ashes of the old?

The Germanic tribes which swept through areas within the sphere of Roman civilization were themselves engulfed by Rome's decadence. But how did the Muslims manage, some centuries later, to absorb the superior civilization they encountered in the Roman sphere, refurbish it and create their own unique culture? Certainly there were important differences between the primitive beliefs of the Germanic tribes and the relatively sophisticated Islamic religion of the Muslims. Note, for instance, that only after Christianity had penetrated to the grassroots could the Germanic tribes resurrect, as it were, the Roman genius, the spirit of "eternal Rome."

Perhaps the same holds true for the turbulent conditions of the late Heian. It was, notably, Kamakura Buddhism which stimulated new signs of life in the cultural decline of that era.

Simply put, we can say that culture and civilization are *ways of life*. The unique life style of the Muslims created a specifically Muslim culture in the Near East, just as the unique life style and thought patterns of the Kamakura warrior class created an entirely new cultural phenomenon in Japan. This is no less true in our day. If our civilization is to mature along humanistic lines, if we hope to prevent its demise, we must resolutely bring to fruition ideas, a religion and a philosophy of life that are unshakably steadfast.

In any event, it seems the time has come for us to bid adieu to days when we could aimlessly and compulsively fritter away the opportunities that now face us.

January 23, 1972

THOUGHTS ON THE LUNAR ECLIPSE

On January 30, 1972, I viewed a rare total eclipse of the moon from Okinawa.

Rotating on its axis once every twenty-four hours, the earth revolves around the sun in a grand elliptical orbit. One cycle takes about 365 days. And the moon revolves around the earth, staying as close as a child clinging to its mother's arm.

When the orbits of the sun, earth and moon bring them into a straight line with our globe in the middle, earth's shadow falls on the moon and we have a lunar eclipse. This unrehearsed cosmic drama of heavenly bodies, featuring the earth's shadow slowly blacking out the moon, was exceptionally beautiful on smog-free Okinawa.

A solar eclipse, by contrast, occurs when the orbit of the moon brings it directly between the sun and the earth. Where the moon casts its shadow on our earth, we have a solar eclipse. As far as those frantically providing the necessities of life are concerned, the exquisite movements of heavenly bodies through outer space are incomprehensibly unhurried. It is nevertheless impossible to view an eclipse without being mysteriously moved by the thought that these bodies follow clearly discernible rhythms.

Heavenly bodies move systematically and silently, never deviating from their orbits. They provide us with changes in the seasons, with the ebb and flow of the tides. But how often has man, forgetting that the regular rhythms of the universe impartially watch over every living thing on earth, strayed from his "orbit" and engaged in the folly of dissension?

Modern scientists, observing the regularities of solar and lunar eclipses, have analyzed the precise orbits of these heavenly bodies. Based on their analyses, we moderns can enjoy an eclipse as an objective spectacle. But the ancients, who viewed the universe with awe and reverence, feared eclipses as ill omens—an understandable reaction in light of their ignorance of the heliocentric Copernican theory. Nor could ancient men be expected to have known anything of Newton's law of universal gravitation.

Thoughts on the Lunar Eclipse

Even in our day, when one would think that knowledge of natural science is universal, there are places where ignorance of these theories and laws still exists. The truth of this is illustrated by a recent news dispatch of tragic bloodletting in Cambodia.

Apparently Cambodians continue to believe that phenomena like lunar eclipses are the work of evil spirits trying to hide the moon. Because of this deeply-rooted belief, I hear that whenever an eclipse occurs Cambodians follow the ancient custom of ringing bells and gongs to chase the spirits away. During the January lunar eclipse a number of Cambodian soldiers spent about an hour firing their automatic rifles at the moon to chase off the evil spirits. Three innocent civilians were killed by stray bullets and several dozen others were wounded. It is an unbelievable story!

This incident reveals how fearful superstition can be. Whenever it is superstition and no more, existing in areas unrelated to people's daily lives, it causes little harm. But whenever superstitions surface in the form of lunacy, as in the sad news from Cambodia, they are a completely different matter; they are disastrous.

Needless to say, superstitions are not limited to eclipses of heavenly bodies. For example, both in politics and in fields of economic activity, there is widespread antipathy toward the Jews. And the superstition that the Aryan race must preserve the purity of their line culminated in the frenzied attempt at genocide in which Jews were not even regarded as human beings.

Or take the superstition that economic growth is the symbol of prosperity. As a result of this belief, we assume that environmental pollution is unavoidable and allow it to dehumanize us, afflicting the innocent with incurable diseases.

How is it that superstitions refuse to die out? Perhaps their tenacity indicates that human beings must believe in something. The ancients stood equally in awe of the sun and of fire. Even in Japan during the prehistoric Jomon period, the *haniwa* figurines set up around the tombs of great men reveal that the people believed in something. In our day, many put faith in such things as materialism and humanism.

Perhaps we can say that signs of humility in men— the admission that there must be unknown worlds and unknown truths beyond our shallow intellect—are the beginnings of faith. Humility may also arise from the intuition that, irrespective of the natural phenomenon involved, everything is ultimately related to human life.

Viewed from a milieu in which science has developed to a high level, the faiths of the past perhaps seem little more than superstition. In societies of the future, where science will be further advanced, some scholars predict that superstition will disappear but religion will survive. Superstition is that which runs counter to the knowledge of modern science or man's good judgment; religion is that which not only harmonizes with science and human judgment but embraces and transcends them.

In that sense, we are forced to say that a faith which justifies depriving people of life or livelihood, and which without reason fears such phenomena as solar and lunar eclipses, is not really faith at all. It makes no difference how complex its dogma or how adorned with theology it might be, such a faith is no better than superstition.

Although we must oppose superstition to the end, one problem we need to investigate anew is whether every thought of the ancients was laced with superstition. In view of the many superstitions existing before scientific knowledge and rationalism were widespread, most modern men tend to discount even ancient man's faith as a kind of superstition. The news from Cambodia is perhaps the best example of how we do this. Actually, however, the truth is that ancient man in his wisdom quite frequently had penetrating insights into the meaning of natural phenomena.

For example, we can see in the Hindu classics that, instead of being especially terrified, men in ancient India regarded solar and lunar eclipses as portents of disturbances on the sun. They feared that sunlight would diminish as a result. This suggests the insight that cosmic dust drifting in outer space or particles in Earth's atmosphere might intercept the sun's light. Even modern scientists would doubtlessly consider either possibility an ill omen.

162

Thoughts on the Lunar Eclipse

In a day when it is possible that such phenomena will occur, it would be perilous to disregard the meaning of cosmic omens sent to us thousands of years ago across distant space.

The movements of the heavenly bodies are intricate and complex. It is a fact, however, that these movements are reliable. They never deceive us. No doubt it is the province of philosophy and religion to give accurate insights into the essential nature of cosmic movements and to make our lives on earth more complete. But what kind of religion, what kind of philosophy, will most effectively touch and renew our present age? Though it cannot be easy, is this not a task to which we must address ourselves?

February 7, 1972

163

THOUGHTS ON THE WINTER OLYMPICS

We have just seen the gay conclusion of the Sapporo Winter Olympic Games, youth's festival of ice and snow.

The 70 meter jump, in which Japanese skiers took the gold, silver and bronze medals, was the highlight of the Games. That was the first happy news I've heard in a long time.

I watched the Games on television. Naturally, I became more involved whenever Japanese athletes with a chance to place participated. I was not particularly acquainted with them, nor for that matter do I especially cheer them even in domestic competition. But whenever a sportsman engages first-class international opponents I somehow seem to feel close to him and find myself driven by the desire to see him win. Perhaps everyone in Japan felt the same during the Olympics.

This feeling seems common to all peoples. For example, I understand that Austrians staunchly supported the skier disqualified in the wake of the stormy debate over amateur status that preceded the Games.

Just the other day newspapers reported that when the skier in question returned to Austria, the Minister of Education met him at the airport. There was a parade to the Minister's official residence where some ten thousand people had gathered despite a drizzle. Among conservative "outs" some politicians even urged awarding the athlete a medal for his sacrificial act. It appeared as though he had returned "in the triumph of victory."

What is the source of such abnormally heated sentiments? Needless to say, they are forced to the surface by the consciousness of relatedness, by a people's shared awareness of belonging to the same country, of knowing they are Austrians or Japanese. Despite the fact that all human beings are brothers on a level beyond racial or national differences, we must recognize that each individual is naturally aware of his relatedness to a race or a nation, and that he has feelings of prejudice toward others.

There are, I suppose, various views as to whether national consciousness is good or bad. Some have, as a matter of fact, stated opinions against the stress on national honor and prestige in the modern Olympic movement. For example, here and there one hears critics call for reforming the system where nation competes against nation; they would put a stop to playing national anthems and raising national colors.

Perhaps it is unnecessary to become overly concerned about the way athletes try so hard to live up to the expectations of their countrymen, or about the way people so fanatically cheer their sportsmen. After all, do we not see a similar phenomenon at annual Field Day celebrations in schools across our nation? I suspect that the parent beaming over his child's participation has very much the same state of mind.

It is interesting that human beings feel so sympathetic toward their own kind. We do not become too concerned about that which seems far removed from our personal interests, no matter how worthy the problem. But if the matter relates directly to us, we feel a powerful attachment. We have this feeling first of all toward whatever we regard as "mine" as opposed to what belongs to others: my family, my native town, my country. We have no trouble feeling close to them. The national consciousness of the man on the street thus seems motivated by sound natural human feelings, which give his nationalism a potential for good.

That is why I think we should actively remonstrate against unnecessarily inculcating the kind of nationalism that molds people's feelings from above. What misery, what tremendous catastrophe, has been wrought by fanatic nationalism! I have firsthand experience of it: relatives killed, my home destroyed. We all know, moreover, that just such narrow nationalism constitutes one of the most implacable barriers to the peaceful solidarity of the world.

But when we look at contemporary young people, it seems that their nationalism lacks the powerful coercive power it had a generation or so ago. I think the reason is that the feeling of sacrifice "for the nation" has been extremely diluted. This may be an indication of the younger generation's tendency to mistrust "the system" whose values they have not accepted. I find this an extremely healthy trend.

In light of this questioning attitude, the nationalism that appears in the Olympic Games certainly seems far from gloomy. Because athletes representing various nations happen to take to the field on a worldwide scale, each fan instinctively becomes aware of his identification with the athletes.

Proof of this can be seen in the Games themselves. Fans do not always root exclusively for athletes representing their own nation, but spontaneously cheer and admire a superior performance, even if the athlete represents a different country. That is why I personally think there is no need to become pessimistic about what this display of nationalism augurs for the future of the peaceful solidarity of our world.

In a sense, a man's values are created in the crucible of interpersonal relationships. If athletes compete only

with their countrymen, neither they nor the fans will feel a strong awareness that they are Japanese. Instead, the basis for cheering athletes is the degree of relatedness the observer feels with them.

When we have an international contest, by contrast, national feelings obviously come to the fore. Consequently, in such competition it is vital that we not deny the natural human tendency to feel related to athletes representing one's homeland. Should we not rather try to direct that feeling into channels that will influence correct human values?

In other words, I wonder if the problem is not to discover the sort of human relations needed in order to build world peace without sinking into narrow nationalism. These relationships will inspire each individual to awareness of a closer connection with all human beings rather than with his countrymen.

If we look dispassionately at the problem, we discover that our civilization finds itself in new circumstances. The situation today demands that we expand awareness of each other as members of the human race. Problems on every side force us to see that our fate is bound up with the fate of all men. These problems include nuclear weapons, environmental pollution, disintegration of the spirit.

Each of these problems compels us to realize that we face new challenges. The issue now is, how can we band together as men in order to reform our values, to change our awareness, to realize that each of us is a part of all humanity?

In former days many believed that institutional reforms, particularly socialist theories of revolution, transcended national consciousness. People expected much of such theories. Looking at recent antagonisms between the Soviets and the Chinese, however, there is reason to wonder whether socialism is able to overcome discontinuities separating nations or even class consciousness.

The problem is that we deal with man's feelings, which cannot be controlled by theories, ideologies or even utopias. If one ignores human feelings, even the loftiest theory will amount to little more than a parcel of empty words.

Men are naturally endowed with a consciousness of kinship. The question is how we might alter that consciousness and raise it to a higher level—to a level where each man can feel kinship with all men, where each can view the whole scene rather than only his own segment of it. I feel quite certain that we must move beyond reform of our theories and our thinking. We must also make reforms in the dimension of life and in the values which form our life style.

February 14, 1972

DEATH OF A JOURNALIST

The eminent journalist Edgar Parks Snow (b. 1905), author of such books as *Red Star over China* (1938), has died. He was sixty-six. Scheduled to accompany reporters covering Nixon's China visit, he passed virtually on the eve of that visit. It was truly regrettable, certainly for Snow himself but also for America and China as well.

Along with such early China observers as Agnes Smedley, I think Snow was one of the few who truly understood China. He may also have been the most influential. By now many of the insights presented in his coverage of China are common knowledge, although they were definitely radical minority opinions when he first announced them. He dedicated himself to China, staking his life on those opinions. He was indeed a journalist whose unprecedented life was blessed with a task fulfilled.

He first went to China in 1928 when he was twenty-two. Subsequently he spent time there as a newspaper correspondent. Near the end of 1935, students from Yenching University staged a demonstration in the streets of Peking, giving impetus to a nationwide anti-Japanese movement. He says in reflections recorded in *Journey to the Beginning* (1958) that plans for the student outbreak were worked over in his living room. He told his wife then that he could not silently stand by and watch a woman he loved being raped, and that Peking was really a lovely old woman.

For Snow, that may have been the most decisive moment of his life. He stepped well beyond the limits allowed an on-the-scene reporter. But his decision to become involved in China's history provided the impetus for putting his life on the line to get the facts. In 1936, after a journey of many hardships, he arrived in Yenan where he met Mao Tse-tung, Chou En-lai, Chu Teh and other Chinese Communist Party leaders. He was the first foreigner to enter the Chinese soviet areas.

He writes that when he left for Yenan he was conscious of having crossed the Rubicon. He was passionately excited about what his trip meant for the future. In those days the soviet areas were wrapped in mystery. There was a confusion of speculations, propaganda and counter-propaganda about them. Those in the soviets were called "Red Bandits." Although Snow was on the scene and observed the arms race which developed between the two sides in the struggle, he never thought of the communists as evil. He wanted to see the soviets with his own eyes.

There were dangers in the trip. But he could not suppress his compelling passion to discover the way things really were. He relates how during the many years of civil war in China thousands of lives had been sacrificed; would it not be worth gambling one Caucasian neck to discover the truth about the situation in China? He was quite attached to the neck in question, but he concluded that even if he had to pay the ultimate price it was worth trying. He wrote that he left for Yenan with the feeling that he was being somewhat histrionic.

I think we can accept this as having been the way he really felt at that moment. *Red Star over China,* resulting from his experience in Yenan, literally awakened the interest of the entire world in what the communists were doing in China. Though Snow was not a communist, his candid sympathy as a human observer permeates every line of his account. He adamantly maintained his objectivity as a reporter. That was the reason he was able to describe in so vivid a manner objects which were in danger of being distorted by superficial observation.

Even in the wake of deteriorating American relations with the Chinese communists following the end of the Pacific War, a time when journalists found it difficult to enter China, Edgar Snow continued to receive preferential treatment. Peking's policy was that American newsmen were not welcome in China. But Chou En-lai explained to Snow that the reason the Chinese made an exception in his case was that they did not welcome him as a journalist but as a writer and a historian. Snow's response was that it made little difference to him, in that "other world called China," whether he was regarded as a historian, a writer or a correspondent. What was essential was to be there, to observe and to write.

Observation is seeing the facts as they are. If only one has the eye for it, anyone should be able to discern the facts. But seeing events as they are is quite difficult. It is not even easy to observe natural phenomena, so how much more difficult the task of observing complex social phenomena in which there are so many elements to distort and cloud one's view, in which there are so many complications?

Whenever ideology, the views of factions, or even the theory of the state is involved, the observer cannot help being aware of them. Unconsciously an observer might frequently be hampered by his awareness. At such times, since he would be caught up in preconceptions and mind-sets, the reporter cannot expect to observe events accurately. Certainly Edgar Snow was not the only journalist in China during this early period of the revolution. I'm sure a good deal of reporting was going on. But other reporters were likely more

constricted by their preconceptions and accordingly unable to penetrate the chaos of the actual situation as Snow did.

If we probe a bit deeper into the problem, it seems uncontestable that the basic necessity if one wants the facts is an observer uninvolved and without preconceptions. It may seem contradictory, but I wonder whether it is not indispensable for such an observer to have something like a view of history—a view in a higher dimension and differing from shallow preconceptions. It seems to me that having such a perspective gives an observer a long-range view of history.

There is no reason to complicate the issue by making a philosophical analysis of history. I wish only to point out that the perspective I have in mind originates in the observer's deep human sympathy for what he observes. Edgar Snow, who opposed groundless reports that communist troops were "tyrannical bandits," was spurred on to search out the truth about the matter because he doubted the reports. And he doubted them on the basis of his instincts as a naive human being. It seems, moreover, that one's understanding of observed events derives from an ability to discern where foreign elements exist.

In our contemporary society, we have a nearly excessive amount of observation and reporting. Beyond the excess, however, I wonder whether our reporting does not try less and less to grapple with a single object and view it continuously over a period of time. One reason may be that the events and problems to be reported change so rapidly that reporters can barely keep up with them. At the same time I wonder whether we have not already been utterly sapped of the energy to make the kind of penetrating observations Snow made in China.

Certainly the death of Edgar Snow marks the passing of a man who indefatigably observed a period of chaos in Chinese history and doggedly pursued the truth about it.

February 19, 1972

IMPRESSIONS

It has been some time since taking excursions turned from being merely a thing almost everybody did to an established way to use leisure time. When a person can get near the verdure of trees and the fresh air and fragrances that waft through them, when he can get away from the tumult and gritty friction of the city, the world of poetic sentiment and history comes alive. For those living in our contemporary urban areas, perhaps excursions to the countryside provide a utopia "hidden in the sheaves," a respite allowing momentary escape from the suffocation of daily life in the city.

But recently I have been so pressed by everyday business that I have had no chance whatsoever to know the joys of the leisurely tourist. And so, whenever I do have time for recreation in a natural setting, I often find myself becoming absorbed in a poetic mood. I let my imagination go and think of the Kiso Road— one of the few places in Japan where traditional landscapes have not completely disappeared. Or of Nara— the ancient capital, the cradle of our nation. I picture myself wandering around such places, strolling through what the poet Basho (1644-94) called "the aftermath of dreams," dreams of dead warriors who carved their niches in history.

One popular route tourists take this year, I understand, covers places mentioned in the *Tale of the Taira,* a mid-thirteenth century historical tale of the rise and fall of a military clan. Last year the favored targets for excursions were apparently the villages of Shiredoko in Hokkaido and Yagyu in Nara. Lately, the young people have been thronging to Guam. Isn't it somewhat ironic that the places tourists flock in escaping the excessive racket of the mass media are the very places they have become familiar with through popular songs, newscasts, and television dramas?

Is it modern man's fate that he cannot, after all, escape entrapment by a gigantic "managed society"? And that the mass media are to pursue him, even into havens where his inborn inclinations for peace and quiet have led him?

Thinking of the *Tale of the Taira* forces us, obviously, to think of Kyoto. A complex tapestry of human relationships unravelled on the dazzling stage of the Imperial court. Shifts in the insatiable power struggles that took place there, together with sounds of the lute which elicit the pathos of those struggles, have been transmitted to us over the centuries by word of mouth.

The Imperial Palace reminds us of the Taira's efforts to become courtiers, of their repeated and inexplicable submissiveness to achieve that end. Beginning as Imperial Guards, the Taira ended up swaggering arrogantly through the hallways of the Palace as relatives of the Emperor. And history tells us that women associated with Kiyomori (1118-81), the leader of the Taira, played out their pathetic roles at Sagano in Kyoto, a spot where beautiful bamboo groves abound. Even a city like Kyoto, which boasts such a bounty of natural freshness, becomes so flooded with tourists in the spring that a person is in danger of being engulfed by waves of human beings.

The feeling of impermanence running through the entire *Tale of the Taira* plays plaintive tunes amid a counterpoint of vivid contrasts: the gaudy splendor and the miserably tragic desolation of the House of Taira. The story begins with the following words:

"The tolling of the Gion Temple bell tolls the impermanence of all things. The color of the blossoms on the twin sal trees reveals the pattern of life: the prosperous must decline. The proud and the haughty disappear like dreams on a spring night. And the brave are scattered meek as dust under the wind."

These words not only announce the basic motif but constitute the conclusion of the story as well. The everyday behavior of those who appear in the story follows with precision the track of the motif: the decline of the mighty is inevitable; those who meet must part. Rather than indicate how the *Tale of the Taira* is based on historical realities, the persistence of the motif rather gives one the impression that we are in the world of fiction, that the story was constructed to harmonize with the theme, "the impermanence of all things."

In the tale we see the faithful delineation of the path of decline followed by the prosperous Kiyomori and other Taira who acted with such haughty insolence. We see the premature death of Kiyomori's heir, Shigemori (1138-79), and the suicide of Kiyomori's grandson, Koremori (1157-84), who threw himself into the sea. The story carries us down to the execution of Koremori's son, Rokudai, in 1198. Throughout these events the particularly detailed description of Kiyomori's tragic heirs is in consonance with the motif stated in the opening sentences quoted above.

We can understand why the tale appends details about Kenreimon'in (1155-1213), the former Empress, if we realize that the purpose is to trace the fate of the various women related to Kiyomori. The former Empress, a daughter of Kiyomori, was the consort of Emperor Takakura and mother of the infant Emperor Antoku; she entered a convent late in life and took the religious name Kenreimon'in. There seems no

doubt that the delicately tragic mood of the impermanence of all things builds up to the destruction of
the Taira clan, which sank like the evening sun that
turns the sky vermillion.

It is obvious, of course, that the "impermanence of
all things" is a Buddhist term. The fundamental meaning of the expression is somewhat different from the
aura of resigned pathos people generally associate
with it. Surprisingly, it does not seem widely known
that this expression contains a philosophical dimension which profoundly probes the natural phenomena
of the entire universe.

The meaning of the term is that it is impossible to
find permanence in any phenomenon under the sun.
What man loves and what he finds agreeable are what
he becomes attached to, what he wishes would be
permanent. But nothing whatsoever can escape mu-
tability. Buddhism teaches that the setbacks and agonies which man suffers in life arise from his lack of
clear insight into the reality of impermanence and from
being attached to things.

That is the reason pioneers in Buddhism have attempted to make clear that a sound understanding of
the concept of impermanence, an awareness of the
change and development of all things, must be achieved
before all else if a man is to live meaningfully. The
original intent of the concept was to inspire men—
neither to find impermanence distasteful nor to flee
the world merely to vegetate but—to discover how

185

they might get the upper hand on this interminably changing world we live in. On that point, it seems to me that those to whom we owe the *Tale of the Taira* created a mood of pathos in the story by ignoring all but one aspect of the impermanence of all things.

Our modern society is troubled by nuclear weapons, environmental pollution, management of the news by the mass media. It seems to me that in such a society something comparable to a feeling of the "impermanence of all things" is taking root among some educated people. To be sure, that feeling might be one phenomenon accompanying the closing decades of an age when human warmth seems to wither a little more each year. But one cannot say that those who vainly drown themselves in world-weariness or those who ignore the world and turn to instant action display an attitude that shows a proper grasp of the significance of the concept of impermanence.

One Buddhist pioneer who goes back several thousand years talked of impermanence. In the final analysis, however, he was pointing out to people the permanent vigor of life which flows deep within life's impermanence. He concluded his explication of impermanence by stressing the fact that the man who looks for the ideal society in another world will not reform the world he lives in.

The arrogance of those with excessive confidence in their own power, of those who have created a society extensively run by machines, will surely defeat them.

They will fall from the heights of triumph to the hell of despair. Like the Taira, they will be transformed into impotent people bound by their own hands and their own feet. The mood of unrest accompanying the closing years of our century will color their decline.

I wonder, however, whether man is not expected to make the attempt to revise his way of looking at his living and breathing world. I wonder whether we are not expected to look from a fresh philosophical viewpoint and wisely try to discover how to take the initiative. How I yearn to tell those who take excursions to places mentioned in the *Tale of the Taira:* If only for a moment you could stroll down the paths suggested by this thought . . . !

February 28, 1972

LESSONS FROM THE
SINO-AMERICAN DIALOGUE

1972! At last it seems that there will be a shift in the historic stalemate in East Asia.

The recent eight-day summit conference between the leaders of China and the United States of America ended the twenty-two year period of antagonism that has existed between these two nations since the end of the Korean war. These talks mark the first celebrated steps toward the opening of an age of renewed dialogue.

The joint communique produced various evaluations. Speaking broadly, however, most commentators viewed the rapprochement in terms of the expectations of the general public. The complexities of politics escape me, but I do know the sentiments of the common people: they lean purely toward a love for peace above all things. That may indicate how simple-minded they are. But at the same time the intrinsic value of the common people is that they can expertly distinguish between something that alleviates and something that aggravates tensions.

Sino-American relations have for many years been antagonistic. They have brought unnecessary tensions and the calamity of war to Asia. Now, at the very least, a road to dialogue between the two nations has been opened. Why shouldn't the common people candidly rejoice over this development and display their true feelings?

I am not a specialist in these matters. All I would like to point out is the obvious fact that the meeting and dialogue took place directly between the top leaders of both nations. And the conferences did not occur just once or twice but were strenuous affairs conducted repeatedly over several days. It seems that the principals continued discussing perhaps until they mutually agreed upon some limited objectives.

Of course, as the catch phrase "Kissinger diplomacy" suggests, there were probably prior negotiations which paved the way. But when the top leaders representing East and West—where interchange had ceased and only antagonisms existed—finally got together, I could not withhold feelings of amazement. And I was also naturally overjoyed because this was something I had for some years advocated and hoped might be realized. It was also truly dramatic that the stage for the rapprochement was not Washington, D.C. but Peking.

Needless to say, this certainly does not mean that China and the United States have been reconciled. Neither have proper diplomatic relations between the two nations commenced, nor have American forces withdrawn from Taiwan. We have merely seen the first step taken toward the solution of these difficult problems. We might rather say that the hard work still lies ahead, and that we should refrain from rashly making excessive evaluations of what these conferences have accomplished.

All the same, however, these talks differ from negotiations for peace in Vietnam conducted in Paris. Negotiators have already met more than one hundred times. The upshot, at this moment anyhow, is a deadlock. This is probably due to the complex nature of the problems involved. For one thing, the war is still underway and the situation is also complicated by the fact that a number of nations are involved. But there are undeniable differences in what has been accomplished in Paris and what was accomplished in the summit meeting at Peking.

I wonder if it is only the frivolous horse sense of an amateur observer that makes one wonder: what if the leaders of the nations involved conducted a summit conference in Paris—following the pattern of the Sino-

191

American talks in Peking—to deal with the problem of peace in Vietnam?

Be that as it may, there is no doubt that the Peking talks truly amount to the dialogue of the century. With regard to the idea of dialogue per se, however, the tensions this dialogue confronted were no different from what we see around us every day. Seen in this light, the Sino-American talks have some valuable lessons to teach us about daily life.

Dialogue has become a cliché these days. Still, human life is unthinkable without it. Or rather is it proper to say that in these troubled times dialogue is our only salvation, for it can bridge gaps between people and transform feelings of distrust for fellow men into feelings of trust.

One often hears these days about the sterility of much dialogue. On many occasions talking about issues does not seem fruitful with regard to problems that crop up in the family, in our local areas or beyond that on the international scene. At times, notably in certain extremely radical student groups, I understand that there isn't even room for dialogue between the leadership and the rank and file. But in less extreme instances, whenever talks lose their viability by breaking down and merely marking time, it is possible that solutions will ultimately be arrived at by force. We have seen this result in the unfortunate incident where radical students and farmers have been opposing construction of the new international airport at Narita across the bay from Tokyo.

Lessons From the Sino-American Dialogue

As far as viability is concerned, the Sino-American talks are certainly a success. What made them successful? In sum, I think it is the feeling of responsibility displayed by the leaders of both countries who regarded themselves as representing their people; they apparently shared the feeling of having millions of citizens entrusted to their care. Had these talks ended in failure, both sides would have left a legacy of regret for later generations. But the feeling of responsibility, shared mutually, has raised the curtain on a new era of hope. It is the tenor of the times that dialogue has allowed leaders to transcend the confrontation of particular national interests.

Antagonism between interests or feelings happens frequently. It results from the bankrupting but the human tendency to adhere tenaciously to one's particular views. In a family dispute, as long as parent and child confront each other only as parent against child and child against parent, they will not find it easy to move beyond their differences and repair the rupture.

But if both sides in such a dispute are aware that they are components of the family, the situation should certainly take a turn for the better. The more highly developed the mutual awareness, the more possible it should be for disputants to tolerate viewpoints and life styles different from their own. It goes without saying that when such awareness is reached dialogue can produce many fruits.

Notice the famous conference that took place in

1867 concerning surrender of the Edo Castle, now the Imperial Palace in Tokyo. The dialogue was between Saigo Takamori (1827-77), who represented the attacking Imperial forces, and Katsu Yasuyoshi (1823-99), who represented the defending Tokugawa forces. Their dialogue produced splendid fruit.

Of course some points in their talks certainly have been embellished in later tellings. Despite that, there is no doubting that the Saigo-Katsu talks have gone down in Japanese history as a famous dialogue. As has been widely discussed since, we cannot be sure to what extent these two men shared a heartfelt concern for the lives of the people in Edo. At the very least, however, both shared at that moment an awareness that they were progressive-thinking Japanese— a category transcending allegiance to the Imperial or the Tokugawa forces. Certainly both men were aware that the problem had to be solved on the basis of such an awareness. That may be what produced the dramatic surrender. . . .

Thus there appears to be hope for any dialogue that occurs between people who share a fairly high level of awareness. This is true whether the dialogue deals with a family spat or with international problems. The hope is that such shared feelings will end the stalemate and allow discussions to move toward a successful conclusion. But how far can we go in heightening the sense of awareness between participants? Perhaps the ultimate we can anticipate is respect for human life. When we reach that level, the milk of humanistic concern for other human beings might even overflow into our society.

In any event, we must deplore all efforts to make dialogue into merely an exchange of words.

March 5, 1972

LITERATURE AND LIBERTY

According to a recent newspaper article, I see that intellectuals in the Soviet Union and other eastern European socialist countries continue to be oppressed. In Czechoslovakia, for example, where officials have been clamping down on the "liberal line" that flowered momentarily, they say that several hundred prominent intellectuals and authors trying to keep that policy alive have been arrested during the past several months.

In response to this development, some eighteen world-famous novelists, poets and sympathizers, including Graham Greene of England and Günter Grass from West Germany, have determined to unite and press for the release of the Czech intellectuals.

Such incidents give us a fresh awareness of the sensitive relation between politics and literature, government and culture. Perhaps it is no exaggeration to claim that the agonies and the tasks which face any human being who confronts the present will cast a pall over him.

Perhaps Aleksandr Solzhenitsyn (b. 1918) of the Soviet Union is the most likely example of an author who stands at the tragic apex of the relations between politics and literature.

Here are the concluding paragraphs of Solzhenitsyn's masterpiece, *One Day in the Life of Ivan Denisovich,* published in the Soviet Union in 1962:

> [*Ivan Denisovich*] *Shukov went to sleep fully content. He'd had many strokes of luck that day: they hadn't put him in the cells; they hadn't sent his squad to the settlement; he'd swiped a bowl of kasha at dinner; the squad leader had fixed the rates well; he'd built a wall and enjoyed doing it; he'd smuggled that bit of hacksaw blade through; he'd earned a favor from Tsezar that evening; he'd bought that tobacco. And he hadn't fallen ill. He'd got over it.*
>
> *A dark day without a cloud. Almost a happy day.*
>
> *There were three thousand six hundred and fifty-three days like that in his stretch. From the first clang of the rail [to announce reveille] to the last clang of the rail [to announce taps].*

Three thousand six hundred and fifty-three days.
The three extra days were for leap years.

(from the Ralph Parker translation)

In this virgin work, Solzhenitsyn describes life at a Siberian concentration camp during the Stalin era; his descriptions are realistic and restrained. The reader is powerfully involved in the narrative, neither because descriptions of conditions at the camp are graphic and revealing nor because they remain above the level of superficial sarcasm or political invective. The reason lies rather in the fact that, as he provides a stage for these particular events, the author has essentially given dimension to the universal condition of man, particularly of contemporary man.

Solzhenitsyn later published such novels as *The First Circle* and *Cancer Ward*. All his works have been an indictment from deep within of the problems of the modern era. The Soviet government, however, appears to have constantly suppressed these works. Most of this author's novels could not be published in the Soviet Union; in 1969 he was expelled from the Soviet Writers' Union.

Even his latest masterpiece, *August 1914,* issued in the summer of 1971 by a publishing house in Paris, has reportedly been lambasted by his government as "anti-Soviet." A recent report, moreover, says that Soviet intellectuals on the eve of emigrating to Israel sent a jointly-signed letter to *The Times* of London in which they reveal a further increase in suppression against such men as Solzhenitsyn.

If we accept the themes and content of these works quite superficially, criticisms that they are "anti-Soviet" do not seem entirely without foundation. But we must say that such criticisms reflect an altogether too intolerant political viewpoint. Even if Solzhenitsyn's works were so obviously unpatriotic and anti-Soviet, it is clearly an error for political authority to suppress literature. Such action will only further lower the government's prestige.

The themes and intent of literature ought really to be understood at a more profound level. For example, Solzhenitsyn himself was probably talking about the essence of literature when he said in an interview:

> When a composition is too realistic and when an author sacrifices "the universal aspects," his composition is already defunct. Conversely, when an author pays too much heed to the timeless and neglects reality, then his work will lose its color, strength and atmosphere. An author forever stands between the devil and the deep blue sea, for he is not allowed to neglect either reality or the timeless.

Literature is something that depicts the timeless problems of man in concrete situations. Or, from the opposite viewpoint, it is something that deals with timeless themes and puts them in bas relief within particular situations. This is, it seems to me, what Solzhenitsyn was driving at.

200

Aleksandr Solzhenitsyn

LITERATURE AND LIBERTY

It is often said that modern literature is "the literature of anxiety." Some people suggest that men who live in a mechanized and excessively rationalized culture become isolated from their fellow men, lose sight of the meaning of life and abandon hope. It is only natural, such people maintain, that literature would deeply reflect the anxiety, despair and decadence of man because it depicts contemporary conditions.

Certainly life seems chaotic. I do not think, however, that the essence of literature is mere description of that ungarnished chaos. No matter how filled with hopelessness, no matter how relentlessly it denounces the emptiness and meaninglessness of life, the literature that deeply affects us contains an undercurrent of hope; it throbs poignantly with the aspiration to seek out and discover meaningfulness in life.

This may be a narrow view, but it seems to me that literature gives us hope in life. I need not add, of course, that this is hardly limited to literature and the arts. Are not all of man's activities a process of creating values which—despite the fact that human existence and life itself are entangled in the chaos of reality—blaze an independent path through confusion?

Solzhenitsyn has said that

Even if society takes an unfair attitude toward authors, I hardly think it a great problem. This becomes a test for the writer . . . . That is one of the risks of the profession. We will probably never see an age when the author's lot will be an easy one.

These words illustrate the mind of an author who struggles toward and attempts to embrace his own vision of truth.

The injustice of the policies which contemporary socialist states take against authors and intellectuals may be reasonable. But genuine literature, by virtue of the fact that it has been created from the very stuff of human nature, cannot help touching constantly on the contemporary social order. Thus it will occasionally produce friction and give rise to opposition. Might we not then say that Solzhenitsyn's life itself is a drama, and that it depicts the essential meaning of literature?

March 12, 1972

THE THROB OF LIFE

I enjoy talking with people. It is extremely pleasant to converse with acquaintances in a relaxed way after completing my daily schedule. Because one is uninhibited on such occasions, the topic of conversation extends to such varied fields as man, society, science and the arts; these talks constitute a precious source of nourishment for me, providing fresh knowledge and an abundance of new concepts. It is already an ingrained habit with me to meet as many different types of people as I can and, while talking with them, to pick up new ideas.

Someone told me the other evening about the following item. The newspaper carried a report from Moscow about a scientific discovery. The article, tak-

205

ing only thirty lines and tucked in a corner of the paper, reported that some micro-organisms two hundred fifty million years old had been revived. These microbes had thrived in the ocean during the Permian period, the last part of the Paleozoic era. Locked in a crystal of potassium ore, the organisms had been dormant for all those years; but in a test tube they came back to life.

Scientists put the Permian period more than two hundred million years in the past. This is when Tibolita and Fusulina swam through the great seas. Reptiles and amphibians had finally begun to appear on the solid land. This period was well before the famed age of the dinosaurs. Of course it is needless to say that it predates the existence of the anthropoid ape, not to mention man himself.

These Permian micro-organisms subsisted in what are now the Ural Mountains. In those days, however, the mountains were under the sea. Perhaps the microbes were by mere chance locked into the potassium; in any event, they had been serenely inactive during the past two hundred million years.

Small sparks of life, no more than faint red spots, they slept through countless vicissitudes and dissensions in history. And now, awakened from their slumber, they are multiplying with lusty vigor in a test tube.

I could hardly help from being astounded at the way such simple forms so tenaciously clung to existence. Embedded in potassium, the environment of these organisms lacked the blessings of life: air, warmth, water, nourishment. They had no choice but to sleep as though they were lifeless. So the inanimate potassium acted as the place of repose and as guardian of these small bits of life. If modern science had not rescued them in the test tube, they might have gone on slumbering for hundreds of millions, even for billions of years. But their slumber had been tranquil, and all along they possessed the potential for activity. If at any given moment the conditions were just right, this potential would initiate a definite pulsing and cause them to brim with vitality and life.

Twenty years ago the "Oga Lotus" bloomed beautifully from a bulb that survived for two thousand years. They say it is still doing well and has been shared with research centers across the land. This news made the world sit up and take note, for it proved that a dormant plant harbored the capability of sprouting. But whether a lotus bulb or a micro-organism, it is quite surprising to think that the sparks of life are concealed in something which at first glance appeared dead. . . . As I pondered these fragmentary thoughts about the mystery of life, I couldn't help but sense that even the hush of darkness enveloping me was somehow throbbing with vitality.

One theory suggests that in our vast universe are several hundred million planets with the same conditions we have on earth. Thus it is obviously conceivable that somewhere in space there would exist living things which have bodies similar to ours. And the beings on such planets likely have intelligence similar or superior to earthmen. This, too, has apparently been conjectured by modern astronomers.

Due to the extreme distances that separate earth from these other planets, however, we have had no contact with such beings. I wonder whether people in those worlds share with us the abysmal agony of sufferings in life and death and whether they, too, repeatedly engage in the mutual strife that is so self-destructive. Or rather do you suppose that the beings on those planets are trying to build a lush paradise dedicated to respect for life?

In any event, scientists have already forecast that there is the potential for generation of life even in environments much more severe than one finds on earth. For example, I understand it is possible for ammonia to be transformed into liquid capable of animated activity even in an environment of some one hundred degrees below zero. And they say that it is even possible for a substance like silicon to take on the character of a living organism when it liquefies in the scorching environment of hundreds of degrees Fahrenheit.

Silicon is an ingredient of rocks. When I heard that silicon might become a living body, I no longer had the power to imagine what sort of mental activity such a living body might engage in. But looking at it simply from the viewpoint of a layman, I have the feeling that there is no choice but to doff our hats in

respect to the mystery of life. Is it not a wonder to conceive of life taking shape even on an intensely frigid or scorchingly hot planet where one would think life is absolutely impossible?

The year before last scientists discovered in a meteor that dropped out of the skies an amino acid clearly different from anything we have on earth. This was noted as initial proof that the basis for the generation of life exists beyond our planet. When one considers the fact that amino acids—substances bursting with the power to initiate life—are floating nearby in the vacuum of cosmic space, it seems as though the universe itself is a mighty womb latent throughout with the germ of life.

The French philosopher Henri Bergson (1859-1941) in his book *Creative Evolution* advocated a splendid metaphysics that conceived of the entire universe in terms of the process of evolution. Near the end of my teens, when I was influenced by Bergson's philosophy, the term *élan vital,* the throb of life, stuck in my mind—as it does now. Perhaps the term represented the cry of the spirit of this thinker who had caught a glimpse of the mysteries of life and the universe.

When Bergson completed writing *Creative Evolution* he described the state of his mind as follows: "Until I wrote the book I was extremely interested in mathematics and physics. I couldn't even say that matter was a huge mystery to me. But after the book it was different. When I focused my attention on life I knew that it was the greatest mystery."

I suspect we moderns need to listen humbly to the impressions of this "philosopher of life." Unless one gives some attention to the mysteries of life and the universe, the aimless waste of lives we see around us will probably play havoc with us as well as with nature and the universe. Well, scientists are giving some attention to the problem. I hear that the Pioneer X probe to Jupiter carries a message to people in space. The possibility of establishing contact with other beings may not be realized for hundreds of years, but it is good to dream about.

The constellations that adorn the skies seem to move inexpressively in their orbits. And yet they establish certain animated rhythms. As I talk with people each evening about the cosmos in which the stars move, I feel I would like the composure to contemplate and humbly view the mystery of life and the profundity of its essential matter. Perhaps the unseen substructure of a truly humanistic attitude lies in taking such a view.

March 20, 1972

AN ANCIENT LEGACY

I like the area around Nara because it impresses me as a place filled with poetry. In contrast to the modern metropolis, where we find less and less of the delicate feelings native to our heritage, Nara exudes the gossamer genius of the *Manyoshu's* rich lyricism.

Nara is in the Yamato area, the center of such vital and animated cultural periods as the Hakuho and Tempyo (7th and 8th centuries). Particularly during the Asuka era, best symbolized by Prince Shotoku (574-622), do we find the simple beginnings in which a distinctive Japanese-type insight begins to assert itself.

An Ancient Legacy

In March, 1972, a brilliantly decorated burial chamber was discovered in the Takamatsu Tumulus located in Asuka, a village near Nara. The discovery is tantamount to getting a glance into the lush culture of distant ancestors across a span of 1300 years. The news was like spring wind that warms the heart after a long winter. Color photographs of the murals published in the newspapers were so vivid one cannot imagine they date from 7th century. A renowned Japanese painter appointed to copy the paintings was said to have been speechless when asked what colors were used to create such splendid hues.

And the murals seem to shimmer in their simplicity with a lively fragrance. So much so that even now one can sense the warmth of the skin on figures depicted on the walls. The figures are dressed in apparel different from what was worn in ancient Japan—did they come from Korea or China?—but the long skirts touching the ground certainly make these garments elegant. One imagines the serene existence of the women depicted on the walls, with their rounded and rouged cheeks. And I even get the feeling that a bucolic scene from ancient times was moving into my line of vision, a scene of women walking through Asuka among nature's greenery.

Certainly these murals are appropriate to the homeland of the earliest collection of Japanese poetry, the *Manyoshu*. Those were the days when even nobility was sufficiently carefree to address a common person,

214

as we see in the first five lines of a poem by the Emperor Yuryaku (418-479) with which the collection begins:

> *Holding a basket, your pretty basket,*
> *Holding a trowel, your nice trowel,*
> *Little girl, digging herbs on the hillside,*
> *May I ask where you live?*
> *Won't you tell me your name?*

At the same time it seems to me that the simplicity of these murals makes an unstated but poignant appeal to contemporary animalistic men who dash off so haphazardly to seek new thrills. The paintings entreat us to restore a sense of poetry to our lives.

Something else in this burial chamber attracted me: the constellations inlaid on the ceiling. This chart of the heavenly bodies, on which the stars are connected by red lines, is said to represent the constellations which ancient man used as his calendar.

I understand that the ancients divided the vast celestial sphere into twenty-eight parts. By investigating the positions of the sun, moon, and the constellations in each part, he tried to ascertain the seasons and the passage of time. These divisions, termed "The Twenty-eight Constellations," were divided appropriately into four groups of seven each, one group for each of the major directions. This represents, I suppose, the wisdom of ancient man who spoke with the stars and journeyed through life with the heavenly bodies.

These constellations had their origin in India. There are also substantial vestiges of them in China. Those found in the burial chamber at Takamatsu probably symbolize the new world into which the deceased would journey. If one gazes up at the flat ceiling and likens it to the dome of the heavens, it seems to have been constructed to look like the wonderful geometrical pattern of stars shining in the night sky. According to one scholar, this seems the largest scale constellation chart of this type in the world.

These constellations amounted to a kind of lunar calendar. But whether solar or lunar, people of those days fixed their calendar by the movements of heavenly bodies, of the sun or the moon. It seems to me that this way of making the calendar illustrates that these people thought to adjust the rhythms of their lives to the rhythms of heavenly bodies.

I wonder, was the calendar influenced by a view which assumed that if only one's confused and complicated patterns of daily life were in harmony with the eternal, the deep-set, the regular rhythms of the macrocosm, those patterns would naturally adjust to the normal rhythms of a microcosm? Or could it be that the idea behind the calendar was the consciousness that even the rhythms of the heavenly bodies have been "programmed" in the innermost rhythms of our own lives? Perhaps the fact that ancient man feared disturbances in the movements of the heavenly bodies as portents of disturbances in society also impelled him

to develop these concepts. Apparently, people in ancient times considered it a catastrophe if the Twenty-eight Constellations were in imbalance.

In our day we regard such views as preposterous. But why should they be? Even modern science demonstrates that our bodies are far more complex and subtle than even the most intricate machine. Resonances may exist that we are totally unaware of.

Everyone remembers in general what happened a day ago. This is not to say, however, that a person remembers everything. The more time passes, a year or a decade, the dimmer the remembrance. But according to medical science we do remember even the most trifling details. Actually, we often hear about cases in which a person, given the occasion, recalls something he thought he had completely forgotten. Or about a person who, in the face of something drastic like imminent death, sees the events of his entire life unfold before him like a kaleidoscope.

We might say, without too much exaggeration, that such memories suggest that whatever a person has experienced, including even the rhythmic movement of heavenly bodies, has been registered in his unconscious. Not only that, we are also told that even the events experienced by our parents, not to mention those which occurred before they were born, have been implanted in our genes.

I recall having read somewhere that the number of possible combinations of brain cells in a single human being exceeds the number of atoms in the entire universe.

If we think about it a bit, we might find that both the vastness of the limitless universe and the permanence of eternal time can be wonderfully condensed in the life of a single human being. To assume that the ancients who constructed the burial chamber at Takamatsu Tumulus conceived of the movements of heavenly bodies as indispensable rhythms in man's life, and, beyond that, to assume that they had sketched the macrocosm of the Twenty-eight Constellations as a world for the dead, makes me feel renewed reverence for the wisdom of ancient man's penetrating insight. At the same time I cannot help feeling disgusted with the imprudence of contemporary man, this stickler for narrow egoism and the immediate, this creature who makes no attempt to exploit the magnificent treasure trove of a life directly tied in with the universe.

As research progresses, the burial chamber in Asuka Village will certainly reveal rich data even about the inner spirit and life of ancient man. I suspect that one of archaeology's main contributions is to study the past in order to rediscover some of the insights of the ancients, insights which modern men have laid aside and forgotten.

Man's agonies and joys have not changed much for millennia. There is probably also a common basis for the wisdom of those who experience agony and joy. The problem facing us is how we in our time can reactivate our long-lost sense of fulfillment—a sense which our distant ancestors achieved through the brilliance of the culture they had inherited. How can we use their wholeness as a mirror to view our own lives?

In any event, I should at least like sightseers in the Nara area to exercise more self control. It is shameful the way their outrageous behavior defaces this area celebrated in the *Manyoshu*.

April 3, 1972

ABOUT THE AUTHOR

Daisaku Ikeda is President of the 15-million member Soka Gakkai International organization. He is a prolific writer, having written over fifty books and hundreds of essays and poems. His popular appeal has made him one of the most widely-read authors in Japan today.

Mr. Ikeda was born in Tokyo in 1928 and experienced severe hardships growing up in a nation torn apart by war. In 1947, he joined Nichiren Shoshu and began studying under his master, Josei Toda, the Soka Gakkai's second president. The following year, he graduated from the Toyo Business School and entered Fuji Junior College, where he earned a degree in economics.

He became the editor of the *Seikyo Shimbun*, a Soka Gakkai publication which has followed the meteoric growth of the organization and is currently the fifth largest daily in the world. In 1960, he was inaugurated as the society's third president, becoming the spiritual leader of the Soka Gakkai's members in over eighty nations.

Mr. Ikeda has traveled extensively around the world in the interests of peace and international goodwill, meeting with international leaders and ordinary people in many nations. He has initiated many cultural and educational exchange programs among universities around the world as well. In 1975, he was awarded an honorary doctoral degree from Moscow State University.

In an age of specialization, Mr. Ikeda's essays concern themselves with the whole of life. His analyses of the world's problems ring with a hope based upon concern for the dignity of human life. His ideas bring the dream of peace in this century within our grasp.

221

MAJOR BOOKS by Daisaku Ikeda

Presidential Addresses, Vols. 1-13. Tokyo: Soka Gakkai, 1961-66. English translation. Vols. 1-5. Tokyo: Seikyo Press, 1962-70.

Collection of Essays and Lectures, Vols. 1-4. Tokyo: Soka Gakkai, 1962-66.

Lecture on Nichiren Daishonin's "Ho-on Sho" (On Appreciation for One's Master). Tokyo: Soka Gakkai, 1964.

Politics and Religion. Tokyo: Hoshoin Publishing Co., 1965.

Science and Religion. Tokyo: Hoshoin Publishing Co., 1965. Translated into English.

Lecture on the Ongi Kuden (Oral Teachings of Nichiren Daishonin), Vols. 1-2. Tokyo: Soka Gakkai, 1965-67.

The Human Revolution, Vols. 1-8. Tokyo: Seikyo Press, 1965-73. Translated into English, French, Spanish, Portuguese and Chinese.

The Family Revolution. Tokyo: Kodansha Publishing Co., 1966. English translation. Los Angeles: World Tribune Press, 1971.

Guidance Memo. Tokyo: Seikyo Press, 1966. Translated into English and Spanish.

Collected Guidance. Tokyo: Seikyo Press, 1967.

Youthful Diary, Vols. 1-5. Tokyo: Youthful Diary Publishing Co., 1967-74.

222

Selected Works of Daisaku Ikeda, Vols. 1-8. Tokyo: Soka Gakkai, 1967-74.

Complete Works, Vols. 1-3. Tokyo: Seikyo Press, 1967-68. Translated into English.

Guidance Quotations. Tokyo: Seikyo Press, 1968.

My Thoughts. Tokyo: Mainichi Press, 1969.

Collected Addresses of President Ikeda, Vols. 1-4. Tokyo: Soka Gakkai, 1970-73.

Collection of My Essays. Tokyo: Yomiuri Press, 1970.

My Vision of Life. Tokyo: Bungei Shunju Publishing Co., 1970.

For the Young. Tokyo: Poplar Publishing Co., 1971.

My Suggestions. Tokyo: Sankei Press, 1971.

To My Young Friends. Tokyo: Bungei Shunju Publishing Co., 1971.

Ode to Youth. Tokyo: Yomiuri Press, 1972.

The People, (Collection of poems in English). Santa Monica, Ca.: World Tribune Press, 1972.

To Young Future Leaders. Tokyo: Kin-no Hoshi Publishing Co., 1972.

Civilization, East and West, (Dialogue with Richard E. Coudenhove-Kalergi). Tokyo: Sankei Press, 1972.

Yesterday, Today and Tomorrow. Tokyo: Yomiuri Press, 1972. English translation. Los Angeles: World Tribune Press, 1973.

The Human Revolution, (Children's Edition), Vols. 1-2. Tokyo: Akane Publishing Co., 1973-74.

My View of Sakyamuni. Tokyo: Bungei Shunju Publishing Co., 1973.

Revolution, Life and Death, (Dialogue with reporter Minoru Omori). Tokyo: Kodansha Publishing Co., 1973.

Dialogue on Life, Vols. 1-3. Tokyo: Ushio Publishing Co., 1973-74.

The Boy and the Cherry Tree. Tokyo: Ushio Publishing Co., 1974. Translated into English.

Essays on Women. Tokyo: Shufu-no Tome Publishing Co., 1974.

Essays on Young Women. Tokyo: Graph Publishing Co., 1974.

Essays on Boys. Tokyo: Seikyo Press, 1974.

Today's Mottos - 365 Days. Tokyo: Poplar Publishing Co., 1974.

My View of Buddhism. Tokyo: Daisan Bunmei Publishing Co., 1974.

The Human Revolution in China. Tokyo: Mainichi Press, 1974.

Daily Guidance. Tokyo: Seikyo Press, 1974.

Dialogue on the Classics. Tokyo: Ushio Publishing Co., 1974.

Russian Sketches. Tokyo: Ushio Publishing Co., 1974.

224

Guidance Memo. Los Angeles: World Tribune Press, 1975.

Dialogue for the 21st Century, (Dialogue with Arnold Toynbee). Tokyo: Bungei Shunju Publishing Co., 1975.

A Personal History. Tokyo: Japan Economic News Press, 1975.

My Views of T'ien-t'ai. Tokyo: Daisan Bunmei Publishing Co., 1975.

Toward the Century of Humanism. Tokyo: Yomiuri Press, 1975.

Hopes and Dreams, Poems by Daisaku Ikeda. Los Angeles: World Tribune Press, 1976.

Advice to Young People. Los Angeles: World Tribune Press, 1976.

INDEX

INDEX

INDEX

Translator's Note

This collection of essays attempts to indicate how traditional principles bear on modern problems. The aim is to communicate a fresh awareness and thus reduce the spiritual and physical suffering of men and women being stripped of their essential humanity by the demonic forces of progress. But Daisaku Ikeda is certainly not against progress. He is against suffering. He aims constantly to get the alienated individual to see reality from a new perspective, to realize that he is part of—and resonates with—the cosmos. . . . These are a few of the reasons I believe that Daisaku Ikeda's secular essays merit translation. Indeed, as a complete (and not always sympathetic) outsider, I must confess that I am frequently impressed by the manner in which the author applies Buddhist principles to the contemporary milieu. It is possible that Christian leaders could learn something from him.

TDistant
THUNDER

by
Peggy J. Herring

Bella
BOOKS

2003

Copyright© 2003 by Peggy J. Herring

Bella Books, Inc.
P.O. Box 10543
Tallahassee, FL 32302

Printed in the United States of America on acid-free paper
First Edition

Editor: Greg Herren
Cover designer: Bonnie Liss (Phoenix Graphics)

ISBN 1-931513-28-7

For Laverne Bell
Because Nice Matters

Acknowledgments

I would like to thank Frankie J. Jones for her comments and suggestions after a first reading of the manuscript. Your vast knowledge and insight into all things "western" were invaluable to me during the course of this project. Blow the dust off that western manuscript you've been wanting to spruce up for years. You aren't getting any younger, you know!

I want to thank Sylvia S. Rodriguez for helping me fine-tune my rusty Spanish.

Thanks to Polly Hawkey for helping select the title and for your enthusiasm for brainstorming.

I also want to thank Martha Prentiss for bringing the term "Lesberado" to San Antonio. That's how I described my main characters for this book and it never failed to make me laugh.

I want to thank Grace Rosales, the school marm, for the great books that proved to be quite helpful and for a fun brainstorming session over some good music and the biggest and best burgers San Antonio had to offer.

A special thanks goes to Laurie McMillen for being my second reader and providing encouragement and support when I needed it the most. Parts of this book were written during some very difficult times for me. I couldn't have gotten through it without you.

Part One

Spring 1888

Chapter One

Leona Trask's mother had died the winter before, when Leo was sixteen, leaving her to help raise her four younger brothers. They had a crop in the field, but no rain for weeks. Leo hated seeing the desperation in her father's eyes every morning as he left to go hunting for something to feed his children.

One morning Leo got up to tend to the fire in their cabin. Her father had already left. She hadn't heard him go, and he didn't come home as the day grew into early evening and then night. The next morning when he hadn't returned, Leo and her brothers scoured the countryside searching for him. Surely he had been thrown from the horse and lay in a field somewhere with a broken leg or worse. Had he met with some sort of terrible accident? If that had been the case, the Trask children would have found him.

Another day passed and nightfall arrived again with no sign of him. Leo fed the boys bacon and milk and made pallets by the hearth so they could all stay close together. Luther, the youngest one, was afraid, so Leo gathered him close until he fell asleep. That night she listened for any sign of her father's return. It was nearly dawn before Leo was able to get any sleep. She was frightened and angry about being abandoned again. This time it seemed worse. When her mother died, Leo had been forced to watch her get weaker and weaker over a short period of time. Her mother's death had almost been a blessing with an end to the ever-present pain that ravaged her frail body. But for Leo to wake up and have her father gone without a word was shocking.

Four days passed before Milton Trask came home. He rode in on a new buckboard loaded with coffee, flour, oats, cornmeal, sugar, and a small bag of hard candy. He passed out new hats for the boys and a sun bonnet for Leo. Then came the real gifts!

For Henry, who was a year younger than Leo, their father brought a new Winchester .44 rifle. For the twelve-year-old twins, Eb and Earl, he brought them their first pair of boots. For Luther, Milton Trask pulled out a shiny new hunting knife that made the young boy's eyes sparkle. Then for Leona he had a beautiful ivory comb, detailed with intricate carvings outlining its edges. Leo was not as forgiving as her younger brothers were. Her anger was not so easily dismissed.

"Where did you get all this, Papa?" Henry asked excitedly as he held his new rifle out in front of him.

Leo wondered the same thing. They had no money and if it didn't rain soon, they would have even less in the future when the crop failed.

"Those boots fit?" he asked Eb as he tousled his son's hair.

The younger boys were squealing after having discovered the candy, but Leo cut her eyes over at Henry and saw the questioning gaze he gave her.

Leo returned to the cabin to fry up more bacon and peel and slice some peaches her father had brought. She would wait until the little ones were tucked in before asking him the questions forming in her head, but much to her relief, Henry's curiosity saved her from having to do it alone.

"Where'd you get all this, Papa?" Henry asked him again once they were all in for the evening and gathered around the table.

"I found work."

Work? Leo thought. There was no work to be found . . . at least no jobs paying this kind of money. He'd only been gone a few days.

"Where at?" Henry asked. "I'd like to work, too. I'm plenty old enough."

Milton got up from the table and plucked his youngest son Luther from his chair and swung him onto his back in a round of horse-play. Leo hadn't seen her father this relaxed and happy since long before their mother died.

"I need you here to look after things with your sister," Milton said to his oldest son. Henry made several attempts to get him to talk about the new job, but the subject was closed.

Over the next few days, the boys chopped wood, carried up extra water from the creek, patched the cabin's roof, and tidied up the barn. The Trask family stayed busy, as if preparing for something, but Leo had no idea what. As the only girl in the family, she was expected to cook, do laundry, and keep the cabin clean. It was an unspoken rule, one Leo despised. Begrudgingly, she made biscuits and peach cobblers and kept the cabin spotless while her father and brothers mended fences, moved the outhouse, and cleaned out the chicken coop. Then one night before Leo banked the coals in the fireplace, her father told her he would be gone for a few weeks on his new job, but that he'd return with more supplies.

"I've talked to Henry already," he said. "You two watch after your brothers while I'm gone."

Leo felt frightened again. Whatever "job" her father had, she didn't like it. The things he had brought with him when he returned this last time cost more than a good crop would have brought in . . . probably even more than a five-year stretch of good crops. Leo had a bad feeling about all of this—especially since her father wasn't giving any details.

4

"Do you have to go?" she asked him. Being without him worried her. What if one of them got sick?

"I'll be back in a few weeks."

"Where will you be? What if we need you?"

"You won't need me. You'll be fine."

"But—"

"Go to the Wilkies' down the road if something happens," he said. End of discussion. He went to bed. When Leo got up the next morning, her father was gone.

So Leo and Henry kept the younger ones busy with chores as the days crawled by. In the evenings they sat around the fireplace where the boys shelled pecans and Leo mended shirts and stockings. She told them stories she remembered their mother telling her when she was younger, and they talked about other relatives they hadn't seen in years.

The days passed and the little homestead in West Texas looked better than it ever had, even though there was still no sign of rain. As the weeks crept by, Leo began to feel less anxious about her father's absence. Being the oldest, she was the one her siblings turned to for everything. Even Henry talked things over with her before making any decision. Leo wondered if she would have to cook and clean up after them for the rest of her life. She worried about the future. Too many things could happen to one of them, and eventually they would run out of supplies. Would Papa be back before the flour ran out? What would she feed them if the chickens stopped laying?

Eventually it got to where Henry came home with a rabbit or a squirrel more often than not when he went out hunting in the mornings. He became a good shot with his new rifle, and was even teaching the twins how to shoot. Leo's skills as a cook improved, even though she longed to be outside in the sunshine instead of stuck in the cabin. *When will Papa be back?* she wondered. *And how long will he stay next time?*

Chapter Two

Cordelia Kincade had spent most of her life sleeping on the ground and making sure she and her father had something to eat. Her mother, a strong willful woman, died in childbirth when Cordy was five. The memory of burying her mother and infant brother was still vivid in Cordy's mind. Her father, Alva Kincade, had never gotten over losing his wife. Cordy spent her formative years watching him succumb to weaknesses that probably would have never surfaced, had her mother been alive. Cordy witnessed the light in her father's eyes grow dimmer with each passing day until there was almost nothing left. He had no ambition, and seemed to always be waiting for his luck to change on its own without him having to do anything to make it happen. Cordy didn't like thinking of her father as lazy. She preferred to think his talents were lying dormant, and just waiting for the right time to show themselves. She assumed the role of the adult at an early age.

After burying her mother and the baby, Cordy and her father drifted from town to town, always camping on a riverbank somewhere and living off the land. Alva did odd jobs in whatever town they were close to at the time. As soon as he had enough money to replenish their supplies, they would break camp and move on.

It was a lonely life, but Cordy learned to be resourceful. By the time she was ten, she could ride and shoot as well as any man. Most wildlife wasn't safe around her. She was able to flush a pheasant or a covey of quail from the thick Texas underbrush. Her father's eyesight wasn't good, so she did all the hunting and gathering. She kept them fed during their travels and developed a great appreciation for the dry South Texas weather and the abundance of food available on the land. When it rained, they had to look for shelter before sleep was possible. Cordy didn't like rain, but she liked being poor even less. She vowed to someday have more than a horse and a saddle. She wasn't sure how she would go about rising above her lot in life, but Cordy was determined. During her travels with her father, she saw the riches of city people and ranchers. If they could do it, she would do it, too.

In the summer, Cordy and her father made their way to the Palo Duro Canyon in North Texas, where the temperatures were cooler and rabbits and prairie dogs plentiful. When the weather started to get too cool, they worked their way south again, down through Odessa and over to San Antonio—eventually ending up in Laredo where they spent the winter. There were huge ranches along the way where Alva Kincade worked as a hired hand, usually just long enough to collect a month's wages.

It was her travels through South Texas in the winter that Cordy enjoyed the most. She learned to speak Spanish during this time. She also discovered how much she liked kissing girls.

One December when Cordy was twelve, she and her father spent a few weeks outside of San Antonio at Mission San José. Other children lived there year round. Food was plentiful and Cordy liked not having to hunt in order to eat. She also liked having a warm, dry place to sleep. Cordy made friends and eventually met a girl a few years older by the name of Elena Gallegos. Cordy helped Elena with her English and in return, Elena taught Cordy more Spanish. They also liked to practice kissing at night when the other children were put to bed.

It was one such winter while Cordy and her father were at the mission that the Kincade luck began to change. Her father had been away from the mission for several days. Cordy was scared. He had never left her before. One night in mid-December, he came to wake her up. It was cold in the small room Cordy shared with the other children, but she and Elena were cuddled in the safety of each other's arms.

"Get dressed," he whispered after startling her awake. "We're leaving."

Cordy didn't ask any questions. She slipped out of Elena's embrace and quietly got dressed. After collecting her few possessions, she tied them into a bundle. Their horses were saddled and waiting outside the gate. Cordy and her father rode away into the cold December night without another word. She assumed they would be back in a few days. At least she hoped so, since she didn't get to tell Elena good-bye. The December night air was cold, and Cordy missed Elena's warmth already.

They rode through the night, traveling south toward Laredo, but this time things were different. Her father had money. *Lots* of money! He also had pocket watches, rings and new boots for both of them. Cordy didn't ask questions. Her father would eventually tell her what he was up to. He bought them new clothes and a Colt Peacemaker pistol for himself. They slept in rooms over saloons with real beds, hot baths and cooked meals. But along with their new and improved financial status came an uneasiness that Cordy didn't quite understand. Alva was more cautious and restless, always looking over his shoulder or sleeping with his revolver on his chest. They did most of their riding at night now and rested during the day. It wasn't long before Cordy learned where the money had come from.

Alva explained that he had recently met two men, the Trask brothers. They were train robbers, and he had been asked to help them on one of their excursions.

"No one got hurt," he added quickly.

Cordy could see the shame and uncertainty in his eyes as he continued.

"I've always been an honest man who had simple needs," he said, "but I'm not getting any younger. I want more now. I want a better life for you."

"By stealing from other people?" Cordy asked. She was trying to understand him, but this was not the man she knew. "Why would you do such a thing? We get by."

"I want more for us. I want more for you."

My father is a thief, Cordy thought. It was that simple. She still loved him, and knew the mundane gypsy-like existence had been taking its toll on him. The reality of what he had done under the pretense of wanting a better life for them confused her. Over the years, Cordy had seen his restlessness and frustration build as they drifted from place to place. She had gotten her aversion to poverty from him, but Cordy imagined settling down again would have been too painful for him. Traveling and running away from his loneliness seemed to work best. But this need to break the law was all new . . . this stealing from others he had gotten involved in. Whoever these Trask brothers were, Cordy had no use for them. They had turned her meek, honest father into a train robber!

Several days passed before any of it was mentioned again. Finally he told Cordy they were to meet the Trask brothers near Sweeny. They found the place and made camp by the river across from a stand of cottonwood trees. The horses were hobbled on a grassy slope where they could graze. A spitted jackrabbit sizzled over the campfire, and the smell of coffee filled the air. It just so happened to be the last of the coffee, too. They were also running low on other things. As Cordy added wood to the fire, two men rode up and stepped down from their horses. Cordy was angry and determined to dislike these spineless cowards, but the Trask brothers were not what Cordy had expected.

They shook Alva Kincade's hand and took off their hats when he introduced them to Cordy. The older one, Jake, told her right away he had a daughter about her age.

"So do I, ma'am," the other one said. He introduced himself as Milton Trask. "My Leona is about your age, too."

As the four of them sat around the campfire, Cordy tended to the roasting jackrabbit and poured them some coffee. Jake pulled out stale biscuits from his saddlebag to share.

Milton Trask was the quiet one, she noticed. Jake was the more personable of the two and seemed to have a story to tell for every occasion.

After everyone got settled, Cordy asked Milton-the-quiet-one why he robbed trains.

"I have five children to feed," he said simply.

"Where are they now?"

"On a farm I'm about to lose if I don't come up with some money soon."

"What about you?" Cordy asked Jake. "You have kids to feed, too?"

"I only got two," Jake said slowly, "but they eat a lot."

That made her father chuckle, which made Cordy angry. She took the jackrabbit off the spit to cool, unable to get over how selfish these men were.

"All three of you like using your young 'uns to justify what you know isn't right," she said. Noticing a quick glare from her father, Cordy turned away so she wouldn't have to deal with him.

"We only rob the rich ones," Milton said.

"How do you figure that?" Cordy asked. From the corner of her eye, she could see the "please be quiet" look on her father's face.

"Poor people don't ride trains," Jake said. "They're like us. They ride horses, get around on a wagon, or they walk."

Cordy had no argument for that and let it go. That night she went to sleep to the sound of mumbling voices and hushed whispers. The next morning when she woke up, her father asked for her help.

"That's all you'll have to do," Alva assured his daughter as they both waited for the coffee to begin to boil. "We jump on the train and you gather up our horses. We'll meet up with you at Possum Creek."

"Possum Creek," Cordy said. "Possum Creek runs for three miles or so."

"We'll be heading south of the trestle. Just make sure you're there with the horses. That's all you have to do."

Cordy was impatient and poured herself some weak coffee. Most of the flavor had been boiled out of the grounds the night before.

"You three have been robbing innocent rich people and then chasing your horses afterward all this time?" she asked. She shook her head and smiled.

Alva took the coffee pot off the fire and set it on the grass so the grounds could settle.

"Jake's son was helping us," Alva said, "but he's not that good with horses. Not like you."

Cordy wondered if her father thought she was buying his lame attempt at flattery. She asked what it was like to jump on a moving train from a galloping horse. Her father claimed not to be able to see well enough to hunt, so how was it he could see well enough to jump on a moving train?

"It's not easy," Alva said. "If climbing on it don't kill me, then jumping off the thing when I'm done probably will someday."

Cordy couldn't imagine him climbing on anything from a moving horse, much less a train going at full speed. His motivation for doing something so dangerous was beginning to open her eyes to just how desperate he was.

"How many more times do you have to do this?" she asked. *Maybe this is just temporary*, she thought. *Maybe he'll come to his senses and things will be back to normal soon.*

"Depends on how much we get the next time."

"We've got more now than we've ever had," Cordy reminded him.

"It's not enough. I want more for you."

Cordy pitched the rest of her coffee into the fire and stood up. "You're not doing this for me. I've got all I need right now."

"Will you get our horses for us afterward?" Alva didn't move from in front of the fire. "Then meet us at Possum Creek?"

Cordy hated what her father was becoming and she hated how their circumstances had driven him to do such things.

"Will you?" he asked louder.

"You're gonna get your fool self killed."

"Maybe. Maybe not. So will you fetch the horses for us? I need to know what to tell them."

"Yes!" she snapped. "Yes, yes, yes!"

He hadn't left her any choice.

It was painful for Cordy to watch the three men ride alongside the train and one by one jump off their horses. She held her breath until all three were safely on board. She hated the thought of one of them slipping off and getting pulled beneath the wheels. Her father surprised her at how coordinated he seemed to be, as if he had done it more than just a few times. Cordy forced herself not to think about what would happen once the three men were actually on the train. Her main focus now had to be getting all the horses to Possum Creek. That in itself would be no easy task.

The riderless horses had veered away from the train and stopped galloping quickly, but they didn't all stay together, nor was the terrain flat enough to keep them in sight. The grass this far south was still green due to a mild winter, and Cordy knew the horses would eventually stop and begin munching on the tender green shoots.

"There you are, boy," Cordy said soothingly as she eased closer to Jake's horse a while later. She had spent time with the Trask horses that morning so they would know her voice when the time came. She gathered the reins and tied it around the end of a rope. She looped the other end of the rope around the pommel on her saddle and listened carefully for signs of the other two horses. Cordy whistled and heard the low whinny of her father's horse close by in some trees. She let out a huge sigh of relief when she found them both grazing together.

"Here we go, boys," she said, and tied the horses to her lead rope and headed southwest for Possum Creek. "They can wait for us there," she said. "They'll be too busy counting their money to wonder where we are."

Chapter Three

"Well, looky here!" Jake said. He came limping out of the brush toward her. He was sopping wet from head to toe. "She's got all three with her!"

Cordy got off her horse and untied the lead rope.

"I told you she could do it," Alva said with a huge smile.

"What happened to you?" Cordy asked Jake, referring to his limp.

Milton came out of the brush to get his horse. "Jumping off the train into the creek wasn't such a good idea," he said.

"I think the possum this creek was named after got me when I hit the water," Jake said.

The other two men chuckled.

"Fools," Cordy mumbled. She led her horse to the creek so it could drink. The men did the same with theirs. "Was it worth it?" she asked her father.

He nodded, but wouldn't look at her. "Nobody got hurt," he said.

"Still don't make it right."

"Leave it alone, Cordy."

To the others she asked, "Is this the only train you rob?"

"Usually," Jake said. He got on his horse and winced at having to put pressure on his ankle.

"There's other trains in this area," she said. "You keep robbing the same one at the same place all the time, you're begging to get caught."

Milton gingerly got on his horse as well. "She's right," he said.

Her father looked at her strangely, but didn't say anything. Later that afternoon, the Trask brothers rode west after making plans with Alva to meet a week later. Cordy and her father rode back to San Antonio to stay at Mission San José until it was time to meet up with Jake and Milton again.

Leaving Elena never got easier, and watching her tease the older boys who lived at the mission made Cordy's heart ache. At night when they were supposed to be asleep, Elena was quick to tell her that the other flirtations meant nothing.

"Those boys are silly," Elena whispered in Spanish. "They only want one thing."

"What is it they want?" Cordy asked. She was relieved when Elena took her into her arms.

"This," Elena said and kissed her. After a while she took her lips away from Cordy's. "Boys will do anything for that." She reached over and cupped Cordy's breast and whispered, "And this." Elena kissed her again and Cordy could feel the most exquisite sensation in her stomach. As their kiss deepened, Cordy thought, *It's not just boys who would do anything for this!*

Thanks to Cordy's keen eye, her observant nature, and her great memory, the next train they held up was easier. Cordy remembered seeing another train late last fall, and reminded her father it didn't go as fast as the one by Possum Creek.

"You'll have a better chance of not getting your fool selves killed on this one," she said.

"How'd you get so smart?" Jake asked her after a moment.

Cordy thought, *How'd you live so long being so dumb?*

So they took the time to watch the other train, and Cordy told them where she thought the best place would be to climb on from a horse.

"It slows down a little going up an incline outside of Morris Station. You've all got good, fast horses."

"I don't know," Milton said. "I'm used to the Possum Creek train already."

"We can't keep robbing the same trains over and over," Jake said. "The kid's right. There's an incline outside Morris Station. The train will be slowing down there."

Cordy listened as they worked out the details on where she would meet them with the horses afterward. If they were going to be successful train robbers, they needed to fine-tune their approach and get their timing down right.

Alva and Milton both had bad ankle sprains this time, and Jake's ankle was still sore from the last train he had jumped from. Cordy seemed to do a lot of head-shaking when she was around them.

"We can rest up at my place," Milton said. "It's about a two-day ride from here."

Much to Cordy's dismay, her father thought it was a great idea. Cordy, however, wanted to go back to Mission San José so she could see Elena again. She didn't openly complain, but her silence was making a point with her father. She hoped he would quit this train-robbing nonsense soon.

The men never talked about the events that took place on the trains they robbed and Cordy never saw any of the loot. There was usually at least a twenty to thirty-minute time difference between the men jumping off the train and the time Cordy got to the designated meeting place with their horses. When Cordy found them, the men were ragged from having to exit the train. Robbing banks or stage coaches sounded like less work and not nearly as dangerous.

After the last heist, they were on their way again and she was glad they moved on at a steady pace. Cordy was always anxious to get away from the train tracks after a robbery. She kept scanning the hillside and half expected a posse to race toward them from the trees on the trail. Her life had changed so quickly. Cordy no longer felt as safe or as free as she had in the past.

"Where's the money?" she asked her father as they rode alongside each other. The Trask brothers rode on ahead of them. Cordy had noticed his puffed-up chest when he got on his horse, but she just wanted to make sure he had been successful this time.

"In my shirt," Alva said.

Cordy glanced at him more carefully and took in the various lumps in his shirt. He was a thin man; keeping the money there made him look more muscular.

"I just take money from the rich ones."

"So do you have enough yet?"

"We have plenty."

"Then let's head back to the mission and rest up there."

"Can't do that. We need to mend somewhere out of the way." He nodded toward the Trask brothers riding ahead of them. "Jake has a plan."

Jake? she thought. Cordy shook her head in disbelief. But Jake was probably the smartest of the three robbers. *And that's not saying much*, she reminded herself.

"Well, how far is this place we're going?" she asked.

"We'll be there late tomorrow."

Cordy was totally unprepared for Milton Trask's homestead when they rode up the following evening. The sun was beginning to set and Cordy was tired and hungry. The four weary riders stepped down from their horses; Cordy was the only one that could move without groaning.

Three young boys poured out of the cabin and ran toward Milton. He scooped up the youngest one in his arms and bent over so the others could hug his neck.

"Papa! Papa!" they shouted.

"You're home! Did you bring us something?"

"Not this time, boys."

Cordy watched as an older boy and a young woman came out and stood on the porch.

"Papa," the older boy said. He gave his father a hug and then broke into a smile when he saw his Uncle Jake.

"Henry!" Jake said. "Look how tall you are now!" He slapped him on the back and shook his hand. Jake stopped when he finally saw the young woman on the porch. "Leo? Is that you?"

She gave him a slight nod. Everyone in the yard turned to look at her. There was a seriousness about her that made Cordy uncomfortable. Leo was a beautiful young woman with a stately, commanding presence. Cordy wondered, briefly, what it would be like to talk to someone her own age again. She missed Elena more than ever before. This Leo person was far from ordinary. Something in her eyes showed intelligence, and something else in her manner demanded respect. Cordy also got the distinct impression that Leo was someone to be avoided if at all possible. There was no humor in her expression, and little joy or relief at seeing her father again.

"Henry," Leo called from the porch. "See to their horses."

Cordy took the reins of her father's horse and hers and followed Henry to the barn. She was glad to be away from the cold glare of the young woman on the porch.

"Name's Henry. What's yours?" he asked.

She removed the saddle from her horse and threw it over a low rail in the barn. A milk cow on the other side of the rail gave her a low moo as she blinked long eyelashes.

"Cordy," she said. She had both saddles off before Henry had even started on his.

Two of the other boys came into the barn. One was carrying a pail of water.

"My name's Earl. That's my brother Eb. We're twins."

Cordy looked at their faces and smiled.

"Earl's the friendly one," Henry said. "Like me. Eb don't ever smile. He's like Leo." He removed the other two saddles and set them on the rail also. "Make sure all the horses get a good drink," Henry told the younger boys. To Cordy he said, "I'll show you around."

"I'll stay with the horses."

"The twins here can take care of 'em."

She allowed Earl to begin unsaddling the horse she was closest to.

"Come on," Henry insisted. "I'll show you around."

Cordy followed him out of the barn and saw no sign of her father, Milton or Jake.

"Where's my Pa?"

"In the cabin, most likely."

"Then show me that first."

She was relieved to see her father sitting at the table. The smell of bacon frying made her stomach growl.

"There you are," Alva said.

Cordy took in the cabin with a quick glance. It was clean and bigger than it looked from the outside. It had a wooden floor. The faint smell of smoke from the fireplace was nice and familiar to her. She could see a loft and a few pieces of furniture, but no clutter anywhere. Cordy noticed a lit lantern in the corner away from the fireplace. It gave off enough light for the entire room. There was a big table and several chairs that dominated most of the cabin space, and a window by the front door and a cook stove on the other side of the huge table. Cordy could see a ladder leading up to the loft, a bed in one corner and another room off to the left. The window had curtains on it and gave the inside of the cabin a warm, civilized feeling. Cordy had lived like this before her mother died. It made her sad to be there now.

"Cordy, this is my daughter, Leona," Milton said. "We call her Leo."

"Welcome," Leo said, without looking at her.

Cordy knew the polite thing to do would be to ask if she could help with anything, but Leo seemed totally unapproachable. Cordy felt more comfortable in the barn with the horses.

"Sit here," Henry said as he pulled out a heavy wooden chair for her. Cordy sat down and took off her hat.

The sound of grease popping in the skillet made the cabin seem more like a home than anywhere Cordy had been in years. She understood why Milton wanted to do whatever he could to keep this place. As she sat down next to Henry at the table, Cordy noticed that biscuits were already in the early dough stage. A smudge of flour on Leo's cheek seemed to soften her a bit.

"I'll get some water," Henry said as he got up again. He smiled at Cordy on his way out the door with a pail in hand. She noticed all the adult Trasks were tall, thin and had thick black hair. Jake's was sprinkled with gray, but he still had a lot of it.

Being inside gave Cordy a mild case of claustrophobia. She was used to being in the open air. She followed Henry outside and sat on the porch steps. A few minutes later he returned with a full pail of water. He set the pail on the porch and sat down.

"How long have you known my father and Uncle Jake?"

"Not long."

"Where did you meet them?"

Cordy glanced at him, but didn't answer. He was about the same age as the boys Elena teased at the mission. *They only want one thing*, she remembered Elena saying.

"Our corn crop's dead," Henry said. "No rain, but we can use it for fodder."

Cordy's stomach grumbled again.

"Got a new rifle," Henry said.

"Use it much?"

"Every day."

The twins came out of the barn and closed the door. As they reached the porch, Earl said, "Fed and watered 'em. I'll tell Uncle Jake the bay needs a new shoe."

"Here. Take this in to Leo," Henry said, pointing toward the pail of water.

Cordy could smell bacon frying inside the cabin. Her stomach growled even louder this time. Breakfast had been jerky and water, and had worn off hours ago.

Earl picked up the water pail and the twins went inside the cabin. A few minutes later, the door opened and Earl came back out again.

"Leo says it's almost time for supper, so don't go wandering off."

Henry stood up, stretched and smiled. "There's nowhere to go wanderin' off to anyway."

"Where you from?" Earl asked Cordy. He had his father's dark brown eyes and an engaging smile.

"All over," Cordy said.

"You got a Ma?"

"No."

"Us either."

A solemn moment passed between the three of them. Finally, Earl said, "I'll go see about the chickens. That fox has been around again."

Chapter Four

Leo's initial relief at having her father and Uncle Jake there was purely selfish—it meant she didn't have to be in charge now. The responsibilities that went along with being the oldest were one thing, but being totally responsible for four other people in her father's absence had been a burden. When Papa left the first time, Leo resented his ability to just leave them alone, while Leo and Henry struggled to keep the farm going and everyone fed. Leo still missed her mother, and ached for the times when they had all been together.

"How are Essie and Frederick?" Leo asked Uncle Jake as she checked on the biscuits. Jake had always been her favorite uncle. There was a playfulness about him unlike any other adult she had ever known. He always had tricks to show, and amusing stories to tell. He was what Leo's mother once referred to as a "charmer." Leo had never been sure whether that was a good or a bad thing.

"They're fine," Jake said. "Essie's married now and Frederick works as a surveyor in San Antonio. We meet up ever so often."

"Married," Leo said under her breath with a cringe. She hadn't seen her cousins in years. Essie was sixteen, Leo's age. They had lived together in Ohio before moving to Texas when the girls, Henry, and Frederick were all small. Playing with her cousins in the first snow in Ohio was one of Leo's best memories. *So Essie is married now,* she thought. *Cleaning, cooking, caring for children and a husband.* Leo couldn't imagine getting married and doing that willingly. She longed for solitude, often having dreams about living alone and having no one but herself to look after.

"Where'd Cordy go?" Milton asked. Little Luther helped his father get his boots off and then Milton showed him his huge, purple ankle.

"How'd you do that, Papa?" Luther asked.

"Landed on it wrong."

"Let's see if mine's any prettier," Uncle Jake said.

Luther hurried over to help Jake get his boots off, too.

"Look at that!" Luther said, his eyes wide with amazement. "You landed on yours wrong, too!"

"Must have!" Jake said.

Leo glanced at the two swollen ankles in question and raised an eyebrow. She would have questions for her father later.

The twins came in with the water pail. Leo motioned for Earl, and he met her in the corner of the room where she was tending to the frying bacon.

"Where's Henry?" she asked in a whisper.

"On the porch talkin' to that girl," he whispered back.

"Go out there and see what you can find out."

"About what?"

"Just ask her some questions."

Earl nodded and went back outside. They didn't come in again until Leo sent Luther to get them all for supper.

❧❧

Leo stayed up late cleaning the kitchen and washing dishes to the chatter of Uncle Jake and his wild tales. Luther fell asleep at the table, his little shaggy head nodding over to the side at an angle that made Leo's neck hurt just looking at him. She saw her father pick him up and hobble barefoot to his own bed in the far corner of the cabin. Milton tucked in his youngest son and kissed him on the brow.

"Cordy can sleep with you," Papa said to Leo a while later. "Jake and Alva can sleep on pallets here by the fire."

"The barn's fine for us," Cordy said from the end of the table. She glared at her father, who nodded.

Leo was relieved not having to share her bed with a stranger.

"There's plenty of room in the cabin," Milton said.

"We'll be fine in the barn," Alva replied.

"I can bunk with the twins," Henry said. "Uncle Jake can have my bed."

Leo told her brother to help Alva and Cordy get settled out there. "Take the lantern and show them the way if that's where they'd rather be."

Henry adjusted the lantern and led them to the barn. Cordy followed him out the door with Alva limping along behind them. Alva left the door open and Leo crossed the room to close it.

"Where'd you two meet up with them?" she asked Uncle Jake. With the lantern gone, they only had the light from the small fire in the fireplace to see by.

"Down south of here," Jake said. "That Cordy's a smart one."

"Not too friendly, though," Leo said.

Jake laughed, but didn't disagree.

In the small bedroom that had once belonged to her parents, Leo loosened the long black hair neatly piled on top of her head. She combed it the way her mother used to when she was a child. Hearing Henry come back in from the barn, Leo went to her bedroom door and looked at him. Henry shrugged, indicating nothing new to report.

Leo thought how nice it was to have Papa and Uncle Jake there with them. She was certain her father would leave them again soon, especially since Jake was with him. Uncle Jake was fun for children to be around, but Leo remembered many nights when her parents argued over the amount of time Papa spent with his brother. Jake's antics never failed to get Milton in trouble with his wife, whether it was the drinking, the improvised sled attached to a horse when there was snow in Ohio, or moving the outhouse forward a few feet after dark. Uncle Jake had a history of irresponsible behavior, Leo was starting to remember. She loved Jake, but didn't like Papa associating with him.

Leo was tired when she crawled into bed, but there were so many unfamiliar sounds in the cabin—like throat-clearing and men coughing—that she had trouble falling asleep. Even with Papa home, the next day would not change for her. More meals to prepare, more people to clean up after, but she could overlook that for now. The thought that the rest of her life would consist of this every day was what disturbed her the most. Something always needed mending or fixed, someone was always hungry or sick. The only time she had to herself was when she was in bed at night . . . when the others were asleep and there was nothing to wash, sweep, scrub or feed. *Do all women hate this as much as I do?* she wondered. *Could Essie possibly enjoy this constant servitude? Will I be stuck here raising kids forever?* At times like this Leo became angry at her mother for dying and leaving them so unprepared for life without her. *Maybe it's time the workload was more evenly shared,* she thought.

Leo formed the plan in her head. She wouldn't put it into action until Papa announced he was leaving again to go back to work—wherever "work" was. Leo and Henry were both aware that things were not as they seemed as far as Papa and a job were concerned.

Every morning Henry and Cordy left to go hunting, so there was fresh meat or fish for dinner. Leo continued to clean up after everyone while the three men sat around the table drinking coffee and telling stories most of the day, under the pretense of letting their ankles heal. Leo had to admit that the two purple ankles, Papa's left and Uncle Jake's right, appeared to be quite painful. Alva Kincade had no visible injuries and could wear both of his boots, so he had no real excuse for sitting around doing nothing all day.

Leo had to constantly remind the three younger boys that just because Papa was home and company was there, chores still had to be done.

"What if I decided not to do my chores today?" Leo asked eight-year-old Luther. "Who would fix your bacon?"

"Henry," he said.

Luther and Leo both laughed. She tousled his shaggy hair. "Wait till I tell him you said that. Now go let the chickens out and give them fresh water. They're depending on you today."

Yes, indeed, Leo thought as she watched her little brother go out the door to begin his chores. She had given the twins a similar speech earlier before sending them to the barn to clean up after the horses and turn the cow out into the corn after milking. Leo also had a list for Henry when he got back from hunting.

Much to her surprise, Leo wouldn't have known Cordy was even there most of the time. She came to the cabin to eat, then was gone again.

"I've been asking her questions to see what Papa's been doing while he was away," Henry told Leo after supper. They were the only two in the cabin. Everyone else was out on the porch.

"What did she say?"

"Not much of anything. She's loyal all the way to the bone," he said. "We'll get more out of Papa and Uncle Jake than Cordy."

"Keep trying. I'll ask Papa if I have to," Leo said, "but I'm not sure how much he'll tell me."

As the days passed, there was more activity outside the cabin. With their purple ankles beginning to heal, the men seemed to become more restless. They helped mend fences, chop wood, and patch the barn where woodpeckers had formed perfectly round holes. The small homestead looked good, but Leo still had an uneasiness deep inside that made her feel afraid and empty. When Papa requested that the twins take his and Uncle Jake's horses out and give them a good run, Leo knew they would be riding out again soon.

Then one night a few evenings later, Papa got out of bed while Leo was combing her hair. In hushed tones he told her he and the others would be leaving in the morning. Henry was to take the younger boys to the creek fishing.

"When will you be back?"

"I don't know this time."

"We need you here," Leo said. She heard the panic in her voice and hated it. At that moment Leo thought she also hated him for wanting to leave them again, but pushed the thought out of her head.

"Here's two hundred dollars," he whispered, and stuffed a roll of bills in her hand. He put his own big hands around Leo's and squeezed firmly. "Send Henry to town for supplies. Be frugal. I don't know when I'll be back with more."

"Two hundred dollars," Leo muttered. She was trembling. She had never seen so much money before. It was more than they would see in two years . . . maybe longer! "Where are you getting this money!" she hissed.

"Just take it and do the best you can for my boys."

He let go of her hand and went back to bed. Leo clutched the huge wad of bills to her chest and couldn't stop shaking.

"They were biting today," Henry said as he held up a stick with several nice fish on it. "Luther caught this big one."

"Eb helped me pull it out!" Luther said with a beaming grin.

"Where's Papa?" Earl asked. The boys looked around the empty cabin. "Where is he?"

"They left," Leo said quietly. She again resented being the one to break the news. "He had to go back to work."

27

Henry went outside and slammed the door, while Luther began to cry.

"Go help Henry clean your fish."

Enough time had passed for Leo to work through some of her anger at her father for leaving them alone again. Her brothers, however, still had that ahead of them. Leo had a plan now. It included keeping them all too busy to miss their father, in addition to spreading the chores around in an attempt to make no one indispensable. She would bring it up at supper and put the plan in action beginning the next day. Leo now knew she was the one who would keep them all together. There was no one else they could depend on.

They were a sad and sorry bunch at the table that evening for supper. Seeing her brothers' long disappointed faces made Leo's anger at her father bubble up inside. In order to give them something new to chew on and take their minds off Papa's absence, Leo laid out her new plan.

"I have a question for all of you," she said. She had watched the younger ones pick at their food long enough. "What would happen if I got sick?"

Luther raised his head and looked at her. "Like Ma?"

"No," Leo said. "Not like Ma. Not as *bad* as Ma. But what if I was a different kind of sick . . . sick where I couldn't get out of bed for a few days?"

"We'd take care of you," Earl said.

Leo nodded, then said, "And who would take care of *you*?" She pointed a finger at each of them. "Who would cook your breakfast? Who would clean your clothes?"

All four boys looked at each other with wide eyes and perplexed expressions. Finally, Luther said, "We'd wait till you felt better."

Leo pursed her lips and checked a bite-size piece of fish for small bones before making her point. "So, Luther. If I was sick for a week, you would wait until I felt better before you'd have any breakfast?"

"No!" he said. Everyone laughed.

"Then who would make your breakfast?"

Luther took his fork and pointed at his older brother and said, "Henry!"

"Me?" Henry said. "Why me?"

Their laughter made Leo smile.

"Me and Earl would hold you up in front of the stove three times a day," Eb said to his sister. Leo glared at him, but the laughter from the others made it hard for her to keep a stern expression.

"Earl and I," Leo said, correcting his grammar the way their mother used to do.

"Whoever," Eb said. He raised his head and smiled at her before returning his attention back to his plate.

"Then I have another question for everyone," she said. "Suppose a bee stung Henry on the face and his eyes got swollen shut for a few days."

The other three boys glanced over at Henry, but were beginning to eat more slowly now.

"When this bee stings Henry," Eb said, "are you still sick in bed?"

Earl and Henry laughed out loud, while Leo took a deep breath.

"I could be," she said. "Let's suppose that's the way it happened. I'm too sick to get out of bed and Henry can't see to cook Luther's breakfast or go hunting." She looked at the twins. "What would you do?"

Henry stopped smiling and met Leo's eyes. His expression changed. It was as though he had read her thoughts. He turned to Earl and asked him what he would do if that situation presented itself.

"I don't know," Earl admitted.

"Eb?" Henry asked.

"I don't know either," he said.

"Luther?" Leo prompted. "What would you do?"

He shrugged and picked at the fried fish on his plate. "Learn how to fry bacon, I reckon."

After supper, Leo outlined her new plan, expecting some opposition and discontent. She was not disappointed.

"That's girl's work!" Eb said in disgust.

"As of right now," Leo said, "there is no girl's work or boy's work. It's all just work."

"So you'll clean out the hen house while I'm doing dishes?" Earl asked incredulously.

"Who do you think cleaned the hen house before you came along?" Leo asked him simply. "But to answer your question—yes. We will all learn to do everyone else's chores and share in the responsibilities of keeping this place going and putting food on the table. Henry will learn to cook and he'll teach us all how to hunt. I'll show you each how to mend a shirt and all of you can teach me how to chop wood."

There was silence around the table before Henry said, "She's right. It won't hurt us to learn to fend for ourselves in case some day we have to."

"Wait till Papa hears about this," Earl mumbled.

Leo sighed. "Papa's probably wishing right now that he knew how to cook."

Chapter Five

Cordy suggested they locate some of the trains going east or even north toward Dallas. She didn't like the idea of doing any of this too close to where they usually traveled or spent a lot of personal time. Jake tended to listen to her suggestions and even asked for her advice on several occasions. The other two were followers and did whatever they were told.

"You three are getting too old for trains," Cordy said. She had a six-foot-long rattlesnake skinned and roasting in several pieces on the spit.

"She's right, Milton," Jake said. "We *are* old for this business. If you broke a leg, we'd have to shoot you." A few chuckles went around the campfire. "You got a better idea than robbing trains?" Jake asked her.

"Banks," Cordy said. "Hit small towns. The only thing you'll have to jump on and off of are your horses. And they'll be standing still while you do it."

"Hmm," he said with a nod. "That's true. My ankle starts to throb each time it hears the word train. What else are you thinking about with these banks?"

"Hit them early just before they open or late as they're closing," Cordy said. "And never hit the same one twice. They'll always be on the lookout for you after that. It'd be too dangerous then."

Alva took a long drink from his canteen, then said, "Won't it look strange for three riders to come up and go in a bank before it opens? Or after it closes?"

Cordy and Jake looked at him. Her father not only wasn't cut out for a life of crime and adventure, he didn't even have good survival instincts or plain common sense. His fast horse was one of the two reasons he'd been asked to join the Trask brothers—the other reason being the way he had bragged to them about his daughter's way with horses and her possible willingness to round them up during a train robbery.

"We'll work out a plan," Jake said, motioning to himself and Cordy.

It was the first indication Cordy could remember where any of the men considered her a part of their operation. She was no longer just the kid who collected horses after a train robbery, or the person who scrounged up a meal and kept them fed. She was becoming a vital part of everything they did.

The decision on what their next job would be led to a lengthy discussion. Alva and Milton didn't want to try robbing a bank yet. Even though train heists were physically punishing, Milton argued that at least it was something he was familiar with.

"On a train, I can pick who I want to steal from," Alva said in agreement. He blew on a piece of rattlesnake that was smoking and still skewered on a thin stick. "The men in their fancy clothes and fat money rolls. Robbing a bank won't give me that choice. I could be taking regular people's money if I'm robbing banks."

"Regular people don't have any money," Milton reminded him.

Jake grunted and then shook his head. "Sounds like another

good reason to rob a bank. If poor people and regular people don't have any money, then only rich people keep their money in the bank."

Cordy snickered at Jake's logic, but noticed the other two said nothing.

"These old bones can't be jumping off too many more trains," Jake said. "You two aren't doing so good either."

Cordy handed him a stick with a nice chunk of cooked rattlesnake on it. He took it from her and inspected it closely.

"What's rattlesnake taste like, Alva?" Jake asked, never taking his eyes away from the toasted hunk of meat on the stick.

"Chicken," Alva said. "Bony chicken. Mostly all ribs."

"Don't seem natural," Jake said as he blew on the snake piece.

"You ever had possum this way?" Cordy asked.

"Possum on a stick?" Jake asked. "Nope. Stewed with turnips and carrots. Now that's good eatin'."

"I'd rather have a snake than a possum," Cordy said. "Easier to clean and no fat to deal with."

"When you two get finished exchangin' recipes, you let us know," Alva said. "We need to decide which train we're gonna rob next."

Cordy and her father rode into a town called Bailey's Fork to get some supplies and look for the train schedule. At the General Store, Alva purchased rifle shells, ammo for his six-shooter, coffee, dried apple slices and jerky. They put most of the supplies in Cordy's saddlebags alongside the rest of her meager possessions. At the small train depot, Alva asked about the train schedule, and while they were there, Cordy saw the wanted poster with the three men on it. The poster had a primitive likeness of Jake, Milton and Alva. With hats pulled down snug on their heads, the wanted poster revealed three scruffy bandits with wild eyes. There was a five hundred dollar reward being offered for them. Cordy felt a sinking sensation in the pit of her stomach. As her father asked the ticket agent a few questions, Cordy looked around slowly before reaching over and snatching the poster off the side of the ticket office.

With shaking hands, she folded the paper up and put it in her pocket. Anxious to get out of town, she tugged on her father's hand and said, "Let's go."

Alva tipped his hat to the ticket agent and he and Cordy got on their horses and rode out of town.

"This don't look nothin' like me!" Jake said. "These wrinkles around the eyes here," he said, pointing to the poster that had been passed around the campfire at least three times already. "This don't look nothin' like me!"

"So you think there's three other men out there robbing trains?" Cordy asked.

There was total silence as they all stared at the small fire burning in front of them. Jake wadded up the wanted poster and tossed it in the fire.

"What did you expect?" Cordy asked. "You can't do this forever. You've all been lucky so far."

"I say we do a bank next," Jake said. He was still pouting about the wrinkles around the eyes on the poster. "That old one was you," he said, pointing to Alva.

"I was the tall one," Alva said. "No wrinkles here on this face."

"Maybe we should do one more train," Milton said. "Away from these parts. Up around Austin or Waco maybe."

Cordy sighed her frustration. *They haven't learned a thing*, she thought.

"Austin's about a four-day ride from here," Alva said.

"Those posters could be all over the state by now," Cordy said. "You can't out-ride them."

"It doesn't matter where those wanted posters are," Jake said. "They don't look nothin' like us anyway!"

"I need more money," Milton said. "I can't quit now."

"Me neither," Alva said.

Cordy looked at her father. She didn't know him any longer. She was afraid for him, but knew he wouldn't listen to her or anyone else. She kept quiet and let them figure it out.

They compromised on the location of the next train to be robbed. Cordy finally let them know that if they wanted her help with recovering the horses, they would need to find a part of the state they hadn't been to yet.

So as not to draw attention to themselves, Cordy and her father rode out two days ahead of the Trask brothers, who would meet them at Onion Creek outside of Austin. Her father was too quiet for Cordy's liking. When he got this way she imagined him to be lost in thought about her mother. She asked him several times when he thought he would have enough money.

"Soon," he said.

"Soon" as in one more train to rob? she wondered. *"Soon" as in a week, a month, a year from now?* It occurred to her more than once that her father didn't care what happened to himself any longer. The light was gone from his eyes and he never talked about his hopes and dreams any longer. He had a weariness about him that worried her. Without him, Cordy would be alone.

"Let's make camp here," he said.

Cordy let him take care of the horses and get a fire going. She took her rifle and set out hunting for their supper, staying close to the river so as not to get lost. Fifteen minutes later she was back with a rabbit. It felt comfortable with just the two of them. Cordy wished things could stay this way forever.

Two days later they reached Onion Creek. It was far enough away from Austin to give the bandits time to do what they needed to do on the train before jumping off and meeting up with Cordy and the horses. While she and her father waited for the Trask brothers to arrive, Cordy had time to get to know the area. There were several places that would be good to hide the horses. She showed her father her favorite one and decided it was the best place to meet them afterward.

Several times she stopped herself from telling him to be careful. She didn't have a good feeling about this. Jake and Milton's arrival eased some of her fears, but only because Jake was so confident about the passengers on this particular train.

"Lots of rich ranchers in this area," he said. "They go to San Antone to sell and buy more cattle. We'll get 'em before they can spend their money."

Cordy wasn't about to get into it with any of them. All she wanted to know was where they were getting on the train and where they wanted her to be with the horses when they got off.

"Did either of you see any wanted posters on the way here?" Jake asked.

"No," Alva said.

"We ain't known in these parts yet." Jake had a twinkle in his eye when he added, "But we will be soon."

Later as Cordy was settling down for the night, she heard her father tell them where she would be with the horses. She also heard him say that this would be his last time stealing from other people.

"I've got enough money now to take care of my little girl," Alva said. "We might go back East. I still have family there."

Finally, she thought. *He's giving it up!* That brought a smile to her face along with a relieved sigh. But then when she thought about what he said about wanting to go back East, Cordy's excitement faded a bit. Texas was her home. She couldn't imagine ever leaving it. But this train-robbing phase was finally coming to an end for them, and she slept well that night.

"Be careful," she said as the three men mounted their horses.

"We're always careful," Jake said.

Alva and Milton never spoke before a heist. Cordy attributed that to nerves. Jake, on the other hand, talked constantly no matter what.

36

Having camped close to the tracks, they had been ready for hours. Jake's horse reared up at the first sound of the train and seemed more anxious to get started than either Milton or Alva were. The men rode off and were racing their horses at full speed by the time the train reached them. Cordy's horse followed at a slower pace. She saw Milton jump on first, then her father and then Jake. It was always such a relief for her to see them all get on the train safely.

As the horses trotted off, Cordy followed them. Jake's horse was the last one to respond to her whistle, and once she found him, Cordy tied the three reins to a rope and led them to the designated meeting place.

After the first two hours and no sign of them, Cordy imagined the three men limping on punished ankles that were probably a nice shade of blue already. But when the third hour passed, she began to worry. *What if all three of them broke a leg jumping off?* she thought. *Or if they got confused about where to meet me?*

She tied the three horses to a tree at the edge of the clearing where the men should have met up with her, then set out riding along the tracks. Cordy searched for them until it was almost dark, but didn't find any trace. On her way back to the horses, she prayed to find her father and his friends waiting for her, but there was no sign of them there either. With darkness quickly approaching Cordy decided to make camp and get the horses watered and hobbled so they could graze.

At first light, she tended to the horses again and led them to the creek two at a time. She was afraid. Cordy had never felt so alone before. Still clinging to hope, she half-expected to see her father and his friends stumble into camp at any moment. After watering the horses and staking them out in fresh grass near the clearing, Cordy rode up and down the tracks again, calling out their names until her throat hurt. Each time she went a little farther than the time before, thinking maybe they had stayed on the train longer than expected.

She even thought perhaps they had gotten disoriented and jumped off the wrong side of the train and gotten lost in the brush.

At the end of the second day—tired, hungry, and frightened—Cordy returned to the clearing again to rest and tend to the horses. She added her own saddle to the semi-circle the other three saddles had formed around the ashes from last night's campfire. Gathering up all the saddlebags, she began going through them, searching for food. In addition to the pocket watches, rings, necklaces and lockets, Cordy found more money than she could hold in her arms, along with six pistols, boxes of ammo and a pile of gold and silver coins. The last saddlebag she went through was her father's, where she found a large stash of bills to add to the pile, a picture of her mother, and some dried apple slices and jerky.

Cordy put a piece of jerky in her mouth with a shaking hand. She held the picture of her mother to her chest. "They aren't coming back," she whispered, as if telling her mother something neither of them had known before.

Chapter Six

It had been almost a month since her father and Uncle Jake left. Even though Leo was still angry that Papa had not returned, she did what had to be done. Leo's resentment of Papa's freedom to come and go as he pleased was ever-present, but Leo's skepticism about the kind of work he was doing gave her just one more thing to worry about. To compensate for her frustration, Leo made the best of a frightening, uneasy situation. Without physically leaving the farm, she devised her own kind of freedom.

The boys resigned themselves to Leo's new way of doing things. The siblings even looked forward to the days when it was Earl's turn for kitchen duty. He had a knack for baking pies and liked experimenting with various herbs and spices their mother had kept stored in the cupboard. On the other hand, Leo and Luther combined their efforts and did their chores as a team. The oldest and the youngest chopped wood together, gathered eggs, cleaned the barn, and cooked two days out of the week. Luther taught Leo how to fish, while Leo taught her little brother how to fry bacon and make jackcakes.

As it turned out, Eb and Henry were not at their best on the days when it was their turn to cook and clean, but after the first two weeks, they finally stopped complaining and got their chores done. With Leo in a better mood, things were more pleasant around the farm.

There were evenings when they sat by the fire and she read to her brothers from old newspapers their mother had collected and saved. In addition, Leo spent part of that time helping the younger boys with their studies. They lived too far from town to attend the small school there. Before becoming so ill, their mother taught the children at home. Leo wanted to give Luther a similar opportunity, but knew her efforts to keep some sort of normal routine in their lives wouldn't be appreciated now. The boys didn't like having to sit still long enough to learn anything, but Leo remained rigid.

"I'm tired from raking hay all day," Henry said as Leo continued to point to his chair at the table.

"Sit," she said. "Luther and I are just as tired from doing everyone's laundry today."

"*I'm* tired of hearing all this complaining," Earl said, fighting back a grin.

Leo passed out slates to the three younger boys and they went over the spelling lesson for the week. To keep Henry involved, Leo had him help when it came to the problem-solving portion of their studies. Eb was forever grumbling about arithmetic.

Henry looked at the younger boys and said, "Now suppose you're buying a three-dollar pig."

"We got pigs already," Eb said. "I wouldn't be buyin' one."

"Suppose you have to buy *another* pig," Henry said with an arched brow. "Then while you're there, you want to buy some chicks."

"Got chicks already, too," Eb said. "Hatched out last week."

Luther giggled, but kept listening to Henry. It was a subtraction problem that involved money and bartering. As Leo watched the boys work through the scenario Henry laid out for them, her thoughts went to the money Papa had given her before he left the last time.

Without knowing when Papa would be back again, Leo was busy thinking ahead and trying to get an idea about where they currently stood. They were already having to hunt in other areas near the cabin in order to find fresh meat. To vary their diet, they were fortunate that fish were plentiful in the creek and had become another staple for them. Leo worried about the garden and the lack of rain, and their next crop when it came time for planting. In the evenings they carried water from the well and kept the garden alive that way. It seemed as though the harder they all worked, the more Leo detested life on a farm. It was a never-ending struggle just to stay alive. She had to admit that the little homestead had never looked better, but there was always something new that needed tending to.

"Luther," Henry said. "Did you get an answer yet?"

Hesitating for several moments, Luther finally said, "Two dollars."

"That's what I got," Earl agreed with a nod.

"Me, too," Eb said.

Henry grinned at Leo sitting at the other end of the table. "Arithmetic lesson is finished."

Leo didn't comment, even though her idea of arithmetic didn't agree with his. "Then let's do some reading," she said.

Eb groaned and Luther slumped in his chair. Leo carefully opened the *Primer* to the middle and then slid the small book across the table to Earl. Leo and Henry knew the book by heart from years of reading it aloud to their mother. The print was large and the pages yellowed with age. For Leo, just touching the book and being close to its musty pages made her think of her mother. Hearing Earl's slow progress through the first paragraph of his reading

41

assignment reminded Leo of her own attempts at trying to master the written word when she was younger.

After finishing, Earl handed the book to Eb, whose low monotone drained the very life out of the story. As if purposely trying to make his short reading assignment as painful for everyone as he could, Eb pronounced all words correctly and ended with absolutely no enthusiasm. He then handed the small book to his younger brother Luther.

"The rest of you can go to bed now," Leo said.

Henry, Eb and Earl scrambled up from the table as if afraid she might change her mind and find something else for them to do. Leo took Luther by the hand and led him closer to the fireplace where the light was better. They sat down, and with her arm around him and Luther holding the book, she helped him as he stumbled over words and sounded them out. When he yawned for the second time, Leo hugged him and put the book away.

Leo, Henry and Luther were at the edge of the woods near the creek practicing with the new rifle. Henry showed them the best way to hit what they were aiming at. Even though Luther was small, he was an extremely good shot. Henry and Leo exchanged wide-eyed looks as Luther repeatedly popped twigs off an old oak tree from forty yards away. After that uncanny display of marksmanship, Luther officially became Henry's new hunting partner.

"Leo! Henry!" a far-away voice called.

"Over here!" Henry yelled.

The three of them started to run toward the voice that had to be one of the twins. Leo felt panic in her heart. Her mind raced with the possibilities of how one of them could have gotten hurt.

Henry reached Earl first and then waved to Leo, letting her know that everything was fine. When she and Luther were close enough, Henry said, "Cordy's here. Alone."

Cordy, Leo thought. She looked over at Henry and saw fear in his eyes. He was ready for whatever needed to be done with the younger boys right then.

"Earl, why don't you and Luther go down to the creek and look for—"

"Is Papa home?" Luther asked.

"Earl," Henry said. "The creek."

"Come on, Luther," Earl said grumpily. "Let's go to the creek."

Leo and Henry didn't speak all the way back to the cabin. They found Eb and Cordy in the barn unsaddling four horses.

"Where's Papa?" Henry asked.

Cordy looked tired and thin. Leo saw the layer of dust on her and wondered how long she had been riding. Cordy's expression was hard, her eyes dark and cold.

"She rode up with all four horses," Eb said, stating the obvious. "I can take care of this."

Cordy slung a saddlebag over her shoulder. With a heavy thud, it hit her back. Cordy looked at Henry, then at Leo, and then back at Henry again.

"We need to talk," she said. "After that I need some sleep." Cordy nodded toward the hay next to the horses. "Here will be fine."

"We have room for you in the cabin," Leo said. "Let's get you something to eat."

"I'll carry that for you," Henry said as he reached for the saddlebag.

"I've got it," Cordy said and brushed passed him.

She's here with four horses, Leo thought as she and Henry hurried to catch up with her. *Where is Papa? Where's Uncle Jake?*

Inside the cabin Leo poured fresh water into a basin. Cordy washed her face and hands, but kept the saddlebag close by her side. When she finished at the basin, she came over to the table and sat down in the chair where Henry usually sat.

"They were robbing trains," Cordy said. Her tone was even and her voice was low.

"What?" Henry said. "*Who* was robbing trains?"

"All of them. Jake, Milton and my Pa," Cordy said tiredly. "I was running down the horses afterward." Her voice dropped to almost a whisper. She explained how the three men were supposed to meet her in a clearing, but never showed up. "I searched for them for two days. I asked around in a few of the towns in the area, but no one knew anything. No one had seen them."

Leo could tell that Henry didn't believe her. Leo herself didn't want to believe her, but the gifts Papa had brought and the money he had given her before he left had to have come from somewhere. There had been too much money for any kind of honest job.

"My father would never—"

"Henry," Leo said.

He stopped and looked at her.

"I believe her," Leo said.

Cordy laughed bitterly. "I don't care whether you believe me or not. It wasn't easy getting them here, but I thought you could use Jake and Milton's horses. And this," she said as she opened the saddlebag and took out a stack of bills that made Henry and Leo gasp. "This is Milton and Jake's cut. They had all this money from other trains they'd robbed. I'm keeping what Pa had."

Leo was stunned, but Henry's face registered disbelief and horror. Leo heard a ruckus outside and recognized Luther's voice as he yelled for Papa. She reached over, snatched up the stack of money and rushed to her room where she had the rest of it hidden.

Since it was Eb's turn for cabin duty, it meant smoked ham slices and beans for supper. That was all he knew how to cook. The cabin was quiet once Leo got Luther settled down. Having Papa and Uncle Jake's horses in the barn without either of the men there was unsettling. She could placate Luther with empty words, but it was Henry who worried Leo the most. Cordy had not brought them good news. Their father and uncle were missing. Leo and Henry were in shock, but Leo attempted to carry on as if everything was fine.

While Leo hid the money, Cordy had returned to the barn to see to the horses. Leo wanted to ask her more questions and get an idea where Papa had been the last time Cordy had seen him. Luther, however, had vocalized everyone's fear as he stormed into the cabin, out of breath from running all the way from the creek. Leo picked him up, wondering when he had gotten so heavy.

"He wouldn't stay at the creek," Earl said, nodding toward Luther who was crying. "I tried to stop him, but he got away from me."

"Let's go get the chickens some fresh water," Leo said to her little brother.

Luther put his arms around her neck and squeezed. "Where's Papa?" he whispered with a sniff.

"He's working," Leo said. Once she got him out on the porch, she set him down and took his hand.

"We gave the chickens fresh water this morning," he said.

"And that means it's not fresh anymore," Leo said. She reached out and tousled his hair. It was a gesture Papa always did when he teased them. Leo felt fear gurgling in her throat. If they were orphans now, she wanted to know . . . she needed to know. Something deep inside told her their lives had changed forever.

Chapter Seven

The younger boys finally went to bed. Supper had been a quiet mixture of stoic chewing and intense thinking for Leo. She couldn't shut her mind off. A few key phrases repeated themselves over and over again in her head. *Papa's gone and gotten himself killed,* was one thought, with the next being, *Now I have four other people to look after on my own.* She didn't want to believe her father was dead. He was a good, caring man. They loved him. They needed him. Leo's resourcefulness and determination to get through things like having a sickly mother or a missing father were not registering. All she could think about was working through this one day at a time, and hoping to somehow come out ahead in the end.

Earlier that evening, Leo felt some semblance of normalcy when Cordy joined them for supper. The girl was so quiet, Leo never knew when she was around. Earl urged Cordy to eat and sleep in the cabin with them.

All the Trasks had been unusually quiet at the table that evening, each lost in his or her own thoughts. Cordy had wasted no time finishing her smoked ham and beans, leaving the table and the cabin with nothing more than a muttered thank you. No one else had anything to say. The tension remained thick long after the younger boys climbed up to the loft to go to bed.

Finally, Henry broke the silence after he and Leo had been sitting alone for several minutes. Keeping his voice low, he said, "We have to do something." He sat with his chair turned toward the fire. Staring at its glowing coals, he had a bewildered, lost look on his face. *The older he gets, the more he resembles Papa*, Leo thought.

"You wait here," Leo said, picking up the lantern and holding it high on her way outside. It was a cool spring evening; the breeze felt good on her face. Striding down the steps and across the yard, she got to the barn and opened the door just enough to slip inside with the lantern. Leo made a low smacking noise with her lips to let the horses and the cow know she was there. In return, she was greeted by the sound of a pistol being cocked. The hair on the back of her neck stood up. She raised the lantern to get a better look at Cordy on the other side of the horses. Cordy was sitting on a pile of hay. Their eyes met and Cordy slowly uncocked the pistol and slipped it in a holster lying beside her.

"I didn't mean to startle you," Leo said.

"It's your barn," Cordy said nonchalantly.

Leo took a deep breath to calm herself down.

"There's a place for you to sleep in the cabin," Leo said finally. The twins still insisted on sleeping with Luther, even though one bed for the three of them was crowded. They kept Papa's things as he had left them and his bed stayed empty. It reminded them that Papa was just "away" and not gone for good. At least that's how it had felt for Leo.

"This is fine," Cordy said. "It's more than I'm used to."

"Suit yourself." Leo moved around to the front of the horses. She was there to seek answers to questions she hadn't formed yet.

Leo needed Cordy's help if they were to ever find out what happened to Papa. She raised the lantern higher and saw for the first time that Cordy had several pistols all around her. The smell of horses and leather mixed with the scent of sweet, freshly cut hay was not unpleasant to Leo. It reminded her of a simpler time in her life . . . a time before there were so many little brothers and she had two happy, healthy parents.

She hung the lantern on a nail sticking out of a beam and watched as Cordy moved her hat out of the way. Her light brown hair reached her shoulders and made her look a lot younger. Leo admired her confidence, freedom and Cordy's uncanny survival instincts. Cordy didn't seem to need anyone, and that was amazing in itself. Cordy had not shared her plans with them, and Leo felt a need to learn all she could about her, and what had happened to the three men. If Cordy decided to leave soon, there would be no other chance.

"I have to ask you some questions," Leo said. Without any encouragement to continue, Leo took a deep breath and asked about the last place Cordy had seen Papa.

"South of Onion Creek. That's where they jumped on the train."

"Where's Onion Creek?"

"West of Austin."

"Do you know where the train was headed?" Leo asked.

"San Antonio and then on south to Laredo. It didn't stop at every podunk watering hole like most do, according to Jake."

The mention of Jake was a sobering reminder that they had more than one person to try and find. Leo was certain that her father and her uncle were together wherever they were. *Frederick's in San Antonio*, Leo thought. Uncle Jake had said his son was now a surveyor there.

"You also mentioned you'd gone to several towns in the area asking about them," Leo said. "Do you remember which ones you went to?"

As Cordy named off ten or twelve towns Leo had never heard of, she got the general idea. Cordy had covered a lot of territory west of Onion Creek.

"So you didn't go to San Antonio?" Leo asked.

Cordy searched Leo's face with her dark, piercing eyes. "I didn't say that."

Leo had never been to San Antonio before, so she couldn't even imagine how big a place it was. "Does that mean you looked for them there?" she asked.

"I went to one of the missions my Pa and I sometimes stay at. I left the other horses there and then went to the jail in San Antonio. No one there knew anything."

Feeling somewhat disappointed, Leo nodded.

"I did what I could," Cordy snapped.

"I'm not saying you didn't."

"Then what *are* you saying?"

"I'm not saying anything!"

"You think it was easy leaving there without them? Wondering when or if they would show up? Looking for blood on the side of the tracks? Calling their names until my throat ached? How easy do you think that was?"

Leo was quiet.

"Each time I went to a town to ask about my Pa, I had to find a place to hide the horses. A place I could remember how to get back to . . . a place where no one could find them and steal them."

Cordy's voice became huskier as she spoke. Leo realized Cordy was in an even worse position than she and her brothers were in now. At least Leo had her family and a place to live. Cordy had nothing but a horse, saddle and a wad of money.

"I should've just turned the horses loose," Cordy mumbled.

Again, Leo felt she wasn't being as friendly or as grateful as she should be. Cordy could have traded, sold or abandoned Papa and Jake's horses. She could have kept their share of the money. Her reasons for returning were her own, but without Cordy they would have no way of knowing where to look for Papa. But even with

49

Cordy's apparent sense of fairness and generosity, there was still something about her that annoyed Leo . . . something that made her uneasy and cautious. No one had ever had such an effect on her before.

"You have any other questions?" Cordy snapped.

"No," Leo said. "Thanks again for bringing the horses." She took the lantern down and went back to the cabin.

Henry was still staring at the coals in the fireplace. He didn't even look up when she came in. Leo put the lantern in its usual place and sat down beside him at the table.

"We both agree that we have to find out what happened to Papa," she said quietly. Henry's nod made her feel a little better. "I have an idea how we can do it."

Henry turned his head to look at her. She saw the same lost expression on his face. Teetering on the very edge of manhood, Leo sensed Henry reining himself in—holding back and afraid to take those few final steps that would transform him out of an adolescent's frame of mind and into the role of a young adult. It was a struggle Leo knew too well. The death of their mother had forced her there at an earlier age. It made her assume a new role almost overnight. It was only natural the loss of their father would do the same to Henry. But as Leo looked at him now, she had an overwhelming need to try and spare him from it. She loved her brother and knew things would never be the same for him again, or for any of them for that matter. Henry and Leona Trask were both adults now, with very little training to prepare them for whatever was ahead. Henry finally took a deep breath and stopped staring into the fire.

"Tell me what you need for me to do," he said.

Leo told him everything Cordy had told her, then launched right in with her own thoughts.

"If they got on the train and were shot or something," she said, "there wouldn't have been any sign of them along the train tracks." These were just words to her. Leo couldn't imagine such a thing actually happening to her father. In her mind, she and her brothers were not orphans. Leo allowed herself to have a sliver of hope and the determination to find answers to what had happened. She cleared her throat and continued. "Cordy said she followed the tracks for several miles and asked about them in all the towns between Onion Creek and San Antonio, but no one had seen them." She paused a moment for all of that to sink in. "The other possibility is . . . they jumped off the train and got hurt or got lost, but Cordy thinks she would've found them near the tracks if that had happened. Or found at least some sign of them."

"That's true, but she found nothing," Henry said. "So you think Papa's dead? That someone shot him on the train?"

Leo shook her head. "No. Maybe for some reason they got on the train and then couldn't rob the passengers right away. Maybe they had to be on there longer than they wanted to. Or maybe something happened and they couldn't get off. They knew Cordy would be waiting for them. Something kept them on the train, otherwise at least one of them would've found a way to get back to her if they could have."

"So what can we do now?" he asked. "Where do we start looking? Texas is a big place, Leo. Papa could be anywhere."

"Not really," she said. "There are only two things that are possible, Henry. They're either dead or in jail. I refuse to believe they're dead. They wouldn't just run off and leave Cordy that way. So I think they're all in jail somewhere."

Leo began to speak slowly and vocalized her plan almost as it came to her. "I want you to ride to San Antonio and find our cousin Frederick. Uncle Jake said he was there working as a surveyor. He'll know where to go to find out certain things if the three of them are in jail or something."

"How do I get to San Antonio from here?" Henry asked. His eyes were wide and she heard a tinge of panic in his voice.

"It's southeast of here," Leo said, making a conscious effort to sound confident and calm. "Probably about a four-day ride."

"Six if I don't know where I'm going."

Leo looked at him as if measuring his willingness to give this his best. "I can go and you can stay here with the boys," she suggested.

"No, I'll go." He sat up a little straighter in his chair as if she had questioned his very manhood. "Who'll do the hunting? There can't be that much ham and salt pork left."

Leo smiled. "We've been preparing for something like this all along, remember? The boys and I will be just fine without you for a few days. Tomorrow I want you and Earl to go to town and get some supplies. Get whatever you think you'll need for the ride to find Frederick. We'll stock up on flour, sugar, and enough shells for the two rifles here, then you can head out for San Antonio the next morning."

"Why can't I go to town with Henry and Earl?" Luther asked after breakfast.

"Because I need you here this morning," Leo said. They were in the barn. Leo noticed Cordy's horse was still there, but she wasn't anywhere around. She was certain Cordy wouldn't be staying with them long.

The boys helped Henry hitch Papa's horse to the wagon. Earl was already sitting high in the seat and fidgeting with excitement. Earlier, Leo had given Henry some of the money Papa had left with her.

"Maybe they'll bring back some peppermint," Leo said as she tousled Luther's hair.

Henry smiled down at his siblings and picked up the reins. "We'll see what they have."

Leo and Luther were chopping up kindling when they saw Cordy in the meadow walking back from the creek. Her hair was wet and hanging loosely at her shoulders. She wore clean clothes and had a wet shirt and another pair of trousers draped over one arm. Tucked under her other arm was her rifle.

Taking a break, Leo wiped the sweat from her brow and leaned on the ax. She had been giving a lot of thought to Cordy's clothes recently. Leo admired the freedom trousers allowed men and boys. She glanced over at the cabin and saw Eb leaning on the homemade broom Earl had constructed several days ago. He was also watching Cordy as she came back from the creek.

The closer Cordy got to the cabin, the more uncertain Leo began to feel. In one way, she couldn't understand how Cordy could be so poised and accepting of the things that had happened. Leo also knew Cordy was different from ordinary people. There was a sense of fairness about her that had served the Trask family well. *Yes,* Leo thought. *She's very different from most people. She hasn't asked for anything in return for her generosity . . . nothing other than a place to sleep in our barn.*

"Mornin'," Cordy said when she got closer to the cabin.

Luther, Eb and Leo returned the greeting. The three of them watched her throw her wet clothes on the fence by the corral, then watched her go into the barn. She came out again with her rifle and headed off toward the field behind the cabin. Leo glanced over at Luther and smiled.

"What are you looking at?" she asked him.

He shrugged and bent down to resume picking up the largest wood chips in the yard. "She's kinda pretty."

"You think so?"

"Yup."

Leo didn't like admitting it, but she was beginning to think so, too.

Chapter Eight

Earl jumped down from the wagon before Henry even had a chance to get it completely stopped. Eb, Luther and Leo were in the yard waiting for them.

"We got us some bargains!" Earl said, scrambling around the back of the wagon. He pulled on a sack of flour and put it in Eb's outstretched arms.

Leo smiled at hearing Earl use the word "bargain" so easily. She had read an article from an old newspaper to them recently where the word "bargain" was mentioned several times. It was nice knowing her efforts to broaden their vocabularies were paying off.

"The drought is forcing some folks to give up their places," Henry said as he jumped down. "There's people in town selling everything they own just so the bank won't take their farms. I've never seen anything like it."

Leo sighed. If Papa hadn't taken up robbing trains, they could very well be in a similar position with a failed crop and no other source of income to depend on.

"What kind of bargains did you get?" she asked. Using Earl's word made her smile.

Henry moved the sugar from the front corner of the wagon, which allowed a piglet to come squealing toward them. "There's a bargain right now," he said.

"See?" Earl said excitedly. "We got him cheap! He was the last one!"

"Luther!" Leo barked. "You're *not* coming in this house with that pig!"

As Luther backed away from the table, he held the animal close to his chest and stuck out his lower lip in a classic pout. "He's just a baby."

"He's still a pig, so out he goes."

Twenty minutes later they were continuing to sort through the things Henry and Earl had brought back from town. There were sacks of flour, sugar, oats and cornmeal piled on the table. The coffee, salt, dried figs and hardtack were stacked on the floor near the fireplace. Earl found the peppermint sticks and proudly waved them around.

"We got one for Cordy, too," he said. "Some are broke already. They were cheaper that way."

Henry looked over at him and laughed. "Another bargain." He picked up a different type of sack and laid it on the table. "Anybody ever heard of pemmican?"

"Nope," Luther said. He was standing next to Leo, who was the only person sitting at the table. She heard something and then noticed he still had the pig in his arms.

"What did I tell you?" She pointed toward the door, and made sure he and the pig left this time.

"What's pemmican?" Eb wondered aloud.

Henry nodded. "Glad you asked! It's good! Earl and I got to try some and I liked it. We can eat it as it is or make a stew with it. The man selling it said Indians eat it all the time."

"Indians?" Luther said from just inside the cabin door. Leo saw him and pointed her finger again. Without her having to say another word, he kept the pig and most of his own scrawny body outside on the porch, but he poked his head just inside the door so he could hear and see what was going on.

"What's it made out of?" Eb asked with a raised eyebrow.

"Buffalo," Henry said, "but you can make it out of other things, too."

"Buffalo," Eb repeated.

Henry opened up the cloth bag that revealed a large hide pouch. He carefully got that open and then cut off several pieces of pemmican and passed them around. Henry also cut a piece for himself and Leo.

"I want some buffalo, too," Luther said, straining his thin little neck around the cabin door so he could see better, but still managing to keep the piglet outside.

Eb stuck the pemmican under his nose and then made a face. "Another one of them bargains? It don't smell too good."

"Neither did that fried pig's innards I saw you eat one time," Henry said with a laugh. "The best thing about pemmican is it doesn't spoil. Cowboys take it on trail drives. Scouts use it. The cavalry uses it."

"And Indians," Luther said. "Let me try it!"

"It'll take some getting used to," Leo said as she chewed without enthusiasm.

"On those winter days when the bacon and ham are gone already," Henry said, "we can have some pemmican stew."

Eb grunted. "Just one more reason to wanna wake up on a cold mornin'." He swallowed the tiny piece he'd put in his mouth and walked to the door to give Luther the rest of it.

Leo wasn't impressed with the taste or the texture of pemmican either, but from the reassuring look Henry gave her, she was pretty sure why he had purchased it. Henry would be eating a lot of pemmican on his journey to San Antonio to look for Papa. And from the expression on Eb's face, he'd be the first one to help Henry pack it up for the trip.

Leo tried to talk Henry into waiting until morning to leave, but he wanted to get started right away.

"I have a better idea where I'm going now since I asked around in town," he said as he saddled Papa's horse. He packed a good supply of pemmican, hardtack, and a full canteen.

Leo gave him a hug and said, "Bring Papa home safely."

Eb was there in the barn with them and gave his brother a pat on the back.

"Once I find Frederick in San Antonio, it'll be easier," Henry said.

Leo was encouraged by his eagerness to get started. She was proud of Henry's confidence. She and Eb watched him ride away, and Leo couldn't help but be envious of him. *Just get on a horse and go*, she thought. *I wonder how it would feel to be able to do such a thing?* A sense of freedom from having no responsibilities was one of the things Leo had always wanted to experience. Being the oldest carried with it the burden of looking after younger siblings. Leo admired Cordy's solitude and resourcefulness. The freedom to just go anywhere and do whatever she wanted was something she thought about all the time now. Having a life where she could be alone with her thoughts and no one but herself to look after seemed to be the ideal life. As Leo watched her brother ride away, she promised herself one day she would do just that. Leona Trask would seek solitude.

Later that afternoon, Leo and Luther were cleaning out the chicken house. Luther was pouting because he hadn't gotten a chance to say good-bye to Henry before he left.

"How long you going to stay mad?" Leo asked him. She wiped

her brow on the sleeve of her dress. It was hot and she had always hated this particular task more than most of the others.

"A long time," he said.

In addition to his pouting about missing out on Henry's departure, Leo had to scold Luther about wagging the new pig around everywhere he went. He was so excited about having it, he hadn't been doing his chores.

"The fish you and Earl caught today will be good for supper," Leo said in an attempt to get him in a better mood.

"Not with Eb cooking," he grumbled.

Leo chuckled and shook her head.

"Henry could've rode by the creek and told us he was leaving," Luther said.

"We didn't want to upset you."

Luther gave her a look reflecting his hurt and disappointment. Leo decided then that in the future they would all make decisions together as a family. Never again would a visit to the creek be used in order to keep unpleasant discussions from being overheard by little ears. *Just because Luther's young doesn't mean he's not affected by any of this*, she thought.

"I'm sorry we didn't try and find you before Henry left," Leo said. "I won't let that happen again. I promise."

"I'm not a baby," he said.

Leo could tell that his anger was subsiding by the way his shoulders began to relax.

"I know," she said. "A baby wouldn't carry a pig around with him everywhere he went," she teased.

With that said, Luther smiled and resumed scraping chicken droppings off the hen house floor.

They hadn't seen Cordy since late that morning. Her horse was still in the barn, so no one worried too much about her. She was free to wander around all she wanted to; it was easy to forget she was even there most of the time. Leo was getting accustomed to Cordy's aloofness. With Henry away, Leo decided the next time she saw Cordy she would make an effort to ask her again to join them in the cabin in the evenings. Leo thought they could all use the company to take their minds off the situation they found themselves in.

By later that afternoon, she and Luther had finished spreading the new chicken fertilizer where the fall garden would eventually be, and took turns loosening the hard, dry dirt to cover it up properly. They saw Cordy at the same time coming across the meadow from the woods. Leo couldn't take her eyes off her. The wooded area to the north of the cabin was filled with all types of wildlife. Many times Leo heard Papa tell the boys about nests he'd seen while out hunting. At certain times of the year he wouldn't hunt there, and as a result the wild fowl population was once again quite abundant.

Carrying a limp male pheasant by its feet, Cordy was graceful as she walked through ankle-high grass toward them. Leo remembered the first time she had seen Papa bringing a pheasant home. Her mother had prepared a fine meal of pheasant and dumplings that evening. The pheasant Cordy had killed was nice and plump, and she carried it the same way Papa had whenever he brought one home. As Cordy came closer to the cabin, Leo glanced over at Luther and smiled at the way his eyes followed Cordy's every move.

"Why don't you wear clothes like that?" he asked his sister.

"Because I don't have any," Leo said as they both stood there watching Cordy walk toward them.

"Would you wear 'em if you had 'em?"

"I might," Leo said.

"Sure would make things easier for you."

She reached over and put her arm on his shoulder. "Papa probably wouldn't like it."

"He's not here," Luther said as he leaned against her.

After Leo and Luther finished covering the chicken droppings and breaking up the soil properly, they took the cow out to pasture and then did the same with the three horses in the barn. On their way back, Leo noticed Cordy had already dressed the pheasant and had its majestic feathers set aside on the porch.

Eb came out of the cabin with an empty pail and drew water from the well. On his way back to the cabin, he nodded at the featherless pheasant and asked, "Is he coming to supper with us?"

Cordy grinned. "He expects to."

"It's my turn to cook and I don't know nothin' about pheasants or prairie chickens."

"Then I guess I'll have to show you," she said.

He climbed the steps on the porch and set the pail down. "You ever heard of pemmican?"

Cordy nodded. "Sure. I've had some before."

"You like it?"

"It's all right."

Leo and Luther went over to the well and got themselves a drink of water. It was the hottest part of the day, and Leo wasn't looking forward to helping Luther clean out the barn next. Luther threw some water on his face, then joined Leo on the porch steps for a short break.

"Where's the other horse?" Cordy asked them.

"Henry took it," Eb said.

"Took it where?"

Leo could feel everyone's eyes on her. She turned and glanced up at Eb and realized he was waiting for her to answer. Henry's whereabouts was no secret, but it felt as though the others thought giving out information was something only she could do.

"He went off to San Antonio to find our cousin," Leo said. "We thought maybe Frederick could help us find Papa and Uncle Jake." So as not to get Luther all riled up again over Henry's departure earlier, she changed the subject. "We have even more room in the cabin now if you're tired of sleeping in the barn."

"You can sleep in Papa's bed," Luther said. "It's the closest to the outhouse."

A chuckle made the rounds and then Cordy nodded. "Thanks," she said.

Eb picked up the pail of water and shuffled back inside the cabin, but not before saying, "I can't be gabbin' out here all day with you people. I've got women's work to do."

That evening after a good meal of fried fish and pheasant—a combination of Eb and Cordy's efforts—Leo and her brothers gathered around the table to listen to stories Cordy had to tell about her time spent at Palo Duro Canyon in North Texas.

"It's the most beautiful place I've ever seen," Cordy said. "The colors there are like a sunset no matter what time of day it is. I never liked leaving there, but the winters are too cold."

Her voice was low. Leo wanted her to keep talking. Cordy's long hair was up in a braid, and the top two buttons on her shirt exposed just a hint of her bare throat. The light from the lantern behind her cast intriguing shadows across her face. She had the Trask family mesmerized. Leo felt something new and exciting in her chest and stomach as she listened to her. She found herself watching Cordy's mouth and lips while she spoke. No one could take their eyes off her.

"Outlaws stay there year round," Cordy said. "We could hear their voices all night long sometimes depending on how the wind blew. They kept to themselves and everyone tended to their own business."

"Any famous outlaws?" Luther asked.

Cordy smiled. "Maybe, but we never saw any. Just heard 'em at night. Lawmen and bounty hunters rode through sometimes, but never found anything. There were too many places to hide, and noise travels differently in a place like that."

Leo was enthralled with Cordy's tale. Cordy also shared stories about her time at Mission San José outside of San Antonio, where she learned to grind wheat at the grist mill and speak Spanish.

"The last time I was there," she said, "my friends were gone and there were new people arriving every day."

"Say something in Spanish," Luther said.

Cordy laughed, then said, *"Tú eres un niño muy bueno."*

Luther laughed delightedly. "What's that mean?"

"Something about you and a pig," Eb said, teasing him. "That's what I heard."

"Me, too," Earl said, nodding his head. "I heard the word *pig*, too."

"It means you're a very nice boy," Cordy said over the laughter. She continued to talk and answer questions. Finally, Leo noticed that Luther's head was bobbing and his eyes kept closing.

"Someone's sleepy," she said.

Luther strained to keep them open, but it wasn't working.

"We've all got another busy day tomorrow," Leo said.

Earl stood up and stretched. "I've got house-mouse duty tomorrow," he said, making everyone laugh again.

"What's house-mouse duty?" Cordy asked.

"I have to cook all the meals and keep the cabin clean," Earl informed her.

"Women's work," Eb added as he looked right at Leo. She returned the stare without amusement, which made him laugh again. He liked teasing her.

Eb picked up Luther and threw him over his shoulder like a flour sack and carried him up the ladder to the loft. Earl headed that way as well.

Leo and Cordy were alone. Leo moved a few of Papa's personal things off his bed and onto the floor. She adjusted the lantern and pushed all the chairs closer to the table as she nervously tidied up a little.

"My room's in there if you need anything," Leo said. "I'll see you in the morning."

Chapter Nine

Leo spent the majority of her time keeping up with the constant repairs needed on the cabin and the farm in general. She had already mastered the art of chopping wood, cutting hay, and shoveling cow, horse and chicken manure. Now she was ready to move on to things like patching the roof, mending fences and tightening up the smokehouse.

As time went on, Leo had less hope of ever seeing Papa again. If he had been alive, Leo was sure they would know by now. She expected to see Henry ride up alone with defeat and disappointment etched in his eyes. In the meantime, she kept the younger boys on a routine of getting up early, tackling the daily chores, and school work in the evenings until they were all too tired to hold their heads up.

Cordy, on the other hand, was finally sleeping in the cabin at night on a regular basis, but they still didn't see much of her. She was up earlier than the rest of them, and usually had the cow milked before the sun made much of an appearance. What Cordy did or where she went the rest of the time wasn't something Leo worried about, but occasionally Earl and Luther would get up early enough to go hunting with her.

Late one afternoon Eb and Leo were going around the smokehouse, putting mud in the cracks on the outside to make it tighter, when Eb asked her what she thought was taking Henry so long to come back.

Leo shrugged. "If he's having trouble finding Frederick, then he might not be getting much cooperation in town. We'll just have to wait and see."

She hoped Henry had enough sense to give up if there were no leads. She missed having him home. He was the one person she had always been able to talk to. Leo needed him to be there so they could prepare the younger boys for the truth about their father.

In the late afternoons, Leo would bring the horses and cow back from the meadow to get them watered and settled in the barn. When it was time to unwind for the day, the boys and Cordy would go on the other side of the garden and do some target practice with her six-shooter. By now, all the Trasks were excellent shots with a rifle, but a pistol took a steady hand, a good eye, and lots of practice.

Leo watched them from the porch and liked the way Cordy talked to her brothers before letting them touch the gun. Earl and Eb took to it right away, but Luther initially had more trouble keeping the pistol steady.

"It's heavy," he said.

"I know," Cordy agreed. "It's heavy for me, too. You just have to keep trying and get used to it."

After a few days of practice, Luther was a better shot with the pistol than either of his brothers.

"Did you see that little weasel hit those targets?" Eb asked Leo one evening as he nodded toward Luther on their way back to the cabin.

"I can *hear* you," Luther said. "Don't be calling me a weasel when I can hear you!"

Cordy and Earl were laughing as they came up to join Leo on the porch. Leo liked hearing laughter again. It had been missing from their lives lately.

"So when do I get to learn how to shoot a pistol?" Leo asked.

Cordy stopped near the steps and looked at her. "Right now if you really want to."

"Of course I want to," Leo said. "I need to know how to do everything around here."

The boys scrambled off the porch, obviously excited about Leo learning how to shoot, too. Leo didn't think she'd be so nervous about getting her first lesson. Luther set up different size blocks of kindling on a stump on the other side of the garden. Leo held the pistol and silently agreed with Luther that it was heavy.

"You'll get used to it," Cordy said, as if reading her mind. "Now hold it with both hands like this," she said, grasping the pistol butt firmly in both hands.

She moved behind Leo and put her arms around her so they were holding the gun at the same time. Leo felt Cordy's breasts pressing against her back. Almost without warning, Leo felt fluttering in her chest and stomach. If Cordy hadn't been helping her hold the gun, Leo was certain she would have dropped it right then.

"Keep it steady like this," Cordy said. Her lips were close to Leo's ear and sent a shiver down her arms.

"Wait," Leo said as she lowered the gun.

"They're just sticks," Eb said. "It won't hurt 'em if you accidentally hit one."

Luther and Cordy chuckled, but Leo was too busy concentrating on taking deep breaths to calm herself down. *She didn't put her arms around the boys this way,* Leo thought. Her body was in turmoil over having been touched like that.

"You ready yet?" Cordy asked.

No, Leo wanted to say—mostly because she didn't want the

others to see how affected she was by having Cordy so close to her. But the thought of *not* having Cordy touch her again was even more out of the question, so she raised the gun and nodded. This time when Cordy moved in closer to her from behind, Leo found herself leaning against her a little so she could feel Cordy's breasts again.

"Keep your arms and hands steady," Cordy whispered in her ear, and again there was a shiver that scampered through Leo's body. "Then aim using the sight. Keep it steady."

Cordy's hands were on Leo's as they both held the pistol. Leo never wanted this moment to end.

"Squeeze the trigger," Cordy said. "Don't pull it or jerk it . . . squeeze it." She straightened their arms more and anchored her feet. "Squeeze whenever you're ready."

Leo took a deep breath and lined up the sight on the gun barrel. She zeroed in on the largest block of wood and squeezed the trigger. The target went sailing in the air and Luther and Eb were impressed enough to exclaim their surprise.

"Looks like we've got two weasels in the family," Eb mumbled.

"Very good," Cordy said. She stepped away from her. "Try the next few on your own."

Leo held the pistol out in front of her and couldn't hide the fact that her hands were trembling. Four shots later, the stump was cleared of kindling and her mind was cluttered with thoughts of low whispers and soft breasts. She handed the pistol back to Cordy and turned and walked toward the cabin. She couldn't have talked now even if she had wanted to. Leo felt flustered and speechless for the rest of the afternoon.

By the time supper came around, Leo thought she had herself more together, but she couldn't stop thinking about Cordy's warm body pressing against her and Cordy's voice in her ear. Even that night as she lay in bed, Leo was in a quandary of heat and confusion. She had never felt this way before, and had no point of reference for the raw emotions racing through her head and her body. When she finally fell asleep, her thoughts drifted to soft, peaceful things with her last conscious thought focusing on holding a heavy pistol and how much she could learn to like target practice.

The next day they had a visitor. A man in a suit rode up and asked for Papa. Leo and Luther had house-mouse cabin duty; the twins were off with Cordy looking for the cow that had wandered away.

"My father isn't here," Leo said to the man. Sweat ran in her eyes, so she used the sleeve of her dress to dab her brow. "Luther," she called to him. He was standing behind her on the porch. "Go inside, please."

He did what he was told, but made no secret of standing by the door with it cracked open.

"Where's your father?" the man asked. He was about Papa's age and had over a day's growth of stubble on his face. As Leo eyed him closer, she noticed his suit was worn at the cuffs and didn't really fit him very well. His boots were scuffed, and his horse wouldn't stay still. Whoever this man was, Leo was immediately leery of him. He introduced himself as Otis Moody, the town banker.

"He's away working," Leo said.

"Away where?"

Leo hesitated. She didn't like this man or his questions. She also didn't like the way he was looking at her.

"Away where?" he asked again.

Leo didn't know what to say. Now she wished she hadn't told him anything at all.

"His payment is late," Mr. Moody said. "When will he be back?"

"What payment?" Leo asked.

"He owes money on the farm."

Leo was stunned. How could they owe money on the farm? They had lived there for years and never owed anyone anything! *The twins were born here*, she thought. *Luther was born here. Why do we suddenly owe money?* Leo posed the question to Mr. Moody.

"Last year he borrowed against the farm," he said slowly.

Why hadn't Papa said anything about that? she wondered.

"I'm here to collect the money," he said.

Leo wasn't intimidated, but was at a loss as to what to say. Once again she felt uncomfortable with the way he looked down at her from his horse. She climbed the steps on the porch, which put them at eye level. She then boldly asked, "When last year did he borrow money?"

"When? Over fourteen months ago. I've given him several extensions on paying this debt. The last extension was up yesterday. I've been expecting him all week. It's unfortunate he's not here now."

"Did he sign papers at the time?" Leo asked.

"Yes."

"Do you have them?"

"Uh . . . not with me right now. They're back at the bank."

"I'll need to see the papers first. I don't recall my father mentioning any loan."

"I can assure you—"

"So when you can return with the proper document, Mr. Moody, then we can discuss this further."

"Are you in a position to take care of this debt?"

The tone of his voice didn't sit well with her. Leo was getting angry now.

"I don't even know how much it is," she said.

"Two hundred dollars."

Leo's gasp at the mention of the amount startled the banker's horse and made it do a nervous little dance.

"Come back with the proper papers," she said after a moment. "My father may be home by then."

After Mr. Moody rode away, Luther came out on the porch. He held Papa's rifle in his skinny little arms and stood next to her.

"He didn't look like a banker to me," he said.

Leo had gotten the same impression. "What makes you say that?"

"His boots. They were all scruffy. *He* looked all scruffy."

"Then who do you suppose he is?"

"I don't know, but I don't think he's a banker."

Leo smiled and tousled his hair. "What are you doing with Papa's rifle?"

"I was gonna use it if he tried to hurt you."

Leo laughed and hugged him.

It was bath night, and instead of hauling water into the cabin like they did in the winter, Leo teasingly suggested they just take turns going to the creek. She was too tired to mess with it.

"That creek's too cold," Earl said. "I'm not getting in it."

"Me neither," Luther said. "Besides, we'll scare all the fish away."

Everyone laughed.

"Have you been down to the creek lately?" Eb asked Leo. "There's not as much water there as usual."

"Maybe it's the drought," she said, then thought about the depth of their well. She made a mental note to check on it tomorrow.

"There could be a beaver dam upstream," Cordy said from the end of the table.

"Do we have beavers around here?" Earl asked.

"Well, I ain't takin' no bath in beaver water either," Luther said.

Leo shook her head. "Then you two go get the tub out of the barn," she said, pointing to Earl and Luther.

"I'd rather take a bath with a beaver than take one after Eb," Earl said on his way out the door. He snickered most of the way to the barn, but from the look on Luther's face, he personally didn't think it was very funny. As the youngest in the family, Luther got the bath water only after everyone else had used it already.

Cordy was a guest, so she was offered the tub first. It was the polite thing to do, so the Trask siblings waited on the porch until she was finished. As the boys talked and played with Luther's pig, Leo listened to the faint sounds of Cordy in the tub. Leo didn't understand what was happening to her, but she knew better than to dwell on it too much or mention these feelings to anyone else. She would think it all through before going to sleep later, but in the meantime Leo had one other thing to take care of first.

The two hundred dollars Mr. Moody claimed Papa owed to the bank weighed heavily on her mind. Leo had reservations about paying anyone anything until they knew more about Papa and where he was. It also concerned her that she knew nothing about the loan. Fourteen months ago they didn't have any more then than they had now, except for the stolen money Papa had given her recently. *Where could Papa have spent two hundred dollars over a year ago?* she wondered. They had nothing to show for it.

The cabin door squeaked open and Cordy came out fully dressed in clean clothes and wet hair piled on her head.

"Who's next?" she asked.

"Leo is," Earl said. "We go by age. I'm the oldest twin," he said, puffing out his chest. It always made Leo laugh when he did that.

She got up and went inside. She closed the door and stared at the tub sitting in front of the fireplace. The cake of soap was on the floor beside it, and suddenly all Leo could think about was Cordy being naked in the water just minutes earlier.

Leo went to her room to get her other dress to change into after her bath. She wasn't sure how to stop herself from thinking so much. She wanted desperately to forget about Cordy's voice in her ear and her breasts against her back. *You have to get over that*, Leo thought. *Whatever it is that's happening to you right now, you have to forget about it.*

She undressed and slipped into the tub. The water was still warm. She leaned back and closed her eyes for just a moment. *I'll be fine*, Leo thought, and then reached for the soap on the floor. Just as she was about to convince herself that her impure thoughts of Cordy would no longer seep into her conscience, she held the soap in her hands and remembered that Cordy had just washed her naked body with it a few minutes earlier. *You have to forget about it*, she thought as she lathered the soap up and began washing her arms. *You have to.*

Chapter Ten

Leo woke up the next morning feeling uncertain. Fate had a strange way of working, and things happened for a reason. Those had been her mother's beliefs, and Leo had adopted them as her own. If Mr. Moody's bank was owed two hundred dollars, then she had to make it good.

She got up to make sure the money was still where she had hidden it. Leo was constantly resisting the urge to check on it each night before she went to bed. The money wasn't going anywhere, she finally decided. The boys never went into her room, and Cordy had money of her own. *Stop worrying so much*, she thought. *If Mr. Moody has the papers Papa signed, then you have to give him the money. It's that easy.* Leo took off her nightgown and dressed for the day. *You have the money to pay the debt*, she reminded herself. *They can't take the farm away.*

❧

There was a line at the outhouse and sleepy yawns and stretches to go with it. On her way back to the cabin, Leo saw Cordy and Eb carrying out dirty bath water from the night before a bucket at a time. They poured it on the garden and eventually had enough water out of the tub to carry it safely. Luther and Eb were on their way to the barn with the empty tub when Leo reminded them she needed it to do the laundry.

"What's left in the garden?" Cordy asked as she sat on the porch steps beside Leo.

Trying not to think about Cordy's closeness, Leo concentrated on her question.

"Mustard and collard greens," Leo said. "Some dill and turnips. Mostly I'm letting it go to seed now. The peas and snap beans burnt up weeks ago. We couldn't keep enough water on it."

"My mother used to love her garden," Cordy said. "It's one of the few memories I have of her."

"Mine did, too," Leo said. She preferred not to talk about her mother. It still made her heart ache and depressed her too much. "It's a lot easier to take care of when we have rain."

Earl came out on the porch and dropped a pile of dirty clothes that had been left near the fireplace the night before. When he went back inside, Leo could smell salt pork frying. It made her stomach growl.

"You and your brothers have a nice place here," Cordy said.

"It's our home. I can hardly remember living anywhere else."

Cordy stood up and looked out across the meadow. She turned around and then glanced over at the barn.

"I'm leaving after breakfast," she said.

Leo felt momentarily confused before an initial stab of panic set in. "Leaving for good? Why?"

Cordy shrugged. "It's just something I need to do. I want to thank you for making me feel welcome here."

"Where will you go?"

"I don't know yet. Maybe back up north to Palo Duro."

Just get on a horse and go, Leo thought. She was surprised at how upset she was over this news. Why should she care one way or the other what Cordy did? Leo cleared her throat and asked, "You can't wait until Henry gets back? He might have news about your father."

"My Pa's dead," Cordy said. "I knew that before I came here."

"Why would you say that?"

"We would've found each other by now. But if I'm wrong, that's just another reason for me to go to Palo Duro. There's a chance he might even be waiting for me there."

Leo didn't know what else to say. So many things were bouncing around in her head at that moment. She had not been friendly or hospitable enough toward Cordy. Then Leo's body reminded her it was Cordy's voice that haunted her at night and Cordy's touch that made her ache with longing. How could she vocalize those feelings now and convince her to stay?

"I'd be interested in buying some of that pemmican you have," Cordy said with a shy smile.

"Take anything you want," Leo said. The disappointment she felt was too overwhelming. Before she said something she would later regret, or even worse—begin to cry—Leo went inside the cabin. She wanted Henry and Papa home now. She wanted her life back the way it was before.

Leo had lost her appetite by the time Earl called them to breakfast. Luther rambled on nonstop about his pig, while Earl and Eb stuffed themselves with jackcakes and honey.

Leo kept her eyes on her plate and chewed her food only as an afterthought. She was wondering when Cordy would tell the boys about her plans to leave, then realized Cordy might not want them to know. Leo's mind continued to race on with a slew of *what ifs*. She didn't feel as though she had a right to ask Cordy to stay. *What if I had been nicer to her in the beginning?* she wondered again. *What if I'd told her how much better it was around here to have another female in the cabin?* Leo was beginning to wonder now why they hadn't become closer while Cordy was there. Why had two young women not bonded at least on some level? They had things in common—they'd lost their mothers, their fathers were train robbers. They had nothing to show for the ten days they'd spent together. *Unless Cordy knows about the feelings you've been having about her,* Leo thought. She glanced over at her sitting at the end of the table and caught Cordy looking at her. Cordy averted her eyes and seemed to be concentrating on what was left on her plate.

Leo took a bite of her virtually untouched jackcake then said, "Cordy has something to tell us."

Cordy shot her a startled look and then resumed eating.

"Don't you?" Leo asked. She was upset and angry. The only thing that was making Leo feel any better was Cordy's obvious discomfort.

"Luther doesn't like surprises," Leo said. "Tell us what your plans are."

Cordy set her fork down beside her plate. "I've decided to leave today."

"Leave?!" Luther said.

"Where are you going?" Earl asked.

Eb didn't say anything, but stopped eating.

"Back up north for the summer."

"Who's gonna teach me how to shoot a pistol?" Luther asked.

"You already know how, you little weasel," Eb said.

"You going to that Palo Duro place you told us about?" Earl asked.

Cordy nodded.

"You won't be scared there with all those outlaws?"

Cordy remained quiet.

"You'll be there alone this time," Leo said. "You've never been there alone before."

Cordy looked right at her and their eyes met for an intense, lingering moment, as though they were the only people in the room. That strange fluttering returned to her stomach as Cordy's eyes searched Leo's face.

"There are things much worse than being alone," Cordy said.

"What kinds of things come to mind?" Leo quietly asked.

"Things like losing someone you love," Cordy said, "or loving someone you can never have. Lots of things."

Her words set off a new round of fluttering in Leo's body. Leo wanted to make Cordy explain what she meant by that, but instead felt paralyzed with emotion and fear.

"Will you ever come back some day and see us?" Luther asked.

Cordy stood up from the table. "Maybe. I will if I'm ever by this way again," she said. "Being here has helped me get my thoughts together. Oh, and when I mentioned earlier about buying some pemmican from you, I really meant that."

"Buy it?" Eb said with a curled up nose. "You can have my share for free!"

Leo couldn't watch her leave. After breakfast she went down to the creek to fetch some water to start the laundry. When she left the cabin, Earl was cutting a nice hunk of pemmican for Cordy to take with her. The boys were busy filling her canteen and making sure her horse was taken care of first.

Leo took her time, bringing back some water and pouring it in a huge pot to boil. She could hear Cordy and the boys in the barn talking as they saddled her horse. Leo refused to get upset. Henry would be back soon and might even have Papa with him. She tried focusing on that as she headed back down to the creek for more water. It wasn't long before she heard the sound of Cordy's horse coming her way.

Leo lifted the pail out of the creek and turned around. It was early in the day, but already getting hot.

"I couldn't leave without seeing you one last time," Cordy said.

Leo squinted up at her on the horse. "Well, now you've seen me."

Cordy looked away. "Yeah, I've seen you."

Leo set the bucket down. She couldn't find the courage to ask

Cordy what she meant earlier about loving someone she could never have. There were so many things about her that made Leo nervous and uneasy. *Why is it you can stare down the likes of a banker coming to snatch the farm, but you can't look a young girl in the eye without feeling foolish?*

"I hope Henry comes home soon," Cordy said. "And I hope he has good news about your father."

"Thanks. So do I." She picked up the bucket and squinted into the sun again to look at her. "I wish you weren't leaving."

"This is best." Cordy sat up straight in the saddle. "You can keep Pa's horse. I don't need it."

"We'll take good care of it," Leo said. She felt a lump forming in her throat, but swallowed hard and managed to say, "You're always welcome here, Cordy."

She nodded and turned her horse around and rode away.

When Leo got back to the cabin, she sent Luther to the creek again for more water. It was Earl's turn to be the house-mouse, but laundry wasn't included as part of those duties yet. Leo was picky about how she wanted the laundry done anyway.

Eb had hitched up the wagon and was off in the woods looking for dead trees or large branches to bring back for firewood. The last time he and Earl had been out there, they had found the beehive with all the honey they'd enjoyed for days afterward.

"I don't like wash day," Luther said as he set the pail of water down by the steps. Leo helped him pour it in the tub and get the laundry started. The pot of water she'd set on the stove earlier was beginning to boil. Luther's job would be to wring out as much water as possible from the wet clothes after Leo scrubbed them good.

"Do you like this more than cleaning the chicken coop?" Leo asked him.

"Yes," he admitted.

"What about moving the outhouse?"

Luther threw his head back and laughed. "Maybe wash day ain't so bad after all!"

Leo and Luther both stopped what they were doing as soon as they saw the two riders coming toward the cabin. Leo felt her pulse quicken at the thought of Henry and Papa finally arriving, but then she saw the hat and Otis Moody's dusty coat. She didn't know the other man with him.

"I thought it was Papa and Henry," Luther said. The disappointment in his voice mirrored her own.

"So did I," Leo said. "Get in the cabin. You and Earl stay there."

"We'll be watchin'," Luther said as he did what she told him to.

She straightened up and left the wet clothes in the tub. Drying her hands on her dress, Leo stayed on the porch so neither of the men would be looking down at her from their horses.

"Mornin', Miss Trask," Otis Moody said with a tip of his dusty hat. The man with him stayed on Mr. Moody's right, away from Leo.

"Good morning," Leo said. "Did you bring the paper my father signed?"

"I sure did." He opened his coat and took out a folded document, then leaned over and handed it to her. Leo unfolded the paper and scanned it for her father's signature.

The entire thing consisted of one short paragraph that was written in longhand—with bad grammar and even worse spelling. The penmanship, however, looked painstakingly clear and precise with a carefully blocked script. Leo also noted that Papa had apparently misspelled his own name and had also printed it instead of signing it in cursive writing, like he usually did. Leo was convinced that her father had not signed this paper, but what her next step should be, she wasn't too sure about yet.

"Who is the gentleman with you, Mr. Moody?" Leo asked.

"One of my bank tellers."

"Does he have a name?"

"You have the money your father owes my bank?"

"My father didn't sign this paper, Mr. Moody. I'm not giving you anything." She carefully folded the document and handed it back to him.

"Then I'll have to bring the sheriff with me next time."

"That'll be fine."

The other man leaned over so he could look around Mr. Moody. "Forget the money," he said. "Tell us where the gold is."

"What?" Leo said. She wasn't sure she had heard him correctly. "Did you say gold?"

"Now Miss Trask," Mr. Moody interjected, "I'm sure we can settle this matter without resorting to any—"

"Who are you?" Leo asked them collectively.

The other man pulled out a gun and pointed it at her. "Give us the money and the gold."

Chapter Eleven

Leo heard the cabin door open. Earl came out with Papa's rifle pointed at Mr. Moody. From her peripheral vision, she could also see Luther with a six-shooter pointed at the other man.

"Drop the gun or I'll blow you right outta that saddle, mister," Earl said slowly.

"And if he don't," came Eb's voice from the side of the cabin, "then I will."

It was only then that it actually registered with Leo that *Luther* was standing beside her with a gun. They didn't own a pistol, but she was glad he had it, wherever it came from.

In a voice as clear and steady as any Leo had ever heard before, young Luther Trask said, "And if my brothers don't blow you two outta them saddles, then I will."

The man tossed his gun to the ground as if it were too hot to hold any longer. Eb was there quickly and reached down to pick it up.

"Get off them horses," Eb said.

The two men slowly did as they were told.

"They ain't bankers, Leo," Luther said.

Leo finally got a good look at the second man, and couldn't believe he had even attempted to pose as a banker. His dark vest had a hole in it and was stained in several places. His coat and trousers were so big there was no way they could've originally belonged to him.

"Put their horses in the barn, Luther," Earl said.

"What are you young 'uns doing with all these guns?" Mr. Moody asked.

"Don't you worry about that," Earl said.

"What are you bumpkins doing in suits?" Eb asked. "Get your hands up over your heads."

Luther led the horses away while Eb and Earl lined up the two men in front of the porch. Earl glanced over at Leo as if to say, "Now what?"

"Make sure they don't have any other weapons on them," she said. "Knives, guns or anything like that." Leo held her hand out to take the rifle Earl was holding. Walking around in front of the men, she turned to Mr. Moody and asked how he knew she had two hundred dollars. "Why that amount in particular?"

He didn't say anything in response to her question or to Earl taking the pistol Moody had stuffed in his belt. Luther came back from the barn and stood next to his brothers.

"Where'd you get that gun?" Leo asked her little brother.

"Cordy gave it to me," Luther said.

"Cordy Kincade?" the other man asked.

Everyone looked at him, including Moody.

"How do you know Cordy?" Earl asked.

"I didn't say I knew her."

"You know her last name," Earl said.

"Shuddup, you fool," Moody snapped at the other man.

Everything was happening so fast, Leo couldn't think clearly. What were they going to do with these two?

Leo thought they might have information about Papa. After all, they knew about Cordy and the two hundred dollars Papa had given her. Then like a lightning bolt zapping her, a thought very disturbing popped into Leo's head. *It sure is an interesting coincidence that Cordy decided to leave just at the time these two "bankers" showed up!* Leo pushed those suspicions out of her mind for the time being. *Cordy doesn't know these two*, she decided quickly, *but that doesn't explain how they know her!*

"Get your boots off," Leo said to the two men. To Earl she said, "Take them out behind the cabin and get them out of their clothes. All except their drawers. And make sure I don't have to see any of that."

"What?!" Moody exclaimed.

"You heard what she said," Earl barked. He took the rifle back from Leo. "Get your boots off."

After the grumbling and grunting to pull off their boots was over, the two men were angry. Moody threw each boot in the dirt once he struggled to get it off.

"You gonna shoot us?" the other man asked after he finally tossed his second boot on the ground.

"We might," Luther said. "That depends on you."

Eb snickered and cut his eyes over at Leo. "Listen to that little weasel."

Leo motioned to the left with her head. "Get moving. If they so much as twitch wrong, shoot them in a leg or something."

Earl nodded toward Moody and his friend. "Let's go."

The two men shuffled off in their stocking feet.

"Get them hands up," Eb barked.

Luther went to follow them, but Leo called him back. "Go to the barn and get some rope. Have the twins tie them up once they're down to their long handles."

He nodded and headed toward the barn.

"Luther," she called.

He stopped and turned around.

"When did Cordy give you that six-shooter?"

"This morning before she left."

"What did she say about it?"

He shrugged. "Nothing. She had a saddlebag full of guns. She gave one to each of us."

So Earl and Eb also have one, she thought. Leo wasn't sure she liked that idea.

"We got to pick the ones we wanted," Luther said proudly.

"Cordy didn't say anything about you boys maybe having to use these guns soon, did she?"

Luther shook his head. "No. All she said was she had extras she'd found."

Leo nodded. "Go get the rope and help your brothers."

So Papa, Uncle Jake and Alva Kincade took guns as well as money, Leo thought. Ha! That worked out pretty well! Luther brandishing a pistol like he knew what he was doing might have been what prompted the "bankers" to drop their guns in the first place.

The boys had the two men tied up in the barn in their underwear. Luther brought their dirty, smelly clothes and dropped them on the porch.

"You gonna do their laundry?" Eb asked.

The laughter came easily. It was a release from the tension and stress.

"What are we gonna do with those two?" Earl asked, nodding toward the barn.

"One of 'em likes to talk," Eb said.

"But that Mrs. Moody won't let him," Luther added.

"They'll get hungry enough to talk soon," Leo said. She didn't have any sympathy for them. They had been there to cheat and rob her.

All four saw the two riders at the same time coming over the hill in the distance. Leo's heart started racing. She wasn't ready to go through this again.

"More bankers?" Earl asked.

"Luther, you get in the cabin," Leo said. "Eb, you watch from the barn door and Earl, you stay with me."

The boys did as they were told.

"If they have guns drawn," Leo said, "shoot them."

Why didn't Cordy leave me a gun, too, Leo thought suddenly, and then as if reading her mind, Luther came back out of the cabin and handed her a pistol.

"Me and the twins picked one out for you and one for Henry," Luther said. He went back inside the cabin and took his place at the door.

The gun felt vaguely familiar in her hand. It didn't seem as heavy as she remembered from target practice.

"Stand behind me," Leo said to Earl.

"Why? I'm not afraid."

"You *better* be afraid! Now get behind me. I don't want the first thing they see when they ride up is you with a rifle."

"Then I'll keep the rifle behind you," he said. "How's it gonna look me standing back there? Like some frilly coward."

As the riders got closer, their horses began to pick up speed. Suddenly, Leo was less certain that it was wise to be standing so boldly in front of the cabin, even though she and Earl had weapons.

"I really hate bankers," Luther said through the crack in the cabin door.

"Me, too," Earl agreed.

"It's Henry," Eb called from the barn. "That's Papa's horse!"

"Is Papa with him?" Luther shouted. He was out of the cabin and scrambling down the steps.

All three boys were at Leo's side as they stood there waiting for the horses to reach them. Finally, Luther said, "It's Uncle Jake with him."

Henry and Jake rode up and hurried down off their horses.

"Where's Papa?" Leo asked.

"I'll tell you all about it," Henry said. He was covered in trail dust. "Get inside." He took the rifle Eb was holding and gave it to Jake.

"What's the matter?" Leo asked him, now even more alarmed than before.

"Eb, take care of the horses," Henry said. "They need water. Earl, you stay with Jake and keep a lookout for riders."

"What's going on?" Leo demanded. "We've got two men tied up in the barn. Are they the ones you're worried about?"

"Which two?" Uncle Jake and Henry asked at the same time.

"Moody's one of them," Leo said. "We didn't get the other one's name yet."

"I bet Gill's the other one," Jake said. "Those two idiots got here before we did?"

"Moody was here alone yesterday," Leo said. "He wanted money he said Papa owed."

"Well, if those two barn rats have been here already," Henry said, "then the smart ones might be out there layin' low and biding their time. Get in the cabin."

"I really do hate bankers," Luther said as he climbed the porch steps.

Leo put her hand on his shoulder, then realized she was still holding the pistol he had given her earlier.

Leo made sure she was sitting close to Luther when Henry told them the news about Papa.

"He's dead," Henry said quietly. "Him and Alva Kincade."

Luther grabbed onto Leo and held her tightly. Earl found her hand and squeezed it hard. At that moment she needed to hold them as much as they needed her.

"Wait until Eb comes in before you say anything else," Leo said. Even though she had expected this, she still wasn't prepared for it.

The way Luther sobbed into her neck made Leo's heart feel like it was breaking. Her eyes filled with tears as she held him.

A little while later Eb came in and leaned the rifle close to the door. He took his usual seat at the table and said, "Papa's not coming home, is he?"

Henry shook his head and then said, "No."

Luther tore himself from Leo's arms and ran to the ladder and scrambled up to the loft. They could hear him sobbing up there and it just seemed to make the whole thing worse.

"What happened to him?" Eb asked. Other than his voice being huskier, he showed no outward signs of emotion.

Henry looked across the table at Leo.

"The twins are old enough," she said. "We'll tell Luther another time."

Henry nodded and began his story.

"I found Frederick the second day I was in San Antonio. He knew a lot of important people and got the information we needed." Henry stopped and looked at the twins. Earl wiped his nose on the sleeve of his shirt, while Eb stared straight ahead. Henry went on to explain that Papa, Uncle Jake and Alva Kincade had been robbing trains in South Texas. "And apparently they were good at it."

Earl and Eb both looked over at him. Earl's mouth hung open, but Eb still showed no emotion.

"There were wanted posters out for them," Henry continued. "The last train they tried to rob had federal marshals on it. Alva and Papa were beat up on the train and the three of them were thrown in jail once they got to San Antonio. All three were lucky they weren't killed then. Anyway, the next day they were tried and then taken to prison. Papa died there a few days later. Mr. Kincade died not long after that. They were both beaten up pretty bad according to Uncle Jake."

Earl reached over and took Leo's hand again. She squeezed it as though her life depended on it. Eb looked up at the ceiling in the direction of the loft. It was the first time she had noticed that Luther had stopped crying.

"So Frederick and I found the prison," Henry said. "As it turns out, some of the prisoners got it in their heads that there was a lot of money left behind. Uncle Jake got to talking and bragging a little about a few things, so other prisoners knew Cordy had been rounding up the horses after each train robbery."

Leo was amazed Henry could be so calm, but he'd had more time to adjust to Papa being dead.

"Uncle Jake is feeling bad about all of this," Henry said. "I think he's starting to remember other things he said to those people."

"Did he mention us?" Leo asked. "Here at the farm?"

Henry nodded.

"Then prisoners could have known I had the money," Leo said.

Henry nodded again.

"How did those convicts get out of prison?" Leo asked. "Or did they get word to friends on the outside?"

"Yeah," Eb said. "How did Uncle Jake get out of prison?"

"There was a fire at the prison while Frederick and I were there," Henry said, "and a lot of the prisoners escaped then. Frederick and I found Uncle Jake in all the confusion, and then Frederick gave us his horse. We've been riding ever since."

Leo let out the breath she had been holding as Henry finished the last part of the story. "So what you're telling us now is that Uncle Jake is the reason Mr. Moody came here for money."

Henry looked her in the eye and said, "Yes. And not only that, Uncle Jake's probably still wanted by marshals for train robbery as well as for escaping from prison now."

Leo was too emotionally drained to be angry at Uncle Jake right then.

"He really feels bad about all of this, Leo," Henry said. "He wouldn't stop riding. He's been so worried about you and the boys and Cordy." He stopped for a moment then added, "He's a different person now. Having to watch Papa die that way has changed him."

Leo felt Earl squeeze her hand again.

"Frederick wants nothing to do with him right now," Henry continued. "Frederick's in a bad position where he works. We're not sure how much danger he's in either. Some of those prisoners who escaped might think he knows something, too. Apparently Uncle Jake bragged about having more money than there really was." Henry took a deep breath. "But Uncle Jake is the only family we have left now. Him and our two cousins are it. Uncle Jake is sorry about what happened. I've never seen him so determined before . . . so sick in his heart about all of this."

After a moment, Henry cleared his throat. "I know this is a shock to all of you, but we're not sure what's going on with those prisoners who escaped."

He put his hands over his face, and when he finally took them away, there were streaks where tears had mixed in with the trail dust on his skin. "We didn't know what we would find when we got here," Henry said with emotion. "We rode as hard as we could." He cleared his throat again and wiped his eyes and nose on his dusty shirt. "Those men in prison are ruthless, and there's no telling how many are looking for this place right now, thinking there's piles of money and gold."

"Gold?" the twins said at the same time.

"Gold," Henry repeated. "Uncle Jake dressed up the story pretty good."

"We don't have any gold," Leo said. It wasn't until Henry mentioned it that Leo remembered the two men in the barn asking about gold.

"I know," Henry said. "But the outlaws don't know we don't have any."

Leo got up from the table and went to Henry and hugged him. Even though he had not returned with Papa, he had done everything Leo and the boys had needed for him to do.

"Where's Cordy?" Henry asked.

"She left this morning," Earl said.

"They're looking for her, too."

"When was the last time you had any sleep?" Leo asked him.

"I can't even remember." He put his arms around Leo and hugged her tightly. "I was so worried about all of you."

"We did fine," Leo said. "Wait till you see those two we have in the barn. Are you and Uncle Jake hungry?"

"I'll eat anything but pemmican," Henry said, sniffing and letting go of her. "I never wanna see any of that again."

Chapter Twelve

"Riders coming," Jake said from the porch.

Leo and Henry scrambled up from the table. Henry grabbed the rifle by the door and went outside.

"How many?" Henry asked.

"Two that I can see," Jake said. "Skirting the tree line."

Leo climbed the ladder to the loft and found Luther on the bed asleep. She gave his shoulder a shake, which woke him.

"Come with me," Leo said.

Luther got up just as the shooting began outside. She grabbed his hand and they climbed down the ladder.

"That doesn't sound like target practice," Luther said.

"Two riders showed up," Leo said. She grabbed the pistol off the table, but the shooting outside had stopped already.

"Did we get 'em?" Jake called from somewhere outside.

"They're down," Leo heard one of the twins shout from the yard.

Leo was scared and angry. She went to the door and shouted, "How many more could be out there?"

"We only saw two, but there could be five or so," Jake said. "That's my best guess. Earl!" he hollered. "You boys see anything?"

"Them two aren't moving," Earl yelled back. Leo could see him at the end of the barn when she stuck her head outside. He held Papa's rifle like he'd been using it his whole life.

"I'm going around the back," Henry said. "They could be anywhere."

Leo and Luther stayed inside the cabin door, while Uncle Jake sat on the porch. Luther never left Leo's side. She kept her arm around his shoulder to comfort him the best she could. Scanning the landscape for movement kept her senses sharp and her body on edge. The cabin only had one window, so staying close to the door was the best way she could see what was happening outside.

Then shots rang out from behind the cabin. Uncle Jake jumped up and went around by the smokehouse to help Henry.

"Let's get all the ammunition together," Leo said to Luther. *Giving us something useful to do might help take our minds off what's going on out there*, Leo thought. She stayed by the door while Luther piled the ammo on the table. He found his pistol and checked to make sure it was fully loaded. When the shooting behind the cabin stopped, Leo stuck her head out the door and yelled for Henry. He answered her right away.

"Me and Jake's fine! We got another one!"

Earl ran up on the porch and Leo opened the door for him.

"Those two up front are dead and look meaner than the two in the barn," he said. He reloaded his pistol and took a handful of bullets and stuffed them in his pocket. He checked the two pistols shoved in his belt, and reloaded them.

"Where'd you get those?" Luther asked, pointing to the spare pistols.

"Got 'em off those dead varmints out there," Earl said. "Where do you suppose prisoners got all these guns?" he asked. "And horses, too?"

"They probably stole them," Leo said.

"Eb is rounding up their horses if he can catch 'em. We don't need other people showing up and seeing rider-less horses everywhere."

"Take some of this to Henry and Uncle Jake," Luther said. He piled a handful of bullets and shells in Earl's hands. The cabin door opened and all three of them swung around with their guns pointing.

"Whoa there!" Uncle Jake said. "Put them things down."

"You scared us!" Luther said.

"I know. I'm sorry." He reloaded his rifle and took extra shells for him and Henry, before disappearing again.

"Go stand by the door, Luther," Earl said. "Shoot anybody you see who isn't one of us."

Leo could see a wild look in Earl's eyes. *We're killing people,* she thought with a sense of sadness. *They're bad people trying to kill us, but they're still people.*

"What are we going to do, Leo?" Earl asked. "We have to sleep sometime. We can't be awake and watching for them forever."

"I don't know."

"Here comes Eb with the other two horses," Luther said.

"It'll be dark soon," Earl reminded her.

"Send Henry in here," she said. "You go take his place in the back."

Earl nodded and left. On the porch Leo heard him tell Eb to put the horses in the barn. A few minutes later, Henry came in.

"It's quiet out there again," he said.

Leo told Luther to keep watch at the door. She motioned for Henry to follow her into her bedroom where she closed the door behind them.

"What are we going to do, Henry?" She relayed her fears about standing watch at night, no sleep and the constant worry about the unknown where it concerned outlaws hounding them for the stolen money and the mysterious gold they didn't have.

"Even if we turned the money over to somebody," she said, "there could be more outlaws to follow who wouldn't believe we didn't have it."

"I know," he said.

"And this thing about the gold."

"I know. I know."

"Then there's Uncle Jake," Leo said. "Will there be lawmen here looking for him, too? A constant stream of bounty hunters picking up his trail leading them here?"

Henry was at a loss for words. He didn't have any answers for her.

"Well, we can't just sit here picking off riders one by one," Leo said after a moment. "What if a neighbor comes over? We could be shooting them thinking they're here after the money! Our home is no longer a safe place, Henry. We can't stay here and defend it without someone innocent eventually getting killed or maybe even one of us getting hurt."

She realized they had to leave the farm.

"We have plenty of horses," she said. "We'll ride the freshest ones and pack things we'll need on the others."

"Leo . . ."

She knew she was right.

"This is our home," she said, with a lump in her throat. "The boys were born here. Our mother is buried here . . . but this isn't the same place it was yesterday, Henry."

He blinked back tears and slowly nodded. Leo could see how tired he was.

"Can we just leave it this way?" he asked.

Leo took a deep breath. "Can we stay here under these conditions?"

"Shouldn't we ask the boys their opinion on this?" Henry asked.

"They'll go along with whatever we want." Her mind was racing with details on what to take and how to pack it.

"We need a quick family meeting," Henry said, "but I'm not sure it's a good idea to leave our positions out there for that."

"Then you talk to the twins and I'll talk to Luther," Leo said. "If we're leaving, we need to get started now."

"Guns, food, clothes, water and grain for the horses get packed first," Henry said. His conviction and determination made her feel better.

"And the money," Leo added. She didn't hate the money, even though it was why they were in this situation to begin with. If the money was the reason they had to leave, then it was going with them.

Besides, they'd need it.

Leo stood on the porch and looked down at the ten saddles lined up on the ground. Henry and Uncle Jake were selecting the six best ones. They had already picked which horses they would be riding and which four would have things packed on them.

Leo and Luther were in charge of gathering their meager wardrobes, food, extra weapons and miscellaneous necessities. As Leo glanced around the cabin at things that had been in her family for generations, she knew she couldn't afford to get sentimental. She had to carefully choose what she needed to take.

They had two hours of daylight left when they were ready to leave. Uncle Jake decided to knock out the two men in the barn and leave them there untied, but naked. Jake was a train robber, not a killer. He also took the clothes off the three dead outlaws sprawled on the ground—the two up front and the one behind the cabin—so when the "bankers" in the barn eventually woke up, they would have no clothes to scavenge off the bodies.

"Just what we need," Eb said. "Nekid bankers following us."

Uncle Jake laughed. "These two won't be following anybody for a while. They'll be waitin' for your neighbors to do some laundry first."

Leo helped Luther set the pigs loose, take the cow out to pasture and made sure the chickens could get out of the coop and fend for themselves. Leo watched Luther set out fresh water for the chickens after he filled all the canteens he could find.

They saddled up with the best tack from the pile. Henry, Uncle Jake, and the twins had one packhorse each to lead. As they rode away from the farm, Leo made it a point not to look back. Her eyes were teary and she was beginning to worry about Luther again. He hadn't spoken since she told him he had to leave his piglet behind. She wasn't sure what to do to help him through this.

"Does anybody know where we're going?" Eb asked.

Leo hadn't wondered about that herself. All she remembered thinking about was getting as far away as possible, as quickly as they could.

"Uncle Jake does," Henry said. "We're following him. Some place he knows called Eagle Canyon."

By the time it got dark, they were tired and hungry. Uncle Jake found a place to make camp and Leo got a hunk of pemmican out of a saddlebag and passed it around.

"Tastes more like buffalo turds than buffalo meat," Eb mumbled.

"How many buffalo turds you ever eaten?" Uncle Jake asked him with a smile.

It was a light moment, and one they all needed.

Uncle Jake built a fire and everyone gathered around it with their saddles as backrests. Guns were kept close at hand. Leo missed her bed and her home already. She glanced over at Luther sitting beside her and put her arm around him. After a while, she got up and motioned to the twins.

"Henry and Uncle Jake need some sleep," she whispered. "The three of us can take turns keeping watch. We don't need any surprises right now."

The twins both nodded.

"I'll take the first watch," Earl said.

"I'll take the second one," Eb said.

"And don't shoot anything until you're sure it's not one of us," Leo reminded them both.

It wasn't long before everyone began to settle down and the quiet voices became soft snoring. Leo had trouble getting comfortable on the hard ground, but despite her discomfort, she slept deeply. Eb had to shake her awake when it was time for her watch. She got up and found her pistol. Leo added dead sticks to the glowing coals. Tomorrow she would have to ask Uncle Jake how far it was to Eagle Canyon. She wanted to know how many more days she had in the saddle and how many more nights there would be sleeping on the ground.

Chapter Thirteen

By the sixth day, they were tired of pemmican and exhausted from riding. Leo wasn't used to sitting on a horse all day. Tempers were short, and morale was a mixture of anticipation about being somewhere new and sadness over the reasons they had to be there.

Even though Uncle Jake had them all lost for several hours as he attempted to get his bearings, he eventually found the right trail that led to Eagle Canyon's entrance. At first, Leo didn't like the idea that there was a trail to this place. To her way of thinking, if people were through there often enough to *make* a trail, then why wouldn't those same people be coming back?

"It's this way," Uncle Jake said when he returned for them the third time.

They all climbed back in their saddles. Leo took the reins to the packhorse Uncle Jake had been leading. They followed him this time, and Leo wondered how anyone could locate this place, once she paid more attention to their surroundings. Everything looked the same to her—the sparse grass, the scrub oaks, the pebbles and rocks underfoot, and the boulders all around them. She felt a bit claustrophobic and irritated, but Leo was encouraged by Uncle Jake's newfound enthusiasm as he started to talk.

"I knew it was here," Jake said. He urged his horse on ahead and had a smile on his haggard face. "You'll see, Leo. This place is just what we need right now."

They finally rounded a corner on the trail and came into a large box canyon with green grass and a stand of trees in the back. Jake held up his hand to stop them, and then Leo saw the two cabins at the edge of the trees about five hundred yards away.

"Wait here," Jake said. He moved his horse out slowly.

Leo was disappointed to have come this far only to have someone else living there. *Now where will we go?* she wondered. She could feel tears on the way, but she was determined not to cry. She didn't have the energy for it anyway.

"You boys stay here," Leo said. "Keep your eyes open, Henry."

She caught up with Uncle Jake's horse, taking in the vast amount of green grass and the trees in the back. Leo didn't get a sense of danger or uneasiness. Eagle Canyon seemed to be a peaceful, welcoming place.

"How big is it?" she asked as they got closer to the first cabin. She didn't see any horses or signs of life anywhere.

"About two hundred acres," Jake said. "Maybe more."

Green grass, Leo thought. *That means it rains a lot here.*

Once they reached the cabin, Leo called out to whoever might be there. "Hello," she said, then stepped down from her horse. It felt good to be out of the saddle. She called out again, then led her horse over to the second cabin. "Anyone home?"

No answer. She turned to look at Uncle Jake. He nodded and got off his horse. He went inside the first cabin, then came out to tell her it was empty. Leo held her breath and pushed the door to the second cabin open. It was empty as well.

She waved her arms for the boys to join them. Henry, the twins, and Luther set their horses off into a trot and were there quickly.

"These cabins have been abandoned for years," Uncle Jake said. "There's an inch of dust everywhere."

"Wonder who built them?" Leo asked.

"Outlaws probably," Jake said. "That's how I knew about this place, but there weren't any cabins here back then."

"I'm not sure it's a good idea for us to be somewhere that another outlaw is coming back to some day," Leo said. "That's why we had to leave our home in the first place!"

"Leo," Jake said. "Whoever built these cabins is probably dead now. No one's been here in years."

The boys were already in and out of both cabins and were back on their horses, ready to explore more of the canyon.

"Stay together," Leo said. "Luther, you make sure you do whatever Henry says."

They rode off and left the packhorses there. Before long all the horses that stayed behind were grazing on the green grass.

"Look at this place, Leo," Uncle Jake said. He opened his arms and turned around in circles. "We can make it ours." He took her by the hand and led her into the first cabin. It was only one room, but bigger than the one on the farm. There was dust everywhere and an old pack rat's nest in the corner. The furniture consisted of a dusty table and a pot with something black and crusty in the bottom. Leo also found a ladle that was dented on one side. Other than the dust, the cabin was dry inside and the fireplace was in fairly good condition.

"The other one's a little bigger and has a couple of bunks in it," she said. "When were you here last?" Leo asked.

"Essie was about seven or eight, so that's about ten years ago, I guess." He lowered his voice as they walked outside toward the second cabin. "I was running with some no-goods then. We'd hold up a few stage coaches and hightail it up this way and hide out 'til it was safe again."

Leo was shocked. For some reason she thought his recent venture into robbing trains had been his first attempt at breaking the law. There had been several years when they hadn't heard from him, but Leo had no idea he'd been involved with other illegal activities.

"I know why you and your brothers have to be here, Leo," he said. "It's because of me."

"That's right."

"I can't change that. I would if I could."

Leo had never seen her Uncle Jake cry before. His eyes blinked rapidly, then he turned away from her.

"I can't change the past," he said. "All I can do is try and make it up to you kids somehow."

"We've lost everything."

Jake nodded. "I know."

Leo was glad to hear the regret in his voice. They walked slowly toward the other cabin and both saw the well at the same time. It was between the two buildings; Leo hadn't noticed it earlier.

"If we've got water, Leo, it's like some kind of sign for us to be here." He went over to the well and dropped a pebble in it. The tiny hollow splash echoed its way back up to them. Jake hugged her then and looked around the place again.

"Tell me what you're thinking," Leo said to him quietly.

"It's been a long time since I've had a home. I'll do my best to make this all up to you and the boys."

Uncle Jake and his two children were all the family they had now. Leo hugged him again. She and her brothers needed him more than ever now.

The nearest town was Gato Pass, about fifteen miles away near the Mexican border and the Rio Grande. By the end of the first two weeks at Eagle Canyon, they had gone there and purchased enough tools to start building a barn and a corral for the horses, and enough other supplies to make life bearable again. The canyon held an abundance of wildlife for hunting and large trees for building. During the first few days, Earl, Leo and Luther slept in one cabin, while Jake, Eb and Henry slept in the other. They ate meals together and had priorities already established for work every day. There was a lot to do, and eventually the hard work paid off as improvements were made to the cabins, and fences were put up and the garden planted.

One evening after a supper of rabbit and dumplings, Luther asked if anyone else ever wondered about how things were at the old farm.

"The chickens haven't had fresh water since forever," he said.

Leo didn't have the heart to tell him that their old chickens probably weren't even alive any longer. She looked at Henry and the twins. She could see it in their eyes—they were all thinking about the farm. Leo herself was doing it off and on each day as she worked in the garden and tended to the horses.

After Luther and the twins went to bed, Leo, Henry and Uncle Jake went outside to talk. Leo posed the question to them about possibly returning to the farm to see if anything of value was still left there.

"How dangerous would it be to go back and just look?" Leo asked.

Henry shrugged. "I don't know."

They both glanced over at Uncle Jake. He shrugged as well.

"I'm not sure you kids should be putting yourselves through that," Jake said. "If others showed up there looking for the money, they probably tore the place all up trying to find it."

Leo nodded. *Was it better to remember the farm the way they had left it?* she wondered. *Or the way strangers had treated it after they'd gone?*

"I could take one of the twins with me and go see what's left there," Henry said. "If there's anything worth saving, we could load up the wagon and bring it back."

"If they left you a wagon," Uncle Jake reminded him. "They

could've burnt the place down to the ground." He shook his head. "Those two I conked on the head in the barn didn't wake up too happy, I'm sure. They probably went through every inch of that place looking for something to wear."

Henry and Jake chuckled. After a moment, Henry asked, "Is it silly to want to go all the way back just to see what's there?"

"I don't think it's silly to want to know," Jake said, "but I'm not sure how safe it would be either."

Leo felt the need to know what happened to the farm. If it had been burnt to the ground with all their belongings inside, she wanted to know about it. When they left, it would've been easier for outlaws to follow them with a loaded down wagon than it would have been to follow them on horseback. Getting everyone away safely had been the main concern.

"I think we should go," Leo said. Ever since Luther had planted the seed, she couldn't stop thinking about it. "I need to see what's there." She looked at Henry. "Can the two of us do it, or do we need to take one of the twins?"

"Uh . . . ," Henry said. "Well, if there's trouble there—"

"If there's trouble there," Leo said, "then we leave, and that's that. I'm not willing to get one of us killed just to save the family Bible or whatever, but if our things are just sitting there waiting for new people to move in . . . well . . . those things belong to us, Henry."

He nodded as they both looked at Uncle Jake.

"What do you think?" Leo asked him.

"You'll never be able to think of any other place as home 'til you go back there and see your farm one last time," Uncle Jake admitted. He nodded toward the cabin where the twins and Luther were sleeping. "The younger ones will adjust to a new place a lot easier than you two will."

"He's right," Henry said to Leo.

"Then do we take one of the twins with us?" Leo asked, "or do you and I go back and see what's left?"

Leo, Henry and Eb made the trip back to the farm in four days. It was easier traveling with fewer people and they knew the way now. The closer they got to the farm, the stranger it felt. When they reached their destination, they camped south of the creek that night and got up before dawn. Leo's back was stiff from sleeping on the ground again, and she felt grouchy and nervous just being there. She thought about the possibility of outlaws living on the farm now or someone even finding them by the creek. All three were on edge.

They kept their voices low even though they were close to a mile away from the farm. The day before, the three of them had ridden with their rifles across their saddles.

"Leo, why don't you stay here with the horses," Henry suggested. "Me and Eb can circle around the cabin and see if anything is moving."

Leo agreed that having them go in on foot would be much quieter and easier. Crawling around in a long dress didn't make a lot of sense.

"If you hear shooting or anything," he said to Leo, "you stay here. We'll find you."

To Eb he said, "Stay low and watch the cabin and the barn. If anybody's there, we all head back to Eagle Canyon. Agreed?"

Leo and Eb nodded.

"How long we gonna watch the cabin once we get close?" Eb asked.

"A few hours," Henry said. "Or until we're certain no one is there."

It was already late in the morning when Eb came to get her. He ran most of the way.

"Nobody's there," he said excitedly, "but they tore the place all up like Uncle Jake said."

Leo was on her horse and leading Henry's before Eb was able to scramble into his saddle.

Leo felt eerily uncomfortable as she rode up in front of the porch. The place no longer had a warm, welcoming feeling about it. The door was gone and the glass from the window was broken and scattered on the porch.

"Is the wagon still here?" Leo asked.

"It's behind the barn," Henry said. He unsaddled two of the horses.

"Eb," Leo said. "You keep a watch for anything that moves out there. Henry and I will load things up."

"We'll take all we can," Henry said on his way to the barn. "Decide what you want. This is the last chance we'll have to get any of it."

Leo felt sick when she went inside. Furniture was turned over and curtains were pulled down. There were bullet holes in the walls and flour spread all over the place. *I thought we packed all the flour,* she thought. Taking a deep breath, Leo set about gathering up what was going with them.

Ninety minutes later, they had the wagon full of what few personal belongings Leo could find for everyone, all the kitchen supplies and utensils, all the beds, the huge table and chairs their grandfather had made, and the tools from the barn.

"Anything else you want?" Henry asked.

"No," Leo said.

"Let's go say good-bye to Mama and get out of here," Eb said.

The three of them walked over to their mother's grave, holding their rifles. Henry and Eb took off their hats and bowed their heads for a moment. When they were finally ready to go, Leo felt both sad and relieved. She didn't even look back as the wagon pulled out on its way to Eagle Canyon.

Another chapter in their lives had closed.

Part Two

Six Years Later

1894

Chapter Fourteen

Cordy woke up and reached for María, but she was out of bed already. For Cordy that was the best part of any day—being able to feel a lover next to her the moment she woke up. It made visiting María that much more special. Cordy was disappointed at missing that feeling again this morning.

The door to the shack opened and María slipped in. There were things about María that reminded her of the childhood friend Cordy had met at Mission San José several years ago. Their features were similar—the long black hair and dark, serious eyes. Cordy's efforts to locate Elena had taken her to many small border towns over the past few years. She often wondered what happened to her. *Elena's probably married with a cabin full of children by now*, she thought.

Cordy loved watching María quietly putter around the shack, tidying things up as she went about her normal routine. *I should come here more often,* Cordy thought. *This is the only place that feels like home to me anymore.* She smiled and stretched under the scratchy wool blanket. *As long as her husband stays gone,* she reminded herself with a smile.

"*Buenas días,*" Cordy said.

María smiled and returned the greeting. Spanish was the language Cordy spoke when she was in Mexico, or close to the border. She liked being known as the *gringa* who robbed banks up north, deep into the state of Texas. She was like a local folklore hero to the children in the villages across the border. Cordy spoke their language and gave them coins. San Benito, a Texas border town where María lived, was Cordy's favorite place to visit. She liked the weather here, and it was the only place where she felt loved.

"Will you stay in that bed all day?" María asked in Spanish.

Cordy stretched again and laughed. "I might." She got up anyway and draped the blanket around her naked body. She went over to the table—one of only four pieces of furniture in the shack—and pulled María up from the squeaky wooden chair. María put down the boot she had been cleaning mud from, and slipped her arms around Cordy's warm body under the blanket.

"You're not finished from last night?" María cooed in her ear.

"I could never be finished with that," Cordy said. She kissed her and felt a rush of desire. She reached for María's breasts and cupped them gently through her dress.

María pulled her lips away and explored Cordy's neck with her tongue and warm breath. "You make me weak from wanting you."

Cordy slowly unbuttoned the top of María's dress and kissed her throat, nibbling playfully along her collarbone.

"Is it safe today?" Cordy asked, wondering if María's husband Francisco would be back anytime soon.

"Yes. We're safe."

"Then come back to bed with me," she whispered. "I want more of what I had last night."

ॐ

Cordy had first met María Montoya two years ago at the well in the middle of the tiny Texas border town of San Benito. Cordy had stopped there to rest and fill her canteen. María had set her bucket down near Cordy and spoke.

"You're in danger," María said.

Cordy looked around and saw no one else in the area.

"Me? Are you talking to me?" she asked in Spanish.

"Yes. There are marshals near by." María pulled up the well's bucket and emptied it into the one she had set by Cordy. "Follow me." She picked up her bucket and walked slowly toward a small shack at the end of town.

Cordy followed her, leading her horse instead of riding it. María told her to tie her horse behind the shack and instructed Cordy to follow her inside. Cordy and María barely got in the shack before three Texas Rangers rode into town and stopped in front of the cantina. Peeking through a crack in the door, Cordy saw their badges as they got off their horses. She slowly looked over at María.

"How did you know those men were coming?"

María shrugged. "I just knew."

"*How* did you know?"

"It's not something I can explain. I just know things."

Cordy smiled, fascinated. *She's beautiful*, Cordy thought as she took in the sight of María's dark eyes and long, dark hair. "What else do you know? Tell me."

"I know you like danger and you are a favorite of the angels."

"Angels?" Cordy said with a laugh. She definitely wanted to hear more. She sat down and removed her hat.

"Wait here," María said. She picked up the bucket of water and poured half into another pail. María went outside and returned several minutes later with the pail empty. "I took care of your horse."

"Thank you."

María dunked a bandanna into the clean water and handed it to her. Cordy used it to wipe the dust off her face and from the corners of her eyes.

"Tell me more about what you know," Cordy said. "You speak to angels?"

María smiled and shook her head. Cordy felt drawn to her. María's smile revealed perfectly straight, white teeth along with a shyness that was endearing. *She's a beautiful woman*, Cordy thought again.

"You live here alone?"

"With my husband," María said.

Cordy felt a pang of disappointment. "Where is he now?"

"Away."

Cordy took the cool bandanna and dabbed the back of her neck with it.

"Away where?"

María shrugged. "He leaves and comes back when he's ready. This time he's been gone for a few weeks."

"What does he do when he's gone?"

"He doesn't tell me."

"That doesn't mean you probably don't know already," Cordy said. "You knew I was in danger before. Why wouldn't you know what your husband does when he's away?"

"I don't care about him or what he does," María clarified.

"I see." Cordy had a tiny shred of hope. She watched as María took out a bowl and put flour in it. Eventually, there were little balls of a doughy substance lined up on a white cloth. Cordy watched in fascination as María made a stack of tortillas in the corner of the shack. María handed one of the tortillas to her. It was almost too hot to touch. María wrapped the remaining tortillas in another white cloth and told Cordy to stay there. María was gone for several minutes, then returned empty-handed.

"The marshals are busy drinking tequila," María said. "It's safe for you to go if you wish."

"What if I'd rather stay here?"

María's shy smile returned, and Cordy was determined to see it more often. She watched as María washed the bowl.

"Would you like that?" Cordy asked. "Would you like it if I stayed here?"

María looked at her, then shyly looked away again. "Yes," she said.

Cordy stood up and felt power and desire. She came around the table and reached for María's hand.

"You're not the one I'm waiting for," María said.

"Who is it you're waiting for?" Cordy asked.

"I don't know yet, but you being here in San Benito is a blessing of some kind. That's the feeling I get."

"Let me show you how good of a blessing it can be," Cordy said with a light chuckle. She leaned closer and touched María's lips with her own. The kiss that followed rocked Cordy's very foundation.

That had been two years ago, and she and María had spent many nights together during that time whenever Cordy came back to San Benito.

Cordy loved having María's warm, naked body on top of her. María had large breasts that fit perfectly against Cordy's less than ample chest. Their lovemaking always left Cordy wanting more. María was just as eager to give pleasure as she was to receive it.

"Tell me again," Cordy whispered in María's ear as they moved against each other. The urgency of flesh on flesh . . . heat and desire mixed with a pulsating rhythm so intricate and demanding it was all Cordy could do to keep from coming too quickly. Touching María this way for as long as she could made everything else in Cordy's life seem trivial. "Tell me again," she whispered desperately.

"Just you," María said in a raspy voice as they began to grind against each other. "It's not like this with anyone else."

No sooner were the words spoken than the connection became more than mere heat and desire. Cordy came alive with a series of intense, molten sensations. She grabbed María's back and hips and they thrashed around as though their bodies were one. Cries of mutual pleasure left no doubt that it had been good, and their murmurs continued on until exhaustion took the place of an unprecedented need.

Cordy barely had the energy to even kiss her afterward, but her lips and tongue had a mind of their own and ignored her fatigue. María always made sure their bodies stayed connected as long as the throbbing between them remained. She raised herself up with her arms and pressed into Cordy, which caused new fringes of desire to surge through both of them.

Afterward, María lay in Cordy's arms where they drifted back to sleep, only to wake up again and start all over. Cordy loved being there with her and thought about María even when she was away leading her usual nomad existence. Cordy often wondered why she couldn't just settle down and be happy in one place . . . be happy with María, but the restlessness always seemed to creep up on her. It was all Cordy knew. It was all her father had left her.

"How long will you stay this time?" María asked.

Cordy kissed her on top of the head. "You tell me since you always know so much," she teased.

"It's you who is restless this time," María said. "Not my husband. You'll need to leave soon. I can see it in your eyes."

"Will I be safe while I'm gone?"

"Yes."

"Then it doesn't matter where I go, does it?"

"You still have to be careful."

Cordy laughed and kissed her.

She liked hitting banks in small towns right as they opened. The town sheriff was usually busy with his breakfast, the bank tellers were slow to get organized, and most customers tended to have other errands to do early. Cordy found this approach to be the most successful.

Usually after a holdup, Cordy would ride for a day and stay off the main roads. Every lawman in South Texas knew who she was and what she looked like, so she saved any socializing for Mexico or

María. Having a good time had become her main focus over the years. She knew how to have fun and knew where to go to find the women who enjoyed such things as well.

Cordy also loved sleeping under the stars with a saddlebag full of money. Having it made her feel happy. She took the money out often just to count it. She loved touching money, sorting it, holding it, and smelling it. She also liked the things money was able to give her—and women had been high on her list of priorities.

María wasn't the only person in Cordy's life. Further into Mexico, Cordy had many female friends and lovers. She bought them clothes and trinkets. She fed and clothed their children. In return, Cordy received love and affection from women who sold themselves to men as well as other women like her. However, Cordy liked to believe they preferred spending their time with her. Despite the adoration they showered her with, Cordy wondered how much these women would love and care for her if there were no presents for them or their children. She didn't waste much time on thoughts like that, though. Spending her money that way gave her another excuse to eventually go rob more banks, and the excitement and danger of that was where the true pleasure was for her.

Two months passed before Cordy returned to San Benito. She robbed a bank in Logansboro the day before and had a small posse chasing her for a while, but she knew the area well and lost them easily. She thought of the chase as a game, and thought herself invincible. She took her time getting to San Benito, making sure no one followed her.

It was late afternoon when she arrived just outside of town. She stopped at the river, watered her horse, then undressed and went for a swim. It felt good to be in the water and out of the saddle. She washed her hair and was glad to have clean clothes to put on afterward.

By the time she got to San Benito, it was getting dark. Cordy was disappointed to see a horse tied up outside María's shack.

Francisco is home, she thought. María had described his horse to her once before. Cordy was surprised she felt no jealousy toward him. He was María's husband and there wasn't much she could do about it.

She looked around and saw several horses in front of the cantina. There was a small church at the other end of the street where María's brother was a priest. Cordy decided if she stayed at the church for the night, she might be able to see María in the morning when she came to the chapel to pray.

Just as she was about to head in that direction, Cordy heard raised voices in Spanish. There was a slap, followed by a muffled scream. Cordy looked around. No one else was in the street. The argument was coming from María's shack.

She got down off her horse and tied it up behind María's place like she always did. Cordy heard a male voice cussing over María's muffled whimpering. Before Cordy could get inside, Francisco slapped María again.

Cordy drew her gun and opened the door. She cocked the pistol and pointed it right at him.

"You hit her again and I'll kill you," she said in Spanish.

Francisco swung around, eyes opened wide, shock and fear on his face. He pushed María away and snatched up his hat; he brushed past Cordy on his way out the door. Cordy watched him jump on his horse and ride off. Once she made sure he was gone, she put her gun away and turned around to see about María.

"Will he be back?" Cordy asked.

"Not tonight," María said. She kept her hand over her mouth, but Cordy could see the blood on her lip and the swelling under her right eye.

"Why did he hit you?" Cordy dunked a cloth in the water bucket and gently dabbed the corner of María's mouth.

"He hates me."

"He hates you? Why does he hate you?"

"I can't give him children."

Cordy didn't know what to say, but a surge of anger brewed inside her.

"He was also angry because I didn't have much money for him."

"He took your money?" Cordy asked calmly. She knew María supplied tortillas to the local cantina every day. It didn't pay much, but it was enough for her to live on.

"How much did he take?"

"All of it," María said. She closed her eyes and a tear rolled down her cheek. "I don't want you to see me this way." She took the wet cloth from her and turned around. Cordy noticed then that María's dress was torn at the shoulder.

"You don't want me to see you what way?" Cordy asked. She moved around in front of her and touched María's chin with the tip of her finger. She put her arms around María and pulled her closer. "I'll kill him if he ever touches you again."

Chapter Fifteen

Leo stayed in her cabin, listening to the rain hitting the roof. Luther had been over earlier to help her put more sod on the roof to patch a leak. The boys would be working on repairs to Luther and Uncle Jake's cabin next if the rain let up anytime soon. Rain was one of the nice things about being at Eagle Canyon. After so many years of drought, Leo appreciated every drop they received.

She liked having the cabin farthest away from the others. Leo finally managed to carve out her own niche at Eagle Canyon. She could be alone anytime she wanted to now, and she treasured those quiet moments. Having spent the first sixteen years of her life looking out for siblings, it was a relief to have them all grown and on their own. Leo was close enough to her uncle and brothers to call for help if she needed something, or she could be totally alone if she preferred. Everyone, including her small niece and nephews, respected Leo's need for privacy. The closest cabin to hers was empty, which made for even more privacy. That one had been built for Luther, but he didn't like living alone, and had moved into Uncle Jake's cabin with him.

There was always plenty to do and not enough daylight to get it all done. Soon there would be another baby arriving. Henry and his wife were expecting their fourth child any day now. The twins, Eb and Earl, no longer lived at Eagle Canyon. They were married to sisters from El Paso and lived there on a ranch. Those who had remained at Eagle Canyon still missed them.

Luther and Uncle Jake were bachelors. Luther was too interested in tending to the animals they owned to be concerned with women yet. The family's self-imposed isolation didn't give him many opportunities to meet women, but Luther didn't seem too worried about it.

A few years after the Trask family arrived at Eagle Canyon, the older boys set out to find wives. The twins met their wives Hattie and Gloria in a saloon in Baker's Creek, about a hundred miles north of the border. Henry met his wife, Dell, after her family was killed by Indians on their ranch near Fargo's Crossing. Henry and Leo had gone there a few times to buy cattle and horses. Even though Luther was seventeen now, he was still the baby and thought of in that way. Leo continued feeling a little guilty about Luther having to leave his pig behind when they left the old farm, so she made sure he had anything he wanted now. That had come in the form of pigs, chickens, goats, cows, sheep, and horses. Apparently, having a wife of his own hadn't occurred to him yet.

Leo pulled her boots off and lay down on her bed. She would be able to enjoy the rain and the distant thunder now that her roof was fixed. Each time she stretched out on her bed, she was glad they had gone back to get the furniture from the old farm. Leo had kept her parents' bed for herself. Sleeping in it made her feel close to them.

The rain had cooled everything off. Leo opened her cabin door and waved at Luther, who was carrying a bucket of grain to the barn. She could hear Henry's three children laughing as they tied Uncle Jake to a tree in their yard. Leo waved at the children, and made a mental note to check on Uncle Jake after awhile in case he wasn't able to get loose. A few minutes later, she saw Henry waving his arms at her. Leo met him halfway across the yard and noticed the weariness in his eyes.

"The baby's coming," he said.

Leo put her hand on his shoulder as she followed him to his cabin. "Keep the children outside and make sure Dell is as comfortable as you can make her."

One of the few things that worried Leo the most about being so secluded was the distance to a doctor if they should ever need one.

"I hate this, Leo," Henry said. "She's hurting bad. Seems like it's worse than the last three times."

Leo had delivered all the Trask babies, learning a little more each time she had to do it. "She'll be fine," Leo said. "Take the kids over to Jake and Luther's place."

She watched him gather up his other three children and take them next door. Both of her brothers were good friends. The squabbles were few, and they knew when to tend to their own business. The biggest challenges they faced were conquering boredom and keeping the homestead flourishing. They were fortunate to be satisfied with having a few trips to the nearest town as a source of entertainment.

Other than supply runs and the occasional shopping spree, they stayed at Eagle Canyon. Uncle Jake was the only one who ever left for any length of time. He liked to visit his daughter Essie and her three young sons, who lived near a small town called Wilson Creek. Essie's husband was ill, and Jake gave them money whenever he was there.

"How's she doing?" Leo asked when she went into the bedroom in Henry's cabin.

Henry was there blotting sweat from Dell's forehead. Dell was on the bed, and Leo had arrived just in time to witness the next contraction.

"You have another boy," Leo said to Henry several hours later as she came out of the bedroom. "He and his mother are doing fine."

The relief on Henry's face made her wish that someday someone special would love her that way. He hugged her fiercely and then shook hands with his brother and uncle, who were there with him. Leo was happy for him, and relieved that her new nephew and her sister-in-law were both doing well.

Henry went in to see his wife and new baby. Everyone else sat back down at the table.

"Do they have a name picked out?" Leo asked Luther.

"Milton," he said. "After Papa."

Leo slowly sat down at the table beside him, and then nodded. "That's a good name for a boy," she said quietly.

"We thought so too," Luther said. "So when do we get to see him?"

Leo spent a lot of time at the barn with the horses. She enjoyed talking to them, feeding them, and brushing them as a form of relaxation. During the day she never thought of herself as lonely, but at night when she came outside and could see the glow of lanterns in the other two cabins and hear the muffled laughter in the night air, it reminded her that something was missing.

She stood in the doorway of her cabin and looked out across the large yard toward Luther and Uncle Jake's place. They were still up, but she couldn't hear them talking. She stood in the darkness and watched lightning streak the sky off in the distance. The smell of rain was in the air and she smiled at the thought of falling asleep to it. Leo was at a point in her life where she was ready for a change. She didn't regret any of the choices she'd made. She had almost given up hope of finding what it was she wanted. She wasn't even sure what it *was* she wanted. But she had her family for support and the horses to keep her company and soothe her soul.

"Henry thinks the little ones are old enough to start learning how to ride," Luther said the next morning.

He had the stable raked and fresh hay in the stalls already. "He's probably right," Leo said. "They're at least old enough to start off with saddles on a bench."

"Then work their way up to riding a sheep?" Luther said with a laugh.

"Now days, I'd rather ride a sheep than eat a sheep," she said. Mutton wasn't anyone's favorite meal any longer.

Leo peeked inside one of the barrels where they captured rainwater. Rain barrels were set up wherever runoff was possible. It was easier to give the animals rainwater than to carry it from the well or the spring. They were fortunate to have water year-round there at Eagle Canyon.

Leo picked up a brush and started in on the first horse again. If she had her way, they would raise more horses. Leo liked stepping outside of her cabin and seeing them in the corral and out back in the pasture. There was enough grass to accommodate several more horses, and enough rain fell in the area to keep the grass green all the time, but Luther and Uncle Jake kept reminding her they already had plenty of horses.

"We don't eat horses," Uncle Jake said. "We need the pastures for cows and sheep. The things we *do* eat."

So she left Luther and Uncle Jake in charge of the farming and ranching aspects of everyday life. Leo had more of a leadership role, where her opinion and ideas were sought and appreciated whenever there was a problem. In return, Leo found that Henry and Uncle Jake were the people she felt the most comfortable with whenever it came to anything personal in her own life. Uncle Jake had changed a lot after his brother died. He had settled down and become more serious. In many respects, they all had.

꧁꧂

Uncle Jake stopped by Leo's cabin later that evening. She was tired from spending most of the day in the saddle helping Henry and Luther move the sheep to another pasture.

"You're holding up better than Luther is," Jake said. "He's asleep already."

"It was a long day," Leo agreed.

Jake sat down at the table in her cabin. "I'm off to see Essie tomorrow. I'll pick up a few things we need on the way back. Anything special you want?"

"No, I'm fine," Leo said. "You have money to give Essie?"

He smiled. "I do. I just wanted you to know where I'll be. Probably won't be gone but a few days."

"You be careful."

"I will."

Leo looked at him and decided his physical appearance hadn't changed much other than what the sun had done to his leathery face.

"There's room for Essie and the boys here, you know," she said. "When the time comes."

Jake nodded. "And it just might come to that soon."

"Does she have friends where she's at? Does her husband's family live near them?"

"Jonathan's sister is staying with them. She's helping with Essie's three little boys." Jake laced his fingers together and set them on the table. "While I'm out there I'll be looking for another bank for us to hit when we're ready."

Leo sighed and then slowly nodded. She didn't particularly like the way they financed their life at Eagle Canyon, but had learned to be realistic. They started off with stolen money, and continued when the money ran low. They sold cattle and horses when they could to subsidize their income, but it was never quite enough to get them through. The banks they robbed were far away. They were all in agreement on that aspect of the "family business" they had chosen. Leo hoped someday they would be able to make an honest living with cattle and horses, but that was still in the future.

"Henry is ready," Jake said. He cut his eyes over at her. "He doesn't like it any more than the rest of us do, but he's ready to do whatever needs doin'."

Leo nodded. "Then look for something easy."

"I will."

Leo was up when Luther came over the next morning. He brought her breakfast and put on some coffee to boil.

"The chicks are hatching out," he said. "I'll round up the kids and take them over to the hen house so they can see them later."

He had two biscuits and some bacon on a plate for her. A red bandanna covered the top of it. One thing Leo was proud of was the way her brothers had turned out to be such good cooks. In the beginning when the boys started spending so much time in saloons and courting the women they found there, the Trasks' "house-mouse" talents hadn't initially been discovered. But not long after Henry got married and brought his new bride home to Eagle Canyon, Dell came to Leo, shocked at how helpful Henry was around the cabin. Leo's complaining back then had eventually paid off for someone. She and her sister-in-law talked about the "house-mouse" days in private—never in front of her brother.

"How many chicks this time?" Leo asked. They had gotten some good laying hens near Dos Diablos last spring.

"Looks like ten," Luther said, setting the plate down on the table for her.

Luther was the one who stayed behind at Eagle Canyon when Leo, Henry and Uncle Jake were off "working," as Henry liked to refer to it. Luther had never been a part of a bank robbery. He made sure things ran smoothly at home and those who stayed behind were too busy to ask many questions.

"I got the benches ready for the kids," Luther said. "The saddles look huge when they sit on them."

"Are we moving the sheep again today?" Leo asked.

Luther nodded. "Henry says they stink too bad being so close to

120

the cabins. We might not have to worry about them too much longer if the eagles don't stop plucking the lambs out of the field."

Leo smiled. As long as she didn't have to smell another lamb chop cooking, lamb-plucking by eagles sounded pretty good to her. It had been decided by everyone that when the last sheep was gone, they wouldn't be getting any others. Luther's interest in them wasn't what it once was either.

Chapter Sixteen

Cordy ventured a little further northeast than usual and hit a bank in Victoria, Texas. From there she took her time riding to the Mexican border and enjoyed herself immensely once she reached Agua Dulce in the vicinity of Laredo. There she bought a new dress for María. Even though Cordy liked spending money, she usually had little to show for it other than memories of a good time.

She stayed in a nice room and stocked up on a few supplies while she was in town. When Cordy eventually got tired of sleeping with a string of women or pampering herself with hot baths in hotel rooms, there was only one place she really wanted to be, so she got back on her horse and headed for San Benito and María Montoya.

Cordy rode for two days, sticking to the back-trails along the Rio Grande. Once she was close to San Benito, she gave her horse a rest just outside of town and waited for it to get dark. When darkness finally set in, Cordy rode into town and tied her horse behind

María's shack. She was relieved there was no sign of Francisco. She took her saddlebag down and knocked on María's door. When María answered, she jumped into Cordy's arms and covered her face with kisses.

"I knew you would come," María said.

Cordy laughed. She no longer doubted María's special gift. She had come to appreciate it. "Is it safe for me to be here?" Cordy asked.

"Yes, it's safe," María said. She closed the door and kissed her again. "I've missed you."

They were all over each other even before making it to the bed. *Why isn't this enough?* Cordy wondered as she struggled out of her shirt and boots. *We love each other and she takes such good care of me. Why can't I just be happy with this?*

Once they were out of their clothes, Cordy lay on the bed and María stretched out on top of her.

"This is how you like it," María said with a smile. Her long black hair was a mass of curls around her head. She was a strikingly beautiful woman, and Cordy felt lucky to be a part of her life.

"I like the way you remember that," Cordy said as she reached up and moved a spray of dark curls from María's eyes. "Yes," she whispered. "This is how I like it." She arched her back and rubbed her breasts into María's. "Who *wouldn't* like this?" Cordy asked before she kissed her again.

All night long they made love, and when Cordy woke up the next morning, María was still there beside her. She snuggled into her arms and kissed María's eyelids, nose, and the corners of her mouth. Cordy loved hearing those waking-up-noises María made. As María yawned and stretched, Cordy took a taut nipple into her mouth.

"You want more this morning?" María asked with a chuckle.

"Yes, I want more," Cordy replied. "Lots more!"

"You can have whatever you want," María whispered. "You can have it all."

❧

They stayed in bed until late in the morning. María propped her head up with her hand and smiled down at Cordy.

"You will meet an old friend soon," María said.

"I will?" Cordy ran her hand along María's bare thigh. "A man or a woman?"

"I'm sure you know more women."

Cordy laughed and kissed her on the nose. "I brought you a present, but you can't have it yet. I want to keep you here as long as I can."

María sat up in the bed. "What did you bring me?"

Cordy pointed to her saddlebag. María put it on the bed and then pulled out the dress. She held it up to her and scampered out of bed and began to dance around the room.

"It's beautiful!"

The dress was yellow and brown and went well with María's skin tone and the color of her eyes. María stopped dancing and lowered the dress, exposing the top of her breasts. The sadness in her eyes was sudden and alarming. "I can't accept this gift. Francisco will not let me keep it."

"Why not?" Cordy asked. She sat up in bed, pulling the blanket up around her.

"I could never pay for something this beautiful," María said. "How would I explain where it came from?"

"Tell him your lover gave it to you," Cordy said matter-of-factly. She got up from the bed and wrapped the blanket around her. "Tell him the gringa who almost killed him gave it to you." Standing in front of her, Cordy leaned closer and kissed her gently on the lips. "Tell him the woman who will hunt him down and shoot off his balls if he ever touches you again gave it to you," she whispered.

María threw her head back and laughed. She put her arms around Cordy and kissed her wildly, crushing the dress between them.

They spent the rest of the day in bed.

"I want you to take this money," Cordy said. She had a handful of bills and gave them to María. As Cordy attempted to pull her boots on, she saw María throw the money on the floor.

"I'm not your whore," she snapped.

Cordy was shocked. "That's not what the money is for!"

"I don't want your money."

Cordy finished putting both boots on and shrugged. "It's not my money anyway. I stole it." She got up out of the chair and caught María by the hand. "You're upset that I'm leaving," Cordy said.

"Yes," María admitted with a sniff.

"This morning you also said it wasn't safe for me to be here now. That means I have to go."

María nodded.

"So are you crying because Francisco is coming home? Or because I have to go?"

"Both."

"I can stay and talk to him again."

María tried to hide the beginnings of a smile. "Talk to him with your gun?"

Cordy laughed. "It's a language he understands. We both speak it well." She bent down and picked up the money. Cordy pressed the bills into María's hand again. "I'm giving you this in case he comes back. You'll at least have something to give him so he won't hit you again."

María reluctantly nodded. "I could use it for that."

Cordy turned around and strapped on her holster. She reached for her hat and the saddlebag. "Money can't buy what I get from you," she said. "We both know that." Cordy kissed her gently on the forehead. "You want me to stay and make sure he behaves himself?"

María shook her head. She kissed her and wiped the tears from her eyes. Cordy left her there, got on her horse, and rode out of town. Their visit had been unexpectedly cut short, and neither had been ready for her to leave this time.

Cordy waited for him on the very edge of town. She finally saw Francisco Montoya riding alone on the road leading into San Benito. With her gun drawn, she moved her horse out of the brush and startled him. Francisco raised his hands and had the same wide-eyed look she remembered from their last encounter.

"Don't shoot me!" he said in English.

"Why shouldn't I?" she asked in Spanish.

As if someone had been operating them with an invisible string, his hands popped up in the air even higher.

"It's no secret she can tell when you're close by," Cordy continued in Spanish. "She tells me everything, you know. Where you are, where you've been, and where you're going."

"She's a witch," he mumbled and then spit on the ground.

"Maybe so," Cordy said, "but she's *my* witch." She cocked the pistol and aimed it at his head. "If you want to live," Cordy said slowly, "you need to ride out of here and never come back."

His horse started walking backward as if it understood exactly what she had said.

"If I ever see you again," Cordy said in a voice that sounded even chilling to her. "If I ever hear that you've been back this way, I'll find you and kill you." Her horse kept pace with his each time his horse moved backward. "María will give me plenty of warning about you. She's good at that. Do you understand what I'm saying?"

The fear in his eyes as he nodded was all the reassurance she needed. He turned his horse around and galloped away. Francisco Montoya would no longer be a problem for María.

Cordy watched Francisco's horse speed by another rider on the road. She chuckled at the determination he had to get as far away from there as possible. When the other rider got closer to her, he tipped his hat. There was something familiar about him, and she turned in her saddle and then stopped her horse. The man had stopped his horse also, and then turned it around as well.

"Cordy?" he said.

Surprised at having a stranger know her name, she drew her gun at lightning-bolt speed. *Is there a bounty out on me?* she wondered. *A wanted poster I don't know about?* Everywhere she went, Cordy made sure to keep an eye out for them.

"It's Jake Trask."

Hearing his name was like having ice water thrown in her face. Jake Trask? Jake was dead! Her father and Milton Trask were also dead!

"Jake?" she whispered. Cordy slowly got off her horse. She was afraid her body would give way and she'd fall out of the saddle.

Jake flew off his horse and stood there holding the reins. "You're all growed up, but it sure looks like you! What are you doing here in these parts?"

Cordy's hands began to shake. She thought she might get sick. She put her pistol back in its holster, but her hand was visibly shaking.

"I thought you were dead," she whispered in a trembling voice. "Is my Pa alive too?"

"Oh, Cordy! I'm so sorry. I forgot you didn't know about your Pa."

Jake took the reins of both horses and led Cordy to the shade of a scrub oak. They sat down for a rest as their horses nibbled at the grass.

Cordy listened to him as he told her about that last train robbery where Alva and Milton had gotten beaten. He told her about their brief stay in prison before her father and Milton died peacefully in their sleep.

"It was right nice of you to take the horses back to Milton's place," he said. "You knew that Henry was out looking for us, right?"

"Yes," she said. Cordy was still in shock at having all this brought up again. She hadn't realized that the wound could be opened so easily. Losing her father was finally catching up with her. Having never heard anything else about her Pa, she liked pretending their paths had just not crossed again, and it was still somehow possible that he was alive.

"Where you headed?" he asked.

"Nowhere really," she said.

"Then come home with me!" Jake suggested. "I'm on my way back from visiting my daughter. My niece and nephews would like seeing you again. They're all growed up, too!"

⋙⋘

It was a long ride to Eagle Canyon, but Cordy enjoyed spending time with Jake. He was a talker and he made her laugh.

"What have you been doing all this time?" he asked. "Thought you'd be all married and settled down by now."

"Nope. That life was never for me," she said. Their horses moseyed along the trail. Cordy felt relaxed and happy. Riding with Jake reminded her of times with her father when she was younger.

"My niece Leo said you might have headed out for Palo Duro after you left their farm."

"I went south to Mexico instead," she said. "When I ran out of money I robbed my first bank near Laredo." Jake's hearty laughter made her smile.

"So are you famous yet?" he asked.

"In some parts I am, but mostly I guess I'm just a nuisance to small banks. I've had to do my business further north these days."

Jake nodded. "I have to admit we've been to visit a bank or two over the last couple of years," he said, "but Leo worries about it a lot."

"Really?" Cordy said. "Leo robs banks?"

"Yes, she does. Leo and Henry don't much like it, but they know it needs to be done." He shook his head. "The twins moved away. We never see them, so it's just Leo, Henry and Luther left. Henry got married and has some little ones now."

Cordy couldn't stop picturing Leo helping with a bank robbery.

128

"What's Leo like these days?" she asked. Cordy had spent many nights thinking about Leo after leaving the farm. *She was nice to look at then*, Cordy thought, *so I wonder what she looks like now!*

"Oh, she's changed more than any of them," Jake said. "She wears britches like you! If you ask me, she spends too much time alone. Don't seem right somehow."

"So Leo robs banks," Cordy said with a laugh. *Leo in britches. I have to see this.*

"She's not afraid of anything." He shook his head again. "She's good at keeping us busy. That's for sure."

"Well, I'm anxious to see everyone again," Cordy said. "I'm glad I found you, Jake."

"Who found who?"

They shared a good laugh.

Chapter Seventeen

Cordy was impressed with Jake's ability to tell one boulder from another as they wove their way through trees and rocks. She had never been this far west before, and she wasn't impressed with what she was seeing.

"You sure you know where you're going?" Cordy finally asked him.

Jake laughed. "You're not the first person to ever ask me that."

A short while later after covering another stretch of identical landscape, Cordy said, "Tell me again why you live here?"

"You'll see soon enough."

To Cordy's amazement, he was right. There was a large cluster of brush and bushes that seemed to move on hinges when Jake got off his horse and pulled it to the side. It was almost as though he had opened a door for her. He took his hat off and bowed.

"After you, ma'am."

Cordy was more amazed when she got around the next huge boulder and caught her first glimpse of Eagle Canyon. There was green grass as far as she could see, and what could only be described as a village about five hundred yards away from the entrance. Cordy saw four large cabins, a huge barn and corral, and several pens for chickens, small sheep, and young goats. She felt as though she had stumbled into some sort of lost world.

"Well?" Jake said as he climbed back on his horse. "You like Eagle Canyon so far?"

Cordy didn't know what to say at first. Words to describe it weren't coming to her right away, but she did managed to mumble, "It's really nice."

A man came riding over from a back pasture. Once they got closer, Cordy realized it had to be Henry. He called out Jake's name.

"I brought an old friend," Jake said. He couldn't stop smiling.

"Cordy?" Henry said. "Is that you?"

"It's me all right," she confirmed with a grin. "My goodness. You're all grown up!"

"So are you," Henry said. "How have you been? I've often thought about that Palo Duro place you used to talk about. Did you ever go back there?"

"No. I never did."

The three of them were now riding toward the cabins.

"I thought Jake was lost for sure trying to find this place."

"He probably was," Henry said. They all laughed.

"We expect to find him wandering around out there some day tugging on the wrong brush pile," Henry said. "Where'd you find her, Uncle Jake?"

"San Benito on my way back."

"Luther will be happy when he finds out you're here," Henry said.

Cordy didn't see Leo anywhere. Then, as though someone had stepped on an ant bed, people began to pour out of the cabins. Cordy saw a woman with three small children at her side. She held a bundle in her arms and Cordy wondered if that could be Leo.

The three riders were surrounded by the children now. Cordy and Jake got off their horses. The chatter was constant while they walked toward the cabins. Cordy got her saddlebag down and threw it over her shoulder.

"I'll introduce you to everyone," Henry said. He touched each child on the head as he told Cordy their names, and then introduced her to his wife Dell.

"Welcome," Dell said. She was about Cordy's height with light brown hair piled neatly on top of her head.

"It's nice to meet you," Cordy said. She looked up and saw two other people coming toward the small crowd that had formed. The young man was tall and wore a broad-rimmed hat, white shirt, and brown pants held up with suspenders. The woman walking beside him was almost as tall and was dressed in black pants, a black shirt, black boots and a nice black hat. Her hair was long and dark, but pulled back loosely away from her face. She was a beautiful woman. Cordy couldn't stop looking at her.

"There's Luther and Leo," Jake said. "Looky here who I found!" he called to them.

That's Leo?! Cordy thought. *Whoa!*

"Cordy Kincade!" Luther said. He hurried toward her and swooped her up in his arms. He swung her around to everyone's delight.

Cordy laughed and hugged him. "It's hard to believe you're the same boy who used to wag a pig around," she said.

Their laughter made her feel warm inside. This was the closest thing she'd ever had to a family. Being there with them was like coming home, and it felt good.

Luther set her back down. Cordy readjusted her hat and the saddlebag she was carrying. She stepped away from him and nodded at Leo.

"It's good to see you again, Cordy," Leo said.

There was no smile. Cordy wasn't getting much indication from Leo that her arrival was anything special. Cordy was disappointed, but then remembered how distant Leo had always been.

"You two been riding long today?" Luther asked.

"Long enough," Uncle Jake said.

"I thought for sure he was lost," Cordy commented again.

"He probably was," Henry said.

Cordy got the grand tour from Luther, Dell and the children. She was aware of Henry and Leo walking behind them. Cordy tried to make an effort to listen to Luther as he explained a few points of interest as they went from place to place, but her thoughts kept straying back to Leo.

"My old cabin is that one over there," Luther said proudly, indicating a nice cabin near the barn. "It's been empty a while now. You can stay there if you like. For as long as you want."

They headed that way first. Luther opened the cabin door, crossed the room and opened another door on the other side. The sudden breeze felt good on Cordy's face.

"It's dusty in here," Dell said. "There's a bunk, a table, and a lantern. We can get it cleaned up for you today."

"All this just for me?" Cordy asked, confused. "Who else lives here?"

"Here in Eagle Canyon?" Luther asked. "Just us."

Cordy stuck her head out the front door and glanced around. "All these houses are for the Trask family?"

Luther laughed. "Sometimes there aren't enough of them!"

"I don't need my own place," Cordy said. She came back inside and continued looking around. "A dry corner of the barn will do me just fine."

"You aren't sleeping in the barn," Luther said. "Tell her, Leo. Tell her she doesn't have to sleep in the barn."

Cordy turned and saw Henry and Leo outside the doorway. Henry picked up his little daughter and held her.

"I'm not used to anything this nice," Cordy said.

"You don't have to stay here," Leo said as she stepped inside the cabin.

Once again Cordy was surprised at how tall Leo was. She was indeed a beautiful woman. Seeing her standing next to her brothers gave a false impression of just how statuesque and imposing she actually was. Both Henry and Luther towered over Cordy and Dell, but not over Leo.

"You can stay wherever you feel comfortable," Leo said. Her eyes were dark and penetrating.

"We'll see how you feel about it later," Henry said. "You can stay with us if you'd rather be around people, unlike someone else we know." He looked over at Leo with an arched brow. "I'm sure Dell would like having someone new to talk to."

"Eagle Canyon is a wonderful place," Leo said. "I think you'll be comfortable here."

Cordy watched Leo turn and leave the cabin. She still wasn't sure if Leo was glad to see her.

A crowing rooster woke Cordy up. She was on a pallet in the main room of Henry's cabin. Cordy, Dell, Henry and Luther had stayed up late the night before. Everyone had been eager to hear stories of Cordy's adventures. She had talked as long as they were willing to listen and ask her questions. She made sure not to mention anything about how she made her living, though.

Once the rooster had her awake, Cordy was up for the day. She folded the blanket and set it on a bench by the table. Slipping quietly out the door, she took care of her early-morning personal business at the closest outhouse. Cordy still couldn't believe they had three of them within walking distance of each other.

The sun hadn't been up long, but already Luther was feeding the chickens. He waved and continued on. Glancing over at Leo's cabin, Cordy wondered if she was still asleep. She also tried to imagine what Leo might be wearing to sleep in. Chuckling to herself at being so silly, Cordy got a sudden whiff of bacon frying. Mornings at Eagle Canyon were full of life. She went to the barn to check on her horse and was surprised to find Leo there.

"Good morning," Leo said as she tightened the cinch on the saddle.

"Good morning. How long have you been up?" Cordy asked.

"Not long. Jake said to send you over to his place first thing." She gave the horse's neck a pat and then murmured soothingly in its ear.

"Where you off to already?" Cordy asked.

"I've got work to do," Leo said.

She got on the horse so gracefully that Cordy was mesmerized for a moment. The straight line of Leo's body was emphasized by the long, dark hair flowing down her back. Cordy watched her nudge the horse forward with the heel of her boot and then ride off behind her cabin.

Cordy offered to help Jake and Luther work on thinning out a thicket of scrub oaks. They were looking for a particular size oak to use for fencing purposes. The Trasks had used the landscape and natural resources to their advantage. Cordy was impressed, and surprised by how quickly she felt comfortable among them.

"Here's one the size we need," Jake said. He put his hand around a tree with a trunk no bigger than Cordy's fist. "Just take the ax and give it a whack as close to the ground as you can, then throw it on the wagon."

After an hour of cutting small oaks, Cordy was better acquainted with an ax than she ever wanted to be. More accustomed to sitting in a saddle all day, she wasn't used to such hard work. She took her hat off and wiped her brow with a bandanna. She wondered what Leo was doing right then. Where had she ridden off to earlier?

She leaned over, picked up the last two small trees she had chopped down, and dragged them to the wagon.

"That's enough," Jake called. "The wagon's full."

"Now what?" Cordy asked. She could hear two squirrels scurring over dry leaves several yards away.

"We take these back to the barn and drop them off for Luther to trim up," Jake said. "Then we'll see what Leo has for us to do next."

"Where is Leo?" Cordy asked.

"She's off with Henry looking for a lost calf."

That sounded like more fun than chopping down trees. This time of year she never worked up a sweat this quickly. She did, however, want to earn her keep. At some point later, Cordy also wanted to check around the premises and find a place to make camp. She preferred sleeping under the stars at night. The hospitality of these people was a bit overwhelming. It reminded Cordy how little they actually knew her.

"This is a good load," Luther said. He climbed up in the wagon, while Cordy and Jake rode on top of the oak pile in the back.

"Me, Leo, and Henry are meeting at her cabin later to talk about our next job," Jake said.

Cordy felt her heart skip a beat. "A bank?"

"Most likely. The only question is where. That's what we'll be discussing."

"Maybe I can help," Cordy said. "You shouldn't be hitting some place I've been to already."

"Can you even *remember* all the places you've hit over the years?"

Cordy threw her head back and laughed. "I remember most of them."

Henry came over to the corral where Cordy and Luther were leaning on the fence watching a mare. Cordy noticed the quality of the livestock they had at Eagle Canyon and knew where a large portion of the Trask's money went. Listening to Luther explain why he liked raising sheep more than goats had made it easy for Cordy's mind to wander. She was still thinking about Leo, but was able to find it amusing to hear him describe his preference for eating lamb chops as opposed to goat ribs.

"Cordy, do you have a few minutes for us?" Henry asked. He leaned against the fence and put his elbows on the top rail.

"I do," she said. Cordy felt certain that it was a monumental step forward to be asked to attend Leo's meeting. Maybe now Leo would see her as someone who could do more than cut down a few trees and shoot the wings off a fly at a hundred paces.

"Luther, how many chicks hatched out?" Henry asked him.

"Ten," Luther said with a laugh. "They look like yellow fur balls with legs."

Cordy and Henry exchanged small-talk on the way to Leo's cabin. He wanted to know how she liked Eagle Canyon so far.

"It's quiet and peaceful," she said. "Are there other things you need help with here?" *Besides chopping down saplings*, she wanted to say.

"There's so much to do I'm not sure where to even begin."

"Did you find the lost calf this morning?"

"Yes! We were afraid coyotes had gotten it."

"I'd probably like working with the herd that way," Cordy said.

"I enjoy that, too. Leo's convinced the key to our future is in raising horses, though. She wants to do that full time and just keep the cattle around as a food source."

"There's always a market for a good horse, so she might be right."

Henry nodded. "Then there's the problem of getting our good horses to buyers who have the money. Leo wants to try getting a contract with the Army eventually."

They had reached Leo's cabin. Henry knocked before going inside. Cordy was nervous about being there, but she felt better when she saw Jake sitting at the table.

"Have a seat," Jake said with a grin.

Leo came out of another room carrying some papers. It was the first time since arriving that Cordy had seen her looking so relaxed. Leo didn't have her hat on, and her hair was loose. The top two buttons of her black shirt were undone, exposing her neck. Cordy felt paralyzed for a moment. She could see Leo's throat, and imagined what it would be like to kiss her there. She looked away before someone caught her staring, but in her head Cordy knew exactly what she wanted to do.

Chapter Eighteen

"These are the last maps you got from Frederick," Leo said as she unfolded one of the papers and laid it out on the table. She sat down next to Jake and put the other maps to the side. "The 'X's' on here mark banks we've been to before. I think we need to go either north or east." Leo looked up to find Cordy gazing at her. "Have you been around any of these places recently?" she asked.

"No," Cordy said. "I've been working more southeast of San Antonio." She pointed at the map and indicated the area near Victoria, Texas.

"So you're not familiar with this area at all?" Leo asked, pointing at a specific place on the map. She had hoped Cordy could give them some insight into the layout of a few towns closer to them.

"No. Sorry. The furthest west I've been is Dos Diablos."

Leo leaned back in her chair. She looked across the table at Henry. "Then let's start talking. What are you thinking, Henry?"

He reached for the map and looked at it closely. "We do too

much business and trading along the border, so that's not the way to go. I'm looking at something west of San Antonio maybe."

Leo agreed with that in principle, but it also meant they'd be away from home an extended period of time. She didn't like leaving Dell, the children and Luther alone for that long. "Uncle Jake?" Leo said. "What do you think?"

"The Hondo area maybe." Jake looked at Cordy. "Did you ever go there?"

Leo saw a flicker of sadness in Cordy's eyes and wondered if she was thinking about her father. It made her seem younger and vulnerable for a moment.

"No," Cordy said. "I've never been to Hondo."

Jake reached for the map and pulled it closer. He pointed to a town west of San Antonio.

"Cattle country," he said. "Ranchers. Nice bank and hills close by to hide in. Thought about robbing the bank there once, but I never got around to it."

"That's quite a ride from here," Henry said.

"Isn't that the point?" Cordy asked. "Have you done anything across the border yet?"

Uncle Jake thumped the map and rested his arm on the table. "We'd stick out pretty good in Mexico."

"That can be fixed," Cordy said, "but once you've robbed a bank over there, you'd have to do all your buying across the border. At least until the money ran out."

"None of us speak Spanish," Leo said. The whole Mexico idea made her uncomfortable. "You can't spend Mexican money if you can't speak Spanish."

"Maybe you wouldn't need to," Cordy said. "They understand guns over there."

Henry voiced his disapproval about robbing banks in Mexico. "And Hondo seems too far," he said.

"Cordy, when was the last time you hit Dos Diablos?" Jake asked.

"Last year about this time."

"They're bound to have more money by now," Henry said.

Robbing banks still didn't sit well with Leo. She was uncomfortable with putting her family in danger and was determined to find a legitimate way to support them. But for now there were too many things that needed tending to. There was at least one more bank robbery in their future.

Leo folded the maps and looked up at Uncle Jake when he touched her shoulder. She knew he loved these planning meetings almost as much as he loved robbing banks, but Leo wanted to make sure he was strong enough to be going with them these days. He wasn't as sharp as he used to be and his eyesight was getting worse. The last two times they'd hit a bank, Leo had insisted Jake stay back to cover her and Henry while they were in town. Leo decided to speak to Henry about it later.

Uncle Jake and Henry walked out talking about Dos Diablos and how easy it would be to also hit a smaller bank on the way back. Leo noticed that Cordy wasn't in a hurry to leave yet. Once they were alone, Cordy asked her when all this would happen.

"Within the next few days," Leo said. "We'd been waiting on Dell's baby to arrive."

"Who's going with you?"

"Me, Uncle Jake and Henry," Leo said. "Luther stays back with Dell and the kids." She was entertaining the idea of asking if Cordy wanted to join them. Leo knew Jake had been hinting about that most of the day, but she wasn't sure how good of an idea it was. They didn't know how Cordy conducted herself in that situation.

Cordy slowly got up from the table. Leo again was annoyed at the thrill she felt seeing her. It brought back all the old feelings Leo thought had gone away years ago.

"I'd like to go along," Cordy said.

Leo picked up the maps from the table. "I'll talk to Henry about it."

Cordy's smile was disarming, but Leo still wasn't sure it was a good idea to have her go with them.

Leo rode alongside the far wall of the canyon looking for anything out of the ordinary. Ever since she had seen an Indian on the ridge two summers ago, they made routine patrols of the entire area several times a day. It kept them familiar with their surroundings, and made everyone feel safer.

She waved at Henry and Luther, who were mending a fence in a pasture to the west. Leo rode over to see if they needed help. She could see Cordy and Jake in the distance at the other end of the fence, taking turns pounding a post in the ground from the back of a wagon.

"How's it looking over there?" Henry asked her.

"Nothing new," Leo said. She got down off her horse and held the post they were attempting to get into the ground. Out of habit, Leo continued to scan the ridge. The Indian sighting had scared her enough to never take security for granted.

"Get your things together," Leo said to Henry. "We're riding for Dos Diablos in the morning."

"Cordy going with us?" Henry asked.

"I don't know yet." Leo and Henry looked at each other. "Come and find me when you're finished here," she said to him.

Henry nodded. Leo got back on her horse and rode off, continuing to scour the landscape and ridge for anything unusual.

It had been a long day and Leo had spent most of it on her horse. She felt almost obsessive about checking the place over. If there had been absolutely any sign of trouble or danger, she would have canceled the trip to Dos Diablos. She was finally beginning to feel better about their decision.

Leo took Luther to her cabin and sat him down.

"Like before," she said. "Keep everyone together and in the same cabin at night."

"I will," Luther said, "and during the day, no one wanders off."

141

He was repeating her previous directions back to her. She smiled at him. "You have the most important job," she said. "Don't ever forget that."

"I know." Their eyes met and Luther held the look. "Everything will be fine when you get back, Leo," he said. He continued looking at her. "You just make sure everyone gets back here in one piece."

"I will."

Leo's cabin was a busy place on into the early evening. Once Henry got there, she was anxious to start preparing herself for the long ride the next day. Henry's calm demeanor was a nice balance for Leo's natural urge to worry too much. Henry poured himself the last of the coffee.

"Does she go with us, or stay here?" Leo asked him as he sat down at the table.

"You and I probably have the same concerns," he said. "There's a lot of things we don't know about her."

Leo nodded. Those had been her thoughts as well. "I personally would feel better having her stay here with Luther, Dell and the children."

"Her and Uncle Jake both."

That would be the ideal situation, Leo thought. She wouldn't worry as much about leaving Dell and the kids if Uncle Jake and Luther were both there at Eagle Canyon.

"If we have doubts about anyone," Leo said, "then they shouldn't be going with us."

"Do *you* want to be the one to tell Uncle Jake he can't go?" Henry asked. "I know I don't."

"I will if it comes to that." Leo drummed her fingers on the table. "Do you want him staying behind because your wife and children are here? Or because he's no longer doing what we need him to do when you're out there robbing a bank?"

Henry shrugged. "He can't see as well as he used to."

142

Leo smiled. She knew Henry was also thinking about the safety of his family instead of Uncle Jake's stamina, reflexes, and eyesight. Jake could out-ride both of them when it came to endurance and distance. He'd been doing it his whole life.

"Jake can see well enough to hold up a bank and shoot at a posse," Leo said, trying to convince herself as well as Henry. "He loves it and he's still good at it. I think he should go with us." She propped her elbow on the back of her chair. "Now what about Cordy?"

"She wants to go."

"I know she does," Leo said. "She's also got more experience at it than any of us, except Uncle Jake." She went over the logistics of the plan, which had Henry and Jake going into town and holding up the bank. Leo would be on the edge of town ready to shoot and provide cover for their escape. Cordy would be stationed a little farther up the road to help with whoever was still following them if Leo couldn't distract them all or at least slow them down.

"We could use her helping you outside of town," Henry said. "Or even outside the bank."

"She has to do what we tell her to or it won't work," Leo said.

"We have no reason to believe she wouldn't. I think we could use an extra gun."

Leo found Cordy at Luther's old cabin. The furnishings consisted of a table, two chairs, and two bunks against the far wall. The door was open and Leo went in to find Cordy standing in the center of the room with her hands on her hips.

"Change your mind about this place?" Leo asked.

"Might have to. Luther's horrified about me wanting to sleep in the barn."

"It's not much," Leo said, "but at least a cow won't be stepping on you in the middle of the night." She pulled out a chair and sat down at the table. "We're leaving in the morning and we'd like for you to go with us."

Cordy smiled and sat down across from her. Leo felt a tightening in her throat and a flutter of nervousness. *She's as beautiful as I remember,* Leo thought. *The rough edges and rugged pretenses are just the way she hides what she's really feeling.*

"I'd like that," Cordy said.

"You've been there before. Tell me about the bank in Dos Diablos," Leo said.

Cordy described what she remembered.

"Once we get there," Leo said, "I'll go in and make sure things are the same. I'll come back to camp and tell everyone what's there now. Jake and Henry will ride in and hold it up. You and I will be positioned on the edge of town. You'll be a little farther away, ready to discourage anyone who gets by me."

"So I won't be going in the bank with them?"

"No," Leo said. "Someone might recognize you."

"So you and I just lay low and shoot at riders following them," Cordy said incredulously. "You need their canteens filled before we go? Maybe I could clean and load their guns for them, too."

Leo didn't like what she was hearing. Cordy's resentment and anger didn't sit well with her either.

"I'm a bank robber and a thief, Leo. I'm good at what I do."

"I'm sure you are," Leo said dryly.

"I've never been caught, never been in jail, and I like doing these things. They might need me going in with them. I can take care of myself just fine."

"I'm sure you can," Leo said, "but here we take care of each other. That's what we do first. We work together. If you can't do that, then you have no place with us in Dos Diablos. It's your decision. Think about it and let me know in the morning."

Leo got up from the table and left before she let her anger get the best of her. Already Cordy was questioning their plans. Leo hoped she didn't regret agreeing to have Cordy come along with them.

⨯

Leo's saddlebag was packed and she had eaten the breakfast Luther brought over. She went to the barn where Uncle Jake was saddling his horse. They grunted a greeting before walking to the trough to water their horses.

One of the rituals the Trask family had before they left on a job was for Henry to spend a few minutes in front of his cabin saying good-bye to his family. Leo and Uncle Jake were usually in a huddle with Luther, giving him last-minute instructions on how to take care of the place. Cordy was on her horse and slowly rode over to where the three of them were. She didn't say anything, and Leo was glad. She was still peeved at how their discussion had ended the evening before.

After a few more minutes, Leo told them all to saddle up. Henry hugged his children and kissed his wife.

"Everybody got their canteens filled?" Cordy asked. "Guns loaded?"

Leo glanced over at her, but didn't say anything. She indeed hoped it hadn't been a mistake asking her to join them.

Chapter Nineteen

It was a long ride to Dos Diablos. The tension stayed with Leo the whole way. They camped by the river outside of town, with plans for Leo to visit the bank the next day. She was nervous and needed rest, but she wasn't as successful at falling asleep as everyone else seemed to be.

Earlier, Cordy had been helpful, but seemed to resent almost everything Leo said or did. There was enough to worry about just getting her brother back to his family safely. Leo didn't need the distraction of someone complaining about gathering firewood or finding a grassy spot for the horses.

Leo's dreams were filled with being chased by something big and fast. Whatever was after her, she managed to stay ahead of it in her dream, but she could feel herself beginning to tire. When she finally settled down a few hours before dawn, her dreams turned into something less agitating. She saw a woman riding a horse bareback with her long, dark hair flowing in the wind. Leo was comforted by the dream and felt surrounded by warmth and softness. When she woke up the next morning, she was more rested and mellow than she thought possible on such a day. The deeds awaiting her were no longer the stress-makers they had been the night before. Somehow Leo knew things would be fine. There was a feeling of success in the air.

She went down to the river and threw cold water on her face to help wake herself up. She saw Henry tending to the horses, and Uncle Jake was coming back from the trees with wood for the fire.

Leo didn't see Cordy anywhere, but all the horses were there. She couldn't worry about that now. Leo needed to focus on riding into town and coming back with an accurate report of what she found there.

She went back to the campsite and took the piece of hardtack Henry gave her. She chewed on it while pulling a soft gray shirt and a long skirt from her saddlebag. Leo wanted to soften her appearance for her trip into town. She didn't want the usual black garments or the pants she wore on a daily basis to draw any undue attention. Keeping a low profile and being observant were her goals this morning. Leo took her clothes and went to the woods to change.

Leo held her horse to a slow clip as she rode into town. She studied every building, business, and water trough along the way. Dos Diablos seemed as small and sleepy as Cordy had described it.

Leo noted where the sheriff's office was in relation to the bank. If Henry and Uncle Jake had to leave the bank shooting, then there might be a problem, but the ride to get out of town was a short one. Leo also liked the landscape along the main street just before getting into town. Just as Cordy had said, it would be easy for two people to seek cover and shoot at anyone following Henry and Jake once they were on the run.

As Leo got off her horse a few buildings away from the bank, she didn't like the way some of the men stopped what they were doing to look at her. She nodded politely and smiled when they nodded back. Usually men averted their eyes when she met a look straight on. She was sure there weren't many women who rode into town on horseback, but Leo felt as though she had compromised enough already by wearing a skirt. Arriving in a buckboard she would have to abandon later didn't make much sense.

Leo went into the General Store and took a slow, deep breath. The older a store was, the more she liked being in it. She loved the way this one looked and smelled—the worn wooden floor, the pickle barrel near the counter, the many spices mixed in with the smell of new leather goods. Leo bought some candy for the children, and watched as the man carefully wrapped it in paper for her.

"Thank you," she said as the merchant gave her the small package. Leo went outside and looked up and down the street. The layout of the town was simple. The main street went right through town and probably led off south into Mexico. Leo had a plan forming as she stood there soaking up everything she saw. The more confusion they could cause once Henry and Uncle Jake were out of the bank with the money, the better their chances were for success.

Leo went into the bank next. There was one door that opened inward. Three people were inside, all in line waiting. She also noticed that the door to the safe was open. There were only two people behind the counter—one middle-aged man in his fifties and another in his late twenties. Someone came in after her, and Leo nodded and left again. She walked back to her horse and took the wrapped candy and placed it carefully in her saddlebag. She got on her horse and rode out of town in the opposite direction she'd come in from. Leo wanted to see what was out there south of town.

By the time she got back to camp it was noon and beginning to get warm already. Uncle Jake and Henry got up from sitting on the ground in the shade and came over to meet her. Leo saw Cordy, but they didn't acknowledge each other.

"Well?" Jake said. He took the reins from her after she got off her horse.

"I need to change clothes, then we'll talk."

Leo got her trousers out of her saddlebag and went to the woods to change. When she got back, all three were waiting for her.

"The safe in the bank was open, but I want to go over a few things first," she said. Leo found a long stick and walked over to a patch of dirt. She knelt down and began drawing the layout of the road, town, and main street. "Now's the time to ask your questions." She looked over at Cordy and said, "Speak up if I'm not making any sense."

Leo finished her primitive drawing in the dirt and pointed the stick at the road leading into town. "Here we have trees on both sides. I'll be here on the left." She looked over at Henry and dragged the stick up the road she had drawn. "You two ride in and stop in front of the bank." She showed them exactly where it was on her diagram. "It should be an in-and-out kind of thing. I saw two men working inside. Like I said, the safe was open already."

Everyone was so quiet it made Leo even that much more confident about what they were about to do. She had their attention and everyone was taking this seriously.

Leo looked at Cordy. "How much money did you get when you robbed it last time?"

Cordy shrugged. "A lot." She reached for the stick. Leo gave it to her. She drew a smaller picture of just the bank.

"Is this right?" she asked Leo.

"Yes."

Cordy pointed to the counter in her small drawing. "One of you should cover the customers, the tellers and the front door. The second person can go behind the counter and collect the money."

Leo nodded.

"And make sure one of you goes into the safe," Cordy said. "Don't send a teller. They usually have a gun in there. They may even have one behind the counter. Everybody's hands stay up in the air."

Leo looked at Henry and Uncle Jake. "Decide now who is doing what. I don't want anyone confused."

"I'll watch the customers, the tellers and the door," Henry said. "Uncle Jake can get the money. That all right with you, Uncle Jake?"

"I'm fine with it!"

Leo moved the point of the stick to the place that indicated the entry into town.

"What if we have Cordy here," Leo said, "and me here?" she said, indicating the north end of the road into town. "I'll pick off anyone following you two in case someone gets past Cordy. That's another thing," she said, looking at Cordy. "Aim for arms or legs. I don't want to kill anyone. I just want their money."

"I have a question," Jake said. "What if several people are after us and you don't wing them all?"

"I'll get on my horse and follow 'em," Cordy said. "I'll eventually get some good shots off." She looked at Leo and said, "so make sure you don't shoot me."

Nervous chuckles went around the circle.

"When we all get away," Leo said, "we'll ride north to Spit Canyon. Everybody know how to get there?"

Each of them nodded.

Leo took the stick and made several lines going north in the dirt. "Split up when you leave Dos Diablos. Lay low in the hills for a day, then meet up at Spit Canyon. Once we're all together again, then we go home."

Leo was nervous, but ready. If there was a lot of money, then Henry and Uncle Jake would both carry it out of the bank. That way if something happened to one of them, there would still be money to take home.

Everyone mounted up. Leo looked over at Henry and Uncle Jake and said, "I'll see you all at Spit Canyon tomorrow."

She rode off with Cordy. They were at the edge of town within ten minutes. Cordy peeled off to the left so she could hide and get settled. Leo stayed farther away from town up the road. She found some rocks near several trees and tied her horse up. She got her rifle out and tried several angles until she found the one that gave her the best shot and maximum protection from being seen. Now all she had to do was wait.

Once Henry and Uncle Jake rode past her on their way into town, Leo's nervousness continued to grow as time slipped by. It had been almost thirty minutes since she had set up. Her rifle was heavy, but she was still focused, ready, and anxious to know what was taking them so long. Just as she was starting to think about riding back into town to see what the problem was, Leo heard the sound of horses and saw Henry and Jake riding out of town. She didn't hear any gunshots. All she heard were galloping horses. Leo didn't flinch or move her rifle from its steady perch on the rock. She waited several more minutes and then heard gunfire coming from the other end of town. That had to be Cordy shooting at riders. Whoever was in charge of getting the bank's money back had finally set out after Henry and Jake. Leo had only heard three shots.

Leo slid her rifle in the scabbard on her saddle and got on her horse. The shooting up the road toward town had stopped several minutes earlier. She rode through the trees and stopped her horse at the very edge of a clearing. There were two men sitting on the ground, holding their bloody shoulders and grimacing. Their horses were close by munching on grass already. Leo swallowed the nausea she felt in her throat once she saw that the wounded men were strangers and not someone she knew. It looked as though everyone had gotten away safely; she saw no sign of Cordy.

Leo urged her horse through the brush and followed the road a ways. Up ahead she saw another man on the ground trying to stand up. There was blood on his arm and he seemed to be disoriented. His horse was close by and Leo could see the shiny badge on his chest.

She stayed in the brush and worked her way back to the road farther up ahead. *Everyone got away,* she thought with a huge sense of relief. Leo rode hard toward Spit Canyon. The hard part was over.

Chapter Twenty

Cordy felt the toe of a boot nudge her. She was reaching for her gun even as her eyes flew open. She relaxed when she realized it was Jake waking her up. It was her turn to stand watch. When she was on the run like this, it always surprised her how much sleep she could do without. An hour snatched here and there was all she needed. The rest of the time she enjoyed being able to sleep soundly almost anywhere for amazingly long periods of time.

She added a little more wood to the fire, keeping her eyes averted from the flames and having no desire to ruin her night vision before her watch. The first ten minutes of a watch were usually the most dangerous. Senses could still be numb and her head groggy from sleep, but the crisp night air worked fast to clear her head.

Cordy glanced over at Jake, who was already fast asleep and beginning to snore. He used his saddle as a pillow. The gray stubble on his chin seemed to always be there lately.

Cordy stood and checked her gun out of habit. As she returned it to the holster, her eyes fell on Leo, who was asleep and wrapped up in a thin blanket, looking so vulnerable and peaceful. Her long dark hair was in her face and covered her eyes. Cordy recognized the uncertainty that began to stir within her whenever she saw Leo, but she knew better than to dwell on it for any length of time.

She went to check the horses, and then crawled up on the huge rock overlooking the gulch at Spit Canyon. The moonlight uncovered the trail that followed the stream below. They were safe now, since finding them at night would be almost impossible in these hills, but Indians could be close by. Leo had insisted on keeping a watch posted so everyone could eventually get some sleep. They were also waiting for Henry to arrive. Henry had gotten separated from them during the ride out of town after the robbery. The Indian factor was what had them more worried now than anything else, since a posse had never followed them from Dos Diablos. The three riders Cordy had winged outside of town had been the first ones to chase them. The bandits would all be back at Eagle Canyon before Texas Rangers could even reach Dos Diablos.

As Cordy scanned the gulch and the tree line below, she finally allowed herself to think about Leo. Their last personal contact had been just as confusing as their first one had been six years earlier. Cordy was certain that Leo was uncomfortably aware of the attraction between them, but she was also sure Leo would never do anything about it. Leo's anger was one of those unpredictable things that Cordy never knew how to deal with. She also didn't like being the person Leo took things out on when something wasn't going right. Cordy remembered the last conversation they'd had.

"This is your final run with us," Leo had told her earlier that day as they watered their horses by a stream. "You need to stay at Eagle Canyon from now on."

"Eagle Canyon?" Cordy bellowed. Her own anger had risen so quickly that it surprised them both. "Why?"

"I have my reasons."

"I'm as good as any of you when it comes to this!" Cordy yelled, waving her hand to include Jake, who was upstream a ways also watering his horse.

"I know you are," Leo said quietly.

Her calm and patience can be so infuriating sometimes, Cordy thought.

Leo climbed up into the saddle in one swift, smooth motion and said, "But I'm not as good when you're with us."

That had been a few hours after the robbery, and there had hardly been two words uttered between them since. Cordy couldn't imagine having to sit idly and listen to them plan a robbery or prepare their strategy for a holdup. She had to be a part of it. She *wanted* to be a part of it. *What does this woman want from me?* Cordy wondered. *What does she expect me to do? Cook? Clean? Be a house-mouse?* Cordy vowed to turn herself in and surrender before letting something like that happen. She was also wondering what Leo had meant when she had said, "I'm not as good when you're with us." *That makes no sense*, Cordy thought. *What kind of thing was that to say? How can she hold me responsible for what she does or the decisions she makes?*

Everything seemed so confusing. *You're a bandit*, Cordy reminded herself. *A bandit and a thief. A good bandit! You deserve to ride with these people. Leo can only take this away from you if you let her. This is the only life you've ever known or wanted.*

Suddenly she saw movement down below on the other side of the stream. Someone was leading a horse, and from her perch on the rock Cordy could see a silhouette clearly in the moonlight. With a hat dangling down his back, it gave her a momentary flicker of hope. She had seen Henry wear his hat that way before.

She lightly jumped down from the rock and went to wake the others. They were alert immediately and scrambled up and had their guns drawn even before Cordy could say anything. Leo scattered the wood from the campfire and smothered the small flames with her boot; coals continued glowing in the moonlight.

"There's a rider," Cordy reported.

"Jake," Leo said, "circle behind him. I'll go the other way. Make sure there's only one." She kicked dirt and rocks at a flame that had leapt up again.

"I'll go with Jake," Cordy said, and started after him.

"You'll stay here," came Leo's low, sharp voice from the darkness. Uncle Jake had already disappeared into the brush. Cordy stopped in mid-stride and turned toward her.

"Why are you talking to me this way?" Cordy asked. She was stunned. "You're ordering me—"

Leo grabbed her by the arm and yanked her closer. "Stay here," she whispered viciously.

Before Cordy could pull her arm away and protest any further, Leo had disappeared into the darkness. Cordy kicked at the ground, kicked a nearby bush in her way, a tree trunk, rocks, and a small pile of sticks that had been gathered for the fire. Finally she slumped against a boulder, furious and humiliated. Right then she made a decision without having to put very much thought into it. In the morning she would climb on her horse and ride back to San Benito. At least there she would get the respect she deserved.

Cordy was up early, long before anyone else. The reunion with Henry last night had become a celebration stretching on into the wee hours of the morning. Cordy's anger simmered down to something short of stubborn determination, but she still wouldn't stay where she was neither wanted nor needed any longer. Mexico had mountains she could hide in, and rich fat businessmen and banks she could rob. Even though living with the Trasks had given her security and a sense of family she never thought she would find again after losing her father, things were different now. Leo was treating her like a child, like something needing to be watched over and taken care of.

It was time to move on.

❧❧

Before they had even gotten to Spit Canyon, Cordy had noticed another change in Leo when they first encountered a small band of Indians on the way. A posse had never materialized, but the Indians were something no one had anticipated. A few miles south of Spit Canyon, someone started shooting at them. Leo gave orders to scatter among the rocks and return their gunfire.

"Who are they?" Leo yelled over her shoulder. "Can anyone see anything?"

"Indians," Jake yelled from a cluster of rocks to Cordy's left. "Up there on the ridge."

"Is everyone all right?" Leo yelled. "Was anyone hit?"

Jake answered her in between gunshots. He was fine and continued shooting. There was just the three of them under fire at the moment.

"Cordy!" Leo yelled.

There was a break in the return fire as everyone began reloading their weapons.

With an edge of hysteria in her voice, Leo yelled, "Jake! Have you seen Cordy?"

"I'm here," Cordy said. She fired off six shots and then reloaded. "Why did you make us stop?" Cordy shouted as ricochets zinged around her. "It's not smart to stop! We should've kept riding until we lost them!"

Leo didn't answer her, but things hadn't been the same for any of them since then. That had been yesterday. They finally got away from the Indians and made their way safely to Spit Canyon.

Cordy tossed the blanket on her horse and rubbed him gently between the ears. She put the saddle on him and pulled the cinch tight around his belly.

"What are you doing?" came a voice behind her. It was the voice that could make Cordy either happy or furious within seconds of hearing it . . . the voice Cordy would always remember no matter where she went or how long it took her to get there. She pulled the cinch on the saddle even tighter. "Where are you going?" she heard Leo ask more firmly.

Again Cordy didn't say anything, but continued saddling her horse. Leo pulled her by the arm and turned her around, "Answer me," she said.

Leo's eyes were searching and angry. She had eyes the color of coal, as dark as her long thick hair. Cordy yanked her arm away and turned her attention back to the horse.

"I'm leaving," she said, and gathered the reins in her hands.

"Leaving for where?"

"Does it matter?" Cordy asked. "I'm no use to you unless there's a fire to be built or canteens to fill." She led her horse away from the others. "I'm a bandit, Leo. That's what I do best."

She could see anger still steady and clear on Leo's face as they glared at each other. "That's who I am," Cordy said simply. "That's all I'll ever be." She looked up, and their eyes met for what seemed like the first time. In that one intense moment, things became much clearer to her. Cordy let go of the reins and moved toward her. Before she had time to think about what she was doing, Cordy kissed her.

It became a deep, passionate kiss, with Leo's hands in Cordy's hair. Her mouth was hungry, persistent, and possessive. Leo's body melted against her easily, naturally. Cordy felt certain that she had somehow, once again, arrived at home.

Leo pulled away from her and looked into her eyes. Leo's hands were still in her hair, and she moved them down to gently touch Cordy's face. "This is why you have to stay," Leo whispered.

Cordy looked away and shook her head. "No," she said with a tremor in her voice. "This is why I have to go."

She stepped back, feeling more alive and confused than she ever remembered feeling before. If her very presence was the thing making Leo so agitated and restless, then Cordy had no choice but to leave. Now that Henry was there, everyone was together again. The Trasks would be riding out for home soon. Cordy knew it was time for her to move on to something else.

She got on her horse and took a deep breath, knowing her decision was the right one. As she picked her way down through the canyon to the stream below, Cordy was grateful Leo hadn't asked her again to stay. Cordy wasn't sure she would have been able to say no.

She rode into San Benito several days later. Cordy still had a saddlebag full of money, even though she hadn't taken her cut from the Dos Diablos robbery. She had found no reason to celebrate lately either. Cordy was tired and wanted to sleep next to someone who cared about her.

She tied up her horse behind María's shack and took her saddlebag down. Francisco's horse wasn't there, so she assumed María was alone. She went around the side of the shack and María opened the door before Cordy could even knock on it.

"I knew you would come today!" María said with a light laugh.

Cordy always loved the reception she got from her.

"Come here to me," María said, and led her to the table. She took the saddlebag from her shoulder and undid the pistol belt around Cordy's waist. "You're tired," María said.

"Are we safe?" Cordy asked.

María smiled. "Yes, we're safe. My husband has not been back since you were last here."

Cordy smiled. *Maybe the coward is gone forever,* she thought.

Part Three

Three Weeks Later

Chapter Twenty-One

Leo had barely spoken to anyone since their return from Spit Canyon. She felt confused and angry and just wanted to be left alone. She had no appetite, and when she tried to sleep, her thoughts were clouded with the memory of Cordy's soft lips, as if their very texture was scorched into her brain. There was nothing Leo could do to escape the loneliness she felt.

Almost everyone at Eagle Canyon stayed clear of her, and Leo didn't care what they thought. She couldn't function and wasn't fit for company. Luther was the only one brave enough to stop by and check on her every day. Leo's foul mood did little to discourage him. As her old house-mouse partner, he was used to seeing her in all sorts of bad moods.

A successful run usually brought high spirits to Eagle Canyon. Everyone else certainly seemed glad to be home. The money had been counted and divided their first night back, with Cordy's share having been equally split between the others. Leo, however, eventually noticed that she wasn't the only one in a somber mood. She attributed that to Cordy's decision not to return with them. Luther and Dell's questions about Cordy's absence only made things worse for Leo. She didn't have any answers for them.

With Leo not sleeping well at night, she was up early every morning and spent more time than usual with the horses. It was the only thing that seemed to soothe her. A few mornings after their return, Leo was in the barn feeding grain to the horses. She started brushing them one at a time, the muscles in her arms evident through her long-sleeve black shirt. Every stroke she gave a horse's coat was done with precision and care. She didn't know what else to do to get into a more reasonable frame of mind. One kiss had turned her into a person she no longer knew.

Uncle Jake came into the barn and leaned against a support beam. He pushed his hat back on top of his graying head and squinted at her.

"I'm going to visit Essie and take her some money," he said.

Leo nodded. "Be careful. Watch out for Indians." She continued brushing the horse and could feel some of the tension easing from her shoulders.

"If you want Cordy back, you'll have to go get her," he said after a moment.

Leo cut her eyes over at him and then looked away again.

"She won't come back on her own."

"She's made her decision," Leo said. She tossed the brush in a corner and dusted off her shirt.

Jake rubbed his whiskered chin and said, "San Benito. Try looking for her there." He turned and walked over to the saddles lined up on a rail. Leo watched him saddle his horse and leave.

San Benito, she thought. The words continued to bounce around in her head all morning. With each passing day, she hoped the pain and longing would begin to fade, but so far it hadn't happened. Something was drawing her to this San Benito place now, and she was ready to at least try and do something about it.

161

What will you say if you do find her? she wondered. *What can you tell her that she'll understand? What can you do that'll make her want to come back?*

She continued to think and worry. Every night while Leo tried to fall asleep, she kept reliving that kiss. Those thoughts were the only things that made her feel human again. As the days dragged on, even being with the horses wasn't helping her any longer. At night while laying in her bed, in the cool darkness of her cabin, Leo made plans to leave Eagle Canyon and set her search for Cordy in motion. She would never have peace in her life again if she didn't at least try and find her. Leo reasoned that she owed it to herself.

I'll leave in the morning, she thought as she turned over and tried to get comfortable under a blanket. *I can't keep going on this way.*

She didn't discuss her plans with anyone, but did tell Henry that she'd be gone for a while. He didn't ask any questions, but told her to be careful.

Putting some hardtack and jerky in her saddlebag, along with another change of clothes, Leo saddled her horse the next morning and left Eagle Canyon. It was the first time she had ever done such a thing—leaving her family this way and going somewhere out on her own, but it was something she had wanted to do ever since she was a child. *Just get on a horse and go*, she thought. *I need to see what it's like.*

The hard ground was appreciated only because it wasn't the back of a horse. Leo slowly stretched out and leaned against her saddle. Even as she glanced up at the stars, her eyes were closing. She couldn't remember ever being so tired.

She had spent three days riding along dusty roads and well-traveled trails on her way to San Benito. Leo would be there tomorrow, and still didn't know what she would say—*if* she saw Cordy again. Even worse, she might have to deal with the possibility she would never see her again. Leo understood if Cordy didn't want to be found, no one would be able to find her. She was hoping Uncle Jake's hunch was right.

Nervous and determined, Leo rode into San Benito the next day. If the small town had any facilities available, she promised her horse some grain once they arrived. She scanned the almost empty street for anything unusual or even friendly. There was no livery stable, so special treats for her horse were out of the question.

Leo was disappointed by what she found there—a cantina close to a small chapel at one end of town, and several empty buildings and a few shacks at the other. There was a well across from the cantina and a few people mingling about. Leo got down off her horse and stretched the weariness from her body.

She saw two women drawing water from the well and Leo headed that way, leading her horse. Asking questions was her only option now since there was no sign of Cordy or her horse, and no real place for someone to seek lodging. The cantina was closed and there was very little movement on the only street in town. Leo wondered what in particular made San Benito such a popular place for people like Cordy and Jake. It seemed no different than dozens of other border towns.

Leo approached the well and let her horse drink from the trough nearby. The two women there were speaking Spanish, and it occurred to Leo that she might not even be able to ask questions if no one understood what she was saying. Her disappointment at not seeing any sign of Cordy was growing by the minute. *Where do I look next?* she wondered.

Leo put her hand on her horse's withers and gave him a pat. One of the women was older and had a throaty laugh. Taking her water bucket, she walked toward the cantina. The other woman was much younger. Leo glanced around the street, looking for anything that would help with her search, but San Benito had next to no activity anywhere else besides the well.

"You won't find her," Leo heard someone say.

Leo turned around and saw only the young woman there near the well. "Pardon me?"

"You won't find her," the woman said again.

"I won't find who?"

"You're looking for a woman."

"How do you know that?"

Her faint smile caught Leo off guard.

"I know things," she said quietly with a shrug. "She was here, but she's gone now."

Leo didn't question that they were talking about the same person.

"Where did she go?"

The young woman picked up her water bucket. "Cordelia never tells me where she goes from here." She looked up shyly and met Leo's incredulous stare. "Come with me. I've been waiting for you."

Leo followed her to the last building at the end of town. She felt a thread of excitement at finding someone who knew Cordy. Leo watched as the woman carried the pail of water, swinging it gently at her side as her long skirt stirred up the dust in the street. The woman stopped in front of an old building and opened the door. She set the water inside, then turned and said, "Tie your horse in the back. I'll show you where."

Leo followed her around the side of the small building. The woman tied Leo's horse to a tree next to another horse that was tied there already. It wasn't Cordy's.

Once inside the building, the woman closed the door. Leo saw a bed, a table, two chairs, a wooden crate standing on end, and an area in the corner where meals were more than likely prepared. She saw nothing there that belonged to Cordy.

"She left yesterday," the woman said, as if reading Leo's mind. "I told her you were coming."

"You told her I was coming? How did you know I would be here?"

The woman gave another slight shrug. "I just know things," she said quietly.

"Do you know where Cordy was headed?" Leo took her hat off; her long dark hair tumbled to her shoulders.

"She has several women from all over who keep her company."

Leo heard no gloating in her voice. It was a simple statement, but one that made Leo uneasy just the same.

"So she could be anywhere," Leo said, resigning herself to the fact that Cordy probably didn't want to be found. Leo had no choice but to return to Eagle Canyon and hope Cordy would eventually come back there. She put her hat on and noticed for the first time that the woman had a rag tied around her left wrist.

"What happened to your arm?" Leo asked.

"It's nothing," the young woman said. "A burn."

"Let me see." Leo could tell that it needed a new dressing. "Let me see," she said again, her voice having a touch of tenderness in it that even she didn't recognize. Leo felt drawn to this woman, as if her connection to Cordy was something important they shared.

"What's your name?" Leo asked her.

"María."

"How did you burn yourself, María?"

Leo took her hat off again and set it on the table. She reached for María's arm. María turned around reluctantly and tossed her long dark hair away from her face. She was a beautiful woman and much younger than Leo first thought.

"A careless accident."

Leo kept her voice even and her hands steady as she slowly removed the dressing from the burn. "How well do you know Cordy?"

"She's here often."

Leo took the corner of the rag and tore away the soiled part. The rest of the bandage was smaller, but still white and usable. Leo finished cleaning around the burn and wrapped it back up.

"You're the one I've been waiting for," María said in a low voice.

"The one what?"

"It doesn't matter."

Leo picked up her hat and put it on again. "If you see Cordy, tell her I was here looking for her."

"We will see her again," María said with a nod. She picked up an empty flour sack and began putting a few things in it. "I'm going with you."

"Going with me? No, I don't think so."

"Yes, I am," María said. "You need me."

Leo's objections to having María ride with her weren't making much of an impression on the woman. María wasn't saying anything, even though she continued to follow Leo on the horse that had been tied behind her building.

Leo was surprised at how well María could ride without a saddle. She thought about a dream she had not long ago. *A woman riding bareback . . .*

Leo's first impressions of María proved to be wrong. Leo wasn't exactly afraid of her, but was cautious about letting her get too close. Occasionally Leo would stop her horse and turn around to see where María was. Inevitably, she would be about 25 yards behind her, with a steady grip on her horse's mane while resting her small sack of possessions against her body. Leo didn't see any harm in letting her ride along for a day or two, but she didn't want anyone to know how to get to Eagle Canyon. Leo decided that María would have to find another place to go once they got closer there.

They stopped for the night in the area around Dos Diablos, near the place Leo had camped with Uncle Jake, Henry and Cordy before their last bank robbery. María gathered wood and made a fire on her own, and had a "something" skewered and roasting when Leo came back from watering their horses. Still, María didn't say anything and mostly kept to herself.

Leo took her time and cooled off by the river once she had taken care of the horses. They were contentedly munching grass where Leo had hobbled them. She slipped the bandanna from around her neck and dunked it in the cold water to wash her face. Eagle Canyon was still over a day's ride, and Leo was looking forward to having a real bath again as soon as she got home.

She stood up and watched the brilliant lavender sky slowly darken. She missed her family and was looking forward to going home. Turning back toward the camp, Leo saw María putting sticks on the fire. Leo took the wet bandanna from around her neck and dunked it in the water again. She walked back to camp and handed the bandanna to her. María looked up at her with relief and gratitude in her eyes.

Chapter Twenty-Two

Leo sat down across from María and leaned against her saddle. It wasn't quite dark yet, but it was cooling off and the warmth of the small fire between them felt good. Camping out never failed to remind Leo about leaving the farm and being with her family out in the open, under the stars. Being alone these last few days had been strange for Leo, and it was nice now to have some company. As she looked across the campfire at María, she felt an unusual mixture of relief and contentment at having her there. Leo liked the way María had taken charge of the campsite right away. It left her free to be alone and take care of the horses as well as collect more firewood. While Leo did her little chores, she was able to get comfortable with her surroundings and examine her feelings about what had happened with Cordy. When Leo initially started out on this journey, her sole purpose was to find Cordy and convince her to return to Eagle Canyon. Now Leo realized she wouldn't have been able to convince Cordy to do anything. Cordy had her own plans, her own way of doing things. Cordy wasn't capable of being in one place long enough to meet the needs of anyone else.

She stretched out her legs and got comfortable. If she didn't run into any problems tomorrow, Leo thought she could make it home by dark. Glancing around the landscape now, she scanned the tree line several yards to her left just to make sure everything was as it should be.

"We'll be safe here tonight," María said quietly.

Even though her voice was low, Leo hadn't expected to hear her say anything. They hadn't spoken since leaving San Benito.

"How do you know that?"

"I just know," came María's reply.

Once again Leo thought about how glad she was not to be alone. She had lawmen, drifters and Indians to worry about. Having another set of ears and eyes to help keep alert and focused just made her feel better.

Silence fell between them again as María took the mysterious "whatever" that was roasting on a spit and pulled off a meaty leg. She handed the stick with the rest of the meat to Leo. The savory smell made Leo's stomach grumble.

They ate in silence and passed the skewered dinner-on-a-stick back and forth until it was gone. As Leo continued to nibble at a bone and cartilage, she watched María across the small fire. Leo still had no idea why she had agreed to let María come with her, but María hadn't really given her a choice. She had gotten on her horse and followed, totally disregarding whatever Leo had to say.

So how long will she follow me? she wondered. *I might have to sneak off in the middle of the night soon in order to get back to Eagle Canyon by myself.* Leo couldn't let someone follow her home. Jake had taken a chance with Cordy by bringing her there. They too could have been followed. The Trask family liked keeping the activity outside the entrance to Eagle Canyon to a minimum.

Leo pulled another bandanna from her saddlebag next to her and wiped her hands on it. She missed Luther's cooking, even though she had no complaints about whatever María had prepared. It had actually been the tastiest "trail food" she had ever eaten.

As it began to get darker, Leo could feel herself winding down for the night. She wasn't giving herself much of a chance to dwell on not being able to find Cordy. It had been unlikely they would meet up again so soon anyway. Leo had known the success of her search would be based on nearly impossible odds. At the time she left Eagle Canyon, it felt necessary for her to be doing something and going somewhere. Leo felt as though making an attempt to locate Cordy and bring her back was enough to satisfy whatever restlessness there was inside. Memories of the kiss they'd shared would never leave her, but Leo was better prepared to deal with it now. Reminding herself over and over again Cordy would never be able to settle down was the determining factor in her decision to move on emotionally. Leo refused to spend the rest of her life thinking and dreaming about something that could never happen or make her happy.

She wondered briefly what type of relationship María had with Cordy. Leo knew since Cordy seldom spent any length of time in one place, it would be hard for her to have roots anywhere. She didn't understand how Cordy could travel so much and never care about settling down. From a distance it seemed like a fun, carefree existence, but Leo had only been away from home less than a week and she was more than ready to go back and resume her ordinary life. Leo also knew she was lucky to have a family that cared about her, as well as a home to go back to.

Leo heard a noise that sounded like something tearing. Looking over at María, Leo watched as she took the bandage off the burn on her wrist and then attempted to wrap it again. With one hand María held one end of the bandage and then tugged on the other end with her teeth and lips.

"Let me help with that," she said as she got up and moved around the fire. She knelt down beside her and carefully reached for María's wrist.

The burn was healing nicely. Leo didn't think it would leave a scar. She folded the clean piece of cloth and wrapped it loosely around the burn.

"Thank you," María said when Leo had finally secured the dressing. She held María's hand and turned it over to inspect it. The white bandage was such a nice contrast against María's brown skin.

"How did you learn to ride a horse that way?" Leo asked. "Without a saddle."

"My husband."

Leo was shocked. She mentally reevaluated the relationship María and Cordy had.

"I never see him anymore," María said, as if reading her mind again. "Cordelia threatened to shoot him if he ever came back."

Leo smiled. It sounded like something Cordy would do.

"Cordelia found a horse for me."

"Found it?" Leo said. She slowly let go of María's wrist. "That probably means she stole it from someone."

María's faint smile made Leo smile, too.

"She probably did," María admitted.

Leo reluctantly got up and moved to the other side of the fire. She watched María get comfortable against the flour sack she had brought with her.

"You said earlier that you knew I was coming," Leo said. She watched as María nodded slightly. "How did you know? What did you see? How did that happen for you?"

"It's something I sense more than something I see," María said quietly. "I can't explain it any other way. It was you I felt. There was something about you that made me sense your closeness."

"You told Cordy this?"

"Yes," María said. "She asked me questions just like you are doing now. She helped me find out who you were."

"How did the two of you figure out it was me?" Leo asked, fascinated by the explanation.

"I was able to describe you, even though I couldn't see a face or anything like that. I also felt your sadness and determination."

171

"You could describe me?" Leo asked. "Tell me what you saw."

"It was just a brief vision," María said, embarrassed to say more.

"Tell me about it."

"I could see a woman," María said. "She was on a horse and she was dressed in black. Cordelia told me it had to be you."

"Did you know when I would be in San Benito?"

"Those kinds of visions get stronger when the subject gets closer to me."

Leo was captivated by María's explanation. "So Cordy knew I was coming and that was why she left."

"Yes."

Leo's hurt resurfaced. As she sat there thinking about what María had said, the hurt slowly began to turn into anger. *Cordy knew you were coming and left before you got there*, Leo thought. *She didn't want to see you again. She's sorry about the kiss.*

"You can't blame her for wanting to leave," María said. "Cordelia has her own demons to deal with."

"I went there to find her . . . to get answers to questions I have."

"Those answers will come to you soon," María said, "and the answers have very little to do with Cordelia. She doesn't make it easy for us to love her."

Leo snatched up the extra bandanna and stuffed it into her saddlebag. *Love*, she thought. *Cordy doesn't give anyone a chance to do anything. She doesn't stay around long enough for anyone to love her!*

Leo woke up to the warmth of the fire. It was daylight already. María had been up long enough to gather more wood and have something else cooking over the low flames.

Leo stretched and searched for the horses that were happily munching on some grass. She got up and went off into the trees to take care of early-morning business. When she returned, she saw María by the river with the horses. Leo liked the way she helped take care of things without being asked to do so.

On her way to the river, Leo organized her thoughts. She and María had to have a little talk before they started out again.

"Good morning," Leo said. She reached over and patted her horse as he continued to drink.

"Good morning."

"Where will you go from here?" Leo asked her.

"Where?" María said. "I'm going with you."

"You can't go with me."

María stood up and straightened her dress. "You will need me today."

Leo's frustration was not helping. She realized now she should have left in the middle of the night like she had considered doing at one time. Reaching up and giving her horse a slow rub between the ears, Leo shook her head at the predicament she now found herself in.

"I can't take you with me," Leo said.

"You have to. Today you will not be entirely safe."

That made the tiny hairs on the back of Leo's neck stand up. Then she had another thought. "Are you telling me these things so I *will* take you with me?"

"There will come a time when you'll be glad I'm with you."

Leo's frustration was returning. "What's that mean?"

María began walking her horse back to the campsite. Over her shoulder she said, "It means I'm going with you and it means you'll need me and eventually be glad I'm there. I can't explain how I know these things. I just do."

Leo rolled her eyes and led her horse back to the campsite. *Maybe I can lose her at some point during the ride back to Eagle Canyon,* she thought.

After the first hour, Leo resigned herself to the fact she wasn't going to get rid of her very easily. She even found herself wondering what she would do if María followed her all the way home. *How will you explain who she is and how you met her? She's a friend of Cordy's,* Leo thought. *That's all they need to know.*

It also didn't sit well with her that María had mentioned they wouldn't be totally safe that day. The closer Leo got to Eagle Canyon, the more anxious she was to get home.

Several hours later, they stopped at a creek to water the horses again. "How's the burn on your wrist?"

"It's fine," María said. "The bandage you made is helping."

Leo had been thinking a lot while she rode. They had barely exchanged two words over the last hour or so, but Leo couldn't stop going over some of the things María had said. She let her horse nibble at the grass while she and María shared her canteen.

"I have a question for you," Leo said. "What did you mean when you said you had been waiting for me? You don't know me. How could you have been waiting for me?"

"I don't know what it means," María said. "It's just a feeling I have . . . a feeling that makes no sense to me either." She closed the canteen and gave it back to Leo. "There's someone or something I've always been looking for. In the beginning I wanted it to be Francisco. Then later I wanted it to be Cordelia. They were the two people in my life who made a difference, but I could tell right away that the connection with them was not what I was looking for."

"Make a difference how?"

"It has to come from the inside," María said as she made a fist and brought it up to her chest. "I can't explain it."

"So you think I can make a difference?"

María rubbed her horse between the ears. "You already have."

"How?" Leo asked. She desperately wanted to understand this woman.

"You don't question me about certain things," María said. "You believe without knowing why and you trust without fear."

Trust without fear, Leo thought. *That's not something I would ever think about me.*

Leo got on her horse and looked over at María. She couldn't stop thinking about what an extraordinary person she was. The things María seemed to just know . . . her quiet, unassuming nature . . . her determination and insight. Leo was fascinated.

"Do you really not have anywhere else to go?" Leo asked.

María got on her horse in one graceful motion, without dropping her sack full of belongings.

"I have everything I own with me right now," María said. "For me, it doesn't matter where I go. But for you, it's best that I follow you."

Chapter Twenty-Three

Leo grew increasingly uneasy each time they drew near another town. She knew she should be telling María they couldn't go any further together, but the words just never made their way out of her mouth. She could see the hills up ahead on the horizon, and soon they would be reaching the trail that led to Eagle Canyon. There would come a point where Leo would have no choice but to let María follow her, so she had to do something soon to discourage her.

Toward noon, they passed the road leading to the last town on their journey. Looking to her right, Leo could see the cluster of old buildings in the distance. There was only one more place to stop and water the horses before they reached Eagle Canyon. Leo's inability to turn this woman away was just as confusing as her willingness to accept some of the things María said. As if needing to move on into another level of the current situation Leo found herself in, she suddenly decided to focus on getting them both where they wanted to be. If María wasn't going away, then Leo had to decide what other choices she had.

A while later, María began riding closer to her. "Someone's up ahead," she said.

"Who is it?" Leo asked. She scanned the horizon and the trees in the immediate area along the roadside, but didn't see anything unusual or out of place. They both had stopped their horses now and were trying to listen.

"I don't know who they are yet," María said, "but I think there are three of them."

"What do they want?"

All of her senses were suddenly on full alert as Leo's eyes slowly moved from the trees to the beginning of the rocks up ahead. They were at the foot of the hills that led away from the river. Another two miles or so and they would have to leave the main road and start up the trail toward Eagle Canyon.

"They want our horses and our guns," María said finally.

"How do you know that?" After a moment, Leo shook her head and said, "Never mind. You just know." She rose up in her saddle in hopes of seeing better, but it didn't do any good. "How far away are they?"

"I can't be sure."

"If we make camp now, will they go away?"

"It's not safe to camp here."

Leo looked over at her to see if she was telling the truth or just plain crazy. María looked the same to her, which Leo found extremely irritating.

"So what do you suggest we do?" Leo asked. "Go back and wait until you feel better about this?"

María turned her head and met Leo's eyes. "You no longer trust without fear, Leona." She gave her horse a nudge in the ribs and set off into a slow trot. Leo followed her, but kept her eyes and ears open.

177

Leo let María ride ahead mostly because María seemed to be insisting on it. They stayed on the main road another twenty minutes before María finally slowed her horse up ahead. Leo felt her breathing quicken; she reached for her pistol just to remind herself where it was.

"What is it?" Leo asked when she finally reached her. It was eerily still and quiet; they were getting close to the Eagle Canyon trail.

"Three of them," María murmured. "Watching us. Not following us yet."

"Yet?" Leo said. She was suddenly afraid and didn't like being on the road exposed this way. She kept looking around as if something big and scary were about to run toward them from the trees.

"How good are you with the gun?" María whispered.

"Good enough."

"Then we walk the horses and draw them out," María said. "We'll look like easy prey, but instead have the advantage."

Leo wasn't sure she liked the idea of being off her horse, but María was already alongside hers. Leo slowly looked around and then got off her horse, too. She gave him a soothing pat and started walking beside him; María stayed several feet ahead of her. Leo noticed how María gradually slowed the pace, and then she heard the swoosh of an arrow fly in front of her. Leo then heard shooting. Her horse reared up as she drew her gun. She aimed and shot at something moving in the trees. Leo's hands were shaking as she spun around to see if there was anything visible on the other side of the road.

Leo calmed her horse and saw María's pistol for the first time. There were two dead Indians lying in the grass and another one at the edge of the trees. Leo had shot that one, and María had shot the other two.

"Are you all right?" María called.

"Yes," Leo said. She was shaking as she gripped her gun. She watched María walk over toward the two dead Indians. She made sure they were dead before going to check the third one. Leo was in shock as she stood holding the bridle of her horse.

She knew we were in danger, Leo thought. *What would have happened if she hadn't been here with me?* A chilling shiver raced through her body.

Leo took a deep breath to steady herself and then put her gun away. She made a clicking noise with her tongue to soothe her horse and get his attention. She gave him another pat and was grateful they were all safe. Leo looked around her horse for María and saw her by the third body near the trees. Leo had a new respect for her. *Trust without fear,* Leo thought. *From now on it'll be more like trust no matter what!*

María got back on her horse and joined Leo, who was still standing in the road.

"Where did you learn to shoot that way?" Leo asked her. The only Indian she had even seen was the one by the trees. María had killed the other two almost instantly as they ran toward them.

"Cordelia taught me," María said.

Leo offered a weak smile. If nothing else, at least they had that in common.

Leo got on her horse. She stared hard at the bodies of the two dead Indians. *How long had they been waiting there like that?* she wondered. *How would I have reacted had María not warned me beforehand?*

She looked over at María who was sitting on her horse, holding the flour sack that contained her meager possessions. Leo's heartbeat was finally beginning to return to normal again and her hands had stopped shaking.

"You'll be safe now," María said.

Their eyes met. Leo didn't think "thank you" quite described how she felt. She was grateful already, and Leo was at a loss for words when it came to expressing it. All of a sudden Leo wanted

María with her. She felt safe and couldn't imagine taking another step alone. Leo, however, did not know how to articulate any of that, so instead she just said, "Let's go."

After negotiating the rocky hillside for over an hour, Leo was excited to see the entranceway to Eagle Canyon. She got off her horse and opened the camouflaged gate made of brush and shrubs. María held the reins of Leo's horse and went through the gate first with both horses.

"Welcome to Eagle Canyon," Leo said as she got back on her horse after securing the gate. They both sat still for a moment and looked at the cabins in the distance.

"It's beautiful," María said. "This is a safe place. I can feel much love here."

It didn't take long before they were seen and riders began coming toward them. Henry and Luther were the first ones there. Leo and María got off their horses again as the men got closer. Leo let her little brother pick her up in a giant hug.

"We missed you!" Luther said after he set her down again.

"It's good to be home." Pointing toward María, Leo introduced her. "She's a friend of Cordy's and she's now a friend of mine. She saved my life today."

Henry shook María's hand, while Luther tipped his hat in her direction.

The four of them began walking toward the cabins. Dell came from the barn area with baby Milton in her arms. The other children were squealing with delight at seeing their Aunt Leo again. Leo couldn't believe how much she had missed everyone.

After all the excitement of their arrival, Leo was anxious to go home and reacquaint herself with her surroundings again. Henry and Dell invited everyone to supper later to celebrate Leo's return and welcome María to Eagle Canyon.

"You can have your own cabin," Luther said to María at one point. "It used to be mine, but I don't live there anymore."

The whole Trask clan followed them to Luther's old cabin. Once inside, María set her flour sack down and looked around.

"Cordelia has been here," María said.

Leo smiled at seeing a few puzzled expressions around the room. "Yes, she was," Leo confirmed. She looked at Luther and Henry and said, "María just knows things."

"What kinds of things?" Luther asked.

"We'll tell you all about it later," Leo said. "Right now I want a bath and some clean clothes."

Luther and Henry brought the tub to Leo's cabin from the barn. The three of them toted buckets of captured rainwater until the tub was full enough to soak in. Leo had another pot of water heating on her stove. She was looking forward to soaking the trail kinks out of her body.

"You mentioned María saved your life," Luther said as he poured another bucket of water in the tub. "What happened?"

She told him about the three Indians who had attacked them. "María shot the first two before I even knew what was happening."

After a moment, Luther said, "She's pretty *and* she can shoot?"

Leo glanced over at him. It had been a long time since a discussion about women had come up between them. The last person Leo remembered him mentioning in such a way had been Cordy when Luther was just a boy.

"Yes," Leo agreed. "María is pretty and I'm lucky she can shoot."

"I'm gonna show her around the place later."

Leo felt a tiny pang of jealousy that shocked her for a moment.

"Be careful, Luther. She's married. I'm not sure how long she'll be staying here."

The disappointment was evident in his face. The statement also forced Leo to think about what she had just said. *How long will María stay here?* she wondered.

"Where's her husband?" Luther asked.

"I don't know. I didn't ask her."

Maybe it's time Uncle Jake took him into town more often, Leo thought. *New chickens and a few ponies aren't enough any longer. Our little Luther is growing up.*

"Uncle Jake isn't back from Essie's yet?" Leo asked him.

"No," Luther said. He took the pot of hot water off the stove and poured it in the tub for her. "Things might not be too good with Essie now."

"I know," Leo said. "Jake could be staying there with her from now on. It's hard to say."

"He'll start robbin' banks on his own again," Luther said. "He's getting old, Leo. I worry about him sometimes."

"Yeah. Me, too."

Leo offered María the bathtub first, but María wanted to spruce up Luther's old cabin instead.

"A bath would be nice after that," María said. "Thank you."

Leo washed her hair and piled it up on top of her head as she soaked in the warm water. Rubbing the cake of soap over her skin felt sinfully good. Leo was surprised at how little she had been thinking about Cordy. The kiss they shared was a less powerful factor now. Something changed once she learned Cordy had known about her impending arrival in San Benito. The fact Cordy chose to leave before Leo got there had lessened all the feelings she had. Cordy was someone who would never take anything seriously. She would go through life looking out for herself. Nothing else was important to her.

Leo was also realizing there was more to life than just watching other people be happy. She had to find what was right for her and make it work somehow. She had helped her family locate a safe place and had them settled for the most part. Now it was time to concentrate on what was best for Leo.

She finished bathing and got out of the tub. She put on her gray shirt and a clean pair of trousers. Leo wanted to walk around the barn and animal pens with the children for a while before going over to Henry's for supper.

Chapter Twenty-Four

After Leo got dressed, she went over to Luther's old cabin and found María and Dell busy cleaning it up. Two young boys had the run of the place, but there was nothing they could get into. Little Milton was asleep on one of the bunks. With the floor swept and the cobwebs out of the corners, the cabin was comfortable-looking. Leo knelt down to give the children a hug.

"Don't forget. I've got a tub full of bath water at my place you can use for scrubbing and cleaning if you need it," Leo said.

Dell took the broom and swept the dust off the table. "Me and my brood would like that bath water before we do much more scrubbing on a cabin!"

"So would I," Maria said.

"Well, help yourself," Leo said. She picked up one of the children and held the other one by the hand. "I'll take them over to the barn to look for the chicks."

Leo liked the fact that María was already making friends. The cabin project would give her something to do over the next few days.

"I'll bring them back," Leo said to Dell, referring to the children. She looked at María, who was standing in the middle of the room with her head tilted to the side, as if listening for something. Her long dark hair was like a spray of curls around her head. María's face and its almost delicate features were quite deceptive, Leo decided. She was indeed beautiful, but there was so much more to her than first impressions allowed. Leo could feel the intensity radiating from María even now, and there was a connection Leo longed to explore.

With her hands on her hips where her dark gray dress hung loosely at her waist, María looked at her. Leo felt her own breathing quicken for just a moment. The nephew she held in one arm put his little blond head on her shoulder and made Leo smile.

"This house is waiting for someone special," María said.

Leo looked into María's eyes, anxious to know everything she was thinking.

"Maybe it's been waiting for you," Leo said.

María laughed, as if they shared a secret. "I'm not the one it's waiting for," she said, "but I can help prepare it for whatever is about to happen here."

Dell wiped her brow on the sleeve of her dress. "María, hon. We can get this place washed up in no time tomorrow, but right now there's a bath at Leo's place waiting for me."

By the fourth time Leo heard a comment about how much better she looked and sounded since being away, Leo found herself apologizing for her previously bad mood before leaving. Both brothers came to spend time with her and the children at the sheep pen where a lamb had been born the day before.

"I don't think I'd be so smiley if I'd had to shoot an Indian today," Henry commented.

"There's no way to explain how good it feels to be home again," Leo said.

"Luther told me about the trouble you met up with getting here," Henry said. He and Leo each had a little boy in their arms while Henry held his four-year old daughter by the hand.

"María said they wanted our horses and our guns."

"How would she know that?" Henry asked.

"I'm not sure how she knows these things, but she certainly seems to."

Leo looked at him and wanted Henry to understand what had happened with María without her having to actually say the words. In her head it seemed as though once words on this subject were spoken, it all tended to sound silly and make no sense. There were things that couldn't be explained away. They just happened . . . they just "were."

"Leo, what's the matter?" Henry asked. "You don't look like yourself."

"Who do I look like?" she asked him with a slight grin.

"I don't know. You look almost . . . " He paused as if searching for the right word. "You look almost happy." With a sheepish smile he added, "I guess I've never seen you that way before."

Leo stopped for a moment to contemplate what he had said. *I do feel happy*, she thought. Dismissing it as another offshoot from the "I'm just so glad to be home" factor, she was able to reason all her good feelings away for the most part.

"I've missed all of you and I'm glad to be home," Leo admitted.

"Tell me where you found María." Henry set a squirming little boy down and held his hand.

"San Benito," Leo said. "Uncle Jake told me to look there for Cordy."

"You never told us why Cordy left to begin with."

"Who knows why Cordy does anything?"

Leo felt her face grow warm. *That kiss*, she thought. *Cordy left because of the kiss.* As if it were happening to her all over again, Leo's mind went back to that place . . . went back to the memory of soft lips and the hint of a tongue touching hers. The heat and passion of Cordy's mouth was unforgettable. "This is why you have to stay," Leo remembered saying to her. And then as if Cordy had misunderstood what Leo wanted from her, Cordy's reply had done nothing but confuse the situation.

"This is why I have to go," Cordy had said.

Even though Leo seldom dwelled on what their last few minutes together had meant to her, she was lost in a myriad of new feelings that made no sense. She looked across the way at María and Dell standing on the porch of Luther's old cabin. *She probably knows I'm thinking about Cordy*, Leo reasoned. *Why shouldn't she know about that? It's obvious she knows everything else!*

The children had fallen asleep on their parents' bed in the other room, but the adults were still wound up over the festivities. Chairs from Luther and Jake's cabin had been brought in and the last piece of apple pie was making its rounds between Henry and Luther.

Those who had heard the account of how the three Indians had attacked them were amazed by the story. As the evening wore on, the questions for María were almost non-stop, which also made Leo feel better. She wanted her family to like María, so Leo wanted to hug Luther and Dell for their constant curiosity and questions. They continued asking about things Leo herself had wanted answers to ever since she'd met María.

"Is it like seeing a picture in your head?" Luther asked. "Did you see three Indians in the woods wanting to hurt you?"

María shook her head. Leo could tell she wasn't accustomed to so much attention. Her shyness was endearing.

"It's something I sense more than see," María said.

"Explain what you mean by that," Dell said. "You can sense things how?"

María took a deep breath. "I sensed darkness or . . . something dark. To me that always means evil or danger. I also could feel different shades of darkness. As if there were three separate elements of evil." Her voice was low and her word selection and descriptions clear.

"How often do you feel these kinds of things?" Luther asked.

"All the time," María said. "My mind rests while I sleep, unless evil lurks closely, then I can't sleep at all."

"Are you ever wrong about something?" Luther asked.

"I think of myself as a receiver of information that is there for all of us," María said. "Some people have learned to use the gift, while others ignore the signs altogether."

Her comment hung in the air for a moment.

"So anyone can do what you do?" Henry finally asked.

"I believe so."

"Those three Indians would've had me all laid out in that road," Luther said. A group chuckle made its way around the table.

"Me, too," Leo said soberly.

"What other things can you do?" Luther asked.

María's shy smile was back. Leo couldn't stop looking at her. "I sense things about each of you."

Dell, Luther and Henry laughed. Leo had no doubts about anything María said now. She was María's strongest advocate. Henry, on the other hand, didn't have much to say. He was too busy finishing off the rest of the pie.

"Like what? Like what?" Dell asked, practically bouncing in her chair.

"There are good people in this room," María said. "I feel the love you all have for each other. It relaxes me to be here with you. My mind can rest." She glanced at Henry sitting at the end of the table. "You," she said, pointing a finger at him. "You love your wife and your children. You worry about her each time she gives birth, but you don't have to."

Leo saw the surprise in Henry's eyes and then the relief on his face.

María turned her head and looked at Leo then. Leo felt an unexpected thrill scamper through her body.

187

"What do you sense about me?" Dell asked. "This is just so much fun!"

"You love your husband," María said.

Dell put her arm through Henry's. He smiled down at her with pie crust crumbs in his mustache.

"You change your mind a lot," María said to her. "You should be more confident about things that matter to you."

Dell lowered her eyes, but didn't say anything. María then pointed to Henry again.

"You are an interesting man," María said.

Chuckling and mumbling went around the table again.

"You feel things deeply," María continued, "but prefer that no one sees that in you. I sense an adventurous side of you, but there are limits to what you will do. You should share more of yourself with your family. They will benefit from your ability to see things another way."

Dell looked up at her husband and brushed the crumbs from his mustache. "You feel things deeply?" she asked him.

"If María says I do, then I guess I do," Henry said.

"She knew about those Indians," Luther reminded them all.

"She knows I love my wife," Henry said as he gave Dell another hug.

"What about me?" Luther asked.

"You," María said with a smile. She put her hands on the table and laced her fingers together. "I sense that you will find love soon."

"I will?" Luther said. His eyes were huge.

"He will?" Henry said.

"When? Where?" Luther asked.

"You have to be patient," María said.

"When? When?" Luther asked excitedly again.

"She said you gotta be patient, Luther," Dell reminded him.

Leo's eyes were fixed on María's hands . . . the long thin fingers and the shape of her nails. Leo wanted to reach across the table and touch her, but a shiver racing down her arms brought her back to reality.

"What about Leo?" Henry asked.

Leo blinked a few times at the mention of her name. Everyone was looking at her now. She noticed María's smile and the connection was again strong between them.

"I sense many interesting things about Leona," María said.

"You've called me that before," Leo said. "How did you know that was my name?"

"I asked Cordelia about you, remember?"

Leo felt another unexpected thrill race through her body.

"What kinds of things do you sense about Leona?" Henry asked. From the twinkle in his eye, Leo could tell he enjoyed calling her by that name.

"Like Luther," María said. "I'm sensing that Leona will find someone to love soon."

There was a loud gasp, then sporadic clapping and laughter.

"That's not likely," Leo said.

María's steady gaze made Leo warm around the collar.

"When you no longer trust, Leona—"

"It's still not likely."

"Now, Leona," Henry said. "If I can feel things deeply, then so can you."

The laughter around the table eased some of the tension Leo was feeling. Her eyes met María's and Leo felt almost wild inside. She didn't know what to do or say. Then there was a child crying in the other room and Dell got up to see which one it was. The lateness of the evening broke up the party and sent them all on their way home.

Chapter Twenty-Five

Leo and Luther held their lanterns high to help them see where they were going. Leo had hoped Luther would take the hints she'd been tossing in his direction, but so far he wasn't having any of it. To Leo it made sense for them to get Luther home first since his cabin was the closest to Henry's, but he had a chivalrous streak that Leo was beginning to find annoying. His string of questions for María weren't doing much to improve Leo's mood either.

"This woman I'm going to meet," Luther said. "Is she older than me?"

"I've told you all I know," María said.

"Have I met her before?"

María laughed. Her patience with him was remarkable. He reminded Leo of a puppy tugging on a pant leg.

"I don't know if you've met her before," María said.

"Will she like me right away?"

"How could she with all the questions you ask?" Leo said.

"Nothing wrong with questions, is there, María?"

Again, María's light laughter traveled in the night air. Leo couldn't believe how irritated she was to have Luther still walking with them. Then she was amazed when he tried to take the path to Leo's cabin right away.

"We'll get María settled first," Leo said.

Luther stopped on the path and then reluctantly followed Leo to María's cabin. Leo went inside and set her lantern on the table. She knelt down in front of the fireplace and stoked the glowing coals. Throwing a small piece of wood on them, flames finally curled around the edges of the stick. The fireplace gave off enough light that María wouldn't need her lantern once Luther and Leo went to their own cabins.

Leo stood up and looked at her little brother. "I can find my way home. Thanks for walking with us."

The disappointment on his face didn't instill any sympathy in her.

"I'll see you two in the morning then," Luther said. "I'm glad you're here, María."

"Thank you, Luther," María said.

He took his lantern and left the cabin. Leo lowered the flame on hers, softening the light in the room.

"My family likes you," Leo said.

"Why does that surprise you?"

"It doesn't surprise me at all. Even though there are several of us here, this can be a lonely life," Leo said. "Having you here is new and different for us." She smiled. "You'll get a lot of attention."

"They also liked Cordelia."

Leo nodded. It felt good to hear Cordy's name and no longer ache inside. Leo was relieved to be past that and able to function again.

"Cordy's the type of person who's easy to like," Leo said. "There's something about her that makes you want to take care of her. Unfortunately, she's unable to let anyone get close enough to do that, though."

"You know her well," María said.

"In a way. But does anyone really know her at all?"

"The same things could be said about you, Leona. Who among your family really knows you?"

Leo took a deep breath. She didn't know how to answer that.

"Don't close off your heart," María said. "Let those who care about you know what's important to you. Trust them enough to share things with them. They'll love you no matter what your choices are."

"How did you get to be so wise at such a young age?" Leo asked, changing the subject.

"Why is it you can talk about anything or anyone but yourself, Leona?"

Leo had no idea why she didn't find this woman irritating, but she didn't. Leo smiled and picked up her lantern.

"It's late and we've had a long day." She glanced at the bunks in the corner and noticed a folded blanket on one of them. "You're all set for the night," Leo said. "Dell can help you get this place fixed up tomorrow." Leo stopped at the door and turned around. "Let me know if you need anything."

"Thank you. Goodnight."

Leo woke up early and stretched under the warm covers. She heard a rooster crowing in the distance and wondered how Henry and Dell were able to put up with it being so close to them every morning. She got out of bed and gave the coals in the fireplace a few pokes before throwing on some sticks. The mornings were getting cooler. It wouldn't be long before another winter was upon them.

Leo got dressed and went outside. She could see Luther and María by the barn feeding the chickens already. *I need to have another talk with him*, she thought. Leo tended to her early-morning business, then went back inside her cabin to begin emptying the tub.

She carried pail after pail of dirty bath water to the fall garden on the side of the barn. It wasn't long before she was able to move the tub out on the porch. Henry came over and helped her carry it.

"What did you think of that fortune telling going on last night?" Henry asked.

They poured the last of the water on the only dry part of the garden.

"Fortune telling?" Leo repeated. "It wasn't anything like that. Everyone asked María questions and she gave them her answers."

Henry smiled. "Don't get your knickers in a knot, Leo. I'm just mentioning it because Dell wants to talk to María again."

Leo felt the tension drain from her shoulders. She wanted everyone to like María. Why that was important, she didn't really know.

"Have Dell to just ask her," Leo said. "María will tell you whatever she knows."

Henry shrugged as he picked up one end of the tub. "I was hoping you'd ask her for us."

"When do you want her to do it?"

"How about now?"

After putting the tub away in the barn, Leo and Henry went over to the sheep pen where María and Luther were. Two of the children were there with them, leaning on the fence pointing at the new lamb.

"Good morning," Leo said to everyone.

María smiled at her. "Good morning."

"You ever had a tortilla, Leo?" Luther asked. "María made some this morning and they were so good."

Leo was suddenly reminded that Luther hadn't come over with breakfast for her like he usually did. *Maybe he didn't cook today because Uncle Jake isn't here*, she thought. Leo then glanced at María and wondered if she had cooked breakfast for Luther instead. Another small pang of jealousy surprised her.

"I have no idea what a tortilla is," Leo said. To calm herself down, she reached over and tousled the blond hair on her two nephews standing there. One grabbed her around the legs to give her a hug, then waved his arms over his head so Leo would pick him up.

To María, Leo said, "Could you go with Henry this morning? He and his wife have some more questions for you."

María nodded.

"I'm going, too," Luther said eagerly. "I might have more questions myself."

Leo handed the little boy in her arms over to Henry. "Don't think about how she knows things," Leo said. "Just listen to what she says."

While the others were on their way to Henry's cabin for another round of María'isms, Leo went to the barn and saddled her horse. She found some jerky in her saddlebag and settled on that for breakfast. As she rode off toward the back of the canyon, Leo had to admit that it felt good being on a horse again. She liked being home.

As she rode and scanned the ridge along the top of the canyon wall as well as the overall landscape in general, Leo tried not to think of María sitting around Henry's table being the center of attention again, and in her own way being entertained by the others. Leo chided herself for seeming to be so fickle. If she didn't know better, she would think there was even more jealousy creeping in than was called for. *How can you be jealous of your own family?* she wondered. Luther's interest in María was at least something Leo felt she could control to a certain extent. She hoped Luther would do whatever she told him to do, and she needed to remind him again that María was married. *Or is it the fact that María enjoys spending time with someone other than you?* she wondered. *Making breakfast for Luther and helping him with his chores*, she thought. *Well, it's obvious you have to stop thinking about this. You're getting irritated already and no one's even done anything to warrant that yet!*

She saw an eagle soaring overhead and wondered if the lambs in the flock were actually big enough to be in the pasture with the other sheep. Leo usually left that decision for Luther and Uncle Jake to make. They did their best to keep the birthing ewes in pens close to the barn, but occasionally one slipped by and had her lamb in the pasture. Leo rode over to where the sheep were gathered to make sure there was nothing out of the ordinary among them. A few minutes later she saw Henry riding along the canyon's perimeter from the other side. They met halfway and stopped where two fenced-in pastures came together.

"So," Leo said. "How's my brother who cares deeply for his family?"

Henry cut his eyes over at her and tried his best to suppress a smile. "She's something else, that's for sure."

"Are they still at your place?"

"That's all Dell can talk about," Henry said. "María will get no rest now."

Leo shook her head. "Luther might be smitten already."

"I'd say so."

Leo had hoped no one else had noticed. She didn't like being angry at her little brother this way. *Are you upset because you're jealous of Luther?* she asked herself again. *What if María starts responding to him? After all, just because she's married doesn't mean a lot. You've just been assuming she and Cordy have had some sort of relationship. Maybe that's not entirely true.*

Leo didn't like all this confusion and speculation. Worrying about a special relationship developing between Luther and María wasn't something she cared about doing.

"See anything unusual?" Henry asked as he glanced around at the canyon's ridge.

"Just an eagle."

"I say we give the eagles all the sheep they can eat."

Leo just laughed. It was good to be home.

❧❦

Leo and Henry rode the back fence-line and replaced another rotten post. She hadn't given him a chance to tell her what had happened at his cabin earlier. Leo didn't want to know and kept changing the subject often enough that he finally got the message.

Later that afternoon, she could see Henry digging a hole in the middle of another pasture. On numerous occasions it had been determined that an outhouse this far away from the cabins would be a good idea. She could only imagine the things Henry was saying with each shovel full of dirt he heaped on a pile.

Leo looked up and saw Luther riding toward Henry in the other pasture. He threw his shovel down and got on his horse. Leo left the rotted post she'd been working on and jumped on her horse also. When she finally reached them, Luther's eyes were huge.

"María says there's someone coming," Luther said.

"How many?" Leo asked.

"More than three. She can't really tell." Luther turned his horse around; Leo and Henry followed him. "She also said they aren't on horses."

"Indians?" Henry asked.

"No," Luther said. "It's kind of strange. She says there's no darkness. Whatever that means."

"How far away are they?" Leo asked.

"Close enough that she's getting a strong feeling about them." Luther shook his head. "I tell you, it's the strangest thing, Leo. How does she know these things?"

Leo nudged her horse and rode on ahead of them. At times like this she missed having the twins there with them. If the Trask family had to defend their homes at Eagle Canyon, having Earl and Eb there with them would help make it easier to do.

Leo went to find María and saw her near the barn. Henry was already at the front gate with his gun drawn, ready for anything. Leo sent Luther, Dell and the children to Henry's cabin.

"You know you have the most important job, don't you?" she said to her younger brother.

Luther got off his horse and nodded. He pulled his rifle out of its scabbard and went inside the cabin. Leo rode over to the barn and told María to ride with her. She leaned over to help her up, and María was on Leo's horse sitting behind her, hanging onto Leo's waist within moments.

Leo turned her head and said, "Tell me what you see or feel about them."

"More than three," María said. Her lips were nearly against Leo's ear, and Leo wished they didn't have to worry about what was out there so she could enjoy having her so close.

"It's a wagon," María said. "I also sense sadness."

"How far away?"

"It's close."

The three of them were at the gate now. As Leo and María got off the horse, Leo already missed having María's arms around her waist.

"Everyone will be safe," María said quietly.

"What does that mean?" Henry asked.

Leo put her gun away. "It means whatever is on its way here doesn't mean to hurt us." She turned to look at María. "It'll be all right if I go out there?"

María nodded. Leo could see the strain and tension around her eyes. She realized this incident had to be even harder on María than it was on the rest of them. Leo took the reins of her horse and got up in the saddle again.

"Open the gate, Henry. You two wait here."

"Leo—"

"Open the gate," she said again. "If something happens to me, blame it on María," she said with a wink and a smile at María.

Henry slowly opened the gate and let Leo out. She could hear the faint creaking of a wagon as it crept up the incline. She slowly wove her way through the brush several feet away from the trail until she could see the wagon a ways up ahead and to her left. It was Uncle Jake trying to get the horses to make the climb. Leo came out of the brush and saw that he wasn't alone. He had Essie, another young woman and Essie's three young boys with him.

"Need some help there?" Leo yelled.

"Whoa!" Jake called to the horses. "Am I ever glad to see you!"

Chapter Twenty-Six

Leo rode back to the gate to tell the other two it was Uncle Jake and Essie in the wagon. "Jake needs some help," she said. "Leave your horse here."

Henry put his gun away and was through the gate quickly. Leo rode back to Henry's cabin to report the news to the others. Tension was always high when strangers were in the area, and she didn't want Luther worried about having to protect Dell and the children on his own.

"Luther!" Leo called once she got there. "It's Uncle Jake and Essie."

Luther came out of the cabin holding his rifle. The relief she saw on his face mirrored her own. Dell came out behind him with big-eyed children latched on to her long skirt. Leo looked over her shoulder to see María coming back from the gate area riding Henry's horse.

"Is Essie's husband with them?" Dell asked. She held the baby close to her chest; Leo could see that Dell had been crying. She had never gotten over her family being killed by Indians, so whenever something like this happened, Luther always had his hands full with Dell's hysteria frightening the kids.

"No, I didn't see Essie's husband," Leo said.

"Poor things," Dell whispered.

María rode up and got off the horse. "They have much sadness," she said. Leo noticed how tired María looked.

Luther took the horse's reins from María and seemed to have recovered from the earlier scare. She loved how her brothers reacted to an emergency.

"María knew they were coming," Luther said to Leo.

"I know."

"We should listen closer to what she says when that happens. What she tells us and the words she uses . . . it's just all very important."

Leo was still surprised that her family was so accepting of María's gift.

"My goodness!" Dell exclaimed. "You should have seen us when María mentioned there was someone coming!"

"I didn't listen," Luther said, sounding angry at himself. "I jumped up and just started moving."

Dell impulsively hugged María. Leo studied her younger brother for a moment and understood his frustration. She imagined Luther had experienced the same feelings of awe and gratitude over María's abilities as Leo herself had encountered. *It's like María said*, she thought. *It all has to do with trust.* Leo realized she trusted María. It was a nice, warm feeling to have for another person.

As she looked down from her horse, Leo also felt a shift in the mood as they waited for the wagon. The excitement of having Jake and Essie there would give them something new to focus on for a while. The Trask family was at its best during a crisis.

❧

Leo had mixed feelings about seeing her cousin Essie again. For Essie to ever be at Eagle Canyon now, it could only mean her husband had died. It was a relief to know that Uncle Jake had been able to convince Essie to come back with him, as opposed to Jake staying in some strange town with his daughter and her kids where a bounty hunter or a Texas Ranger might eventually find him. Even after all these years of being on the run, it wasn't safe for Jake to be out and about on his own.

As the wagon stopped in front of Henry's cabin, Uncle Jake got off the back and set two of his grandsons on the ground. He looked as though he had aged ten years since Leo last saw him. She decided right then to find less strenuous things for him to do from now on. She wanted him around for a long time. *I'll discuss it with Henry,* Leo thought. *We need to take another look at the workload around here again anyway.*

Essie was sitting beside Henry in the front of the wagon. Even though she appeared to be more weary and haggard than her father, she was still beautiful. Luther was around at the back of the wagon and helped the other little boy out. Essie's children ranged in age from about four to six. There was a young blond woman with them. Uncle Jake helped her down from the wagon. Leo wasn't sure if she was clinging to the boys or if they were clinging to her. Leo noticed the wagon was packed with furniture and all of their worldly possessions. There was barely room for anything else. It was amazing how they had traveled so far under such conditions.

Leo got off her horse. Essie saw her and managed a tired smile. Essie's hair was long and dark, piled neatly on her head. She was tall like Leo, and they looked enough alike to be sisters instead of cousins.

Henry helped Essie down from the wagon and Leo gave her a heartfelt hug. They hadn't seen each other since they were children. As Leo held her, she could feel the sadness almost radiating from Essie's body. *If only there was something we could do to make this easier for her,* Leo thought. She felt helpless to do anything for any of them other than offer comfort and support.

"I'm sorry something like this had to happen before we could see each other again," Leo said.

Essie seemed to almost wilt in Leo's arms, as if she were suddenly exhausted.

"Welcome to Eagle Canyon," Leo said.

Leo was proud of everyone for the way they pitched in to help. By the time she and Essie let go of each other, Luther had Essie's three little boys by the hand and they were all headed toward the pen to see the newborn lamb. Leo motioned for Dell to join them. She introduced everyone and then pointed to both of her brothers and told Essie who they were.

"How'd we all get so old?" Essie asked with a tired smile as she dabbed at her eyes with the back of her hand.

"This is María," Leo said. "She's new to Eagle Canyon, but like you, we're glad she's here."

"They have a very nice cabin for you and your children," María said with a shy smile.

Leo saw the young woman that had arrived with them. She was standing shyly at the back of the wagon. Leo walked toward her and smiled.

"I'm Leona Trask. Essie's cousin," she said. "Come and join us. What's your name?"

"Sarah!" Essie said. "I'm sorry for my bad manners." She walked toward the young woman and reached for her hand. "This is Sarah Wagner," Essie said to Leo and the others. "She's Jonathan's sister. Sarah came to live with us to help me care for him when he got so sick."

"Welcome, Sarah," Dell said.

Leo could see how painfully shy the young woman was. Leo thought it best to just keep everyone busy and let them find their own place among all the new names and faces.

"María said just yesterday that Luther's cabin was waiting for someone special!" Dell said. "This woman has such a gift! You wouldn't believe some of the things I've seen and heard since she's been here."

Leo motioned for Henry to climb back up in the wagon. "Let's get this over to Luther's old place. We can all pitch in and help Essie get settled."

By the time Leo got her horse unsaddled and watered, almost everyone was over at the cabin that had been designated for Essie and her boys. Leo came out of the barn and saw Luther, Henry and Uncle Jake unloading the wagon. Dell was on the porch with Essie and Sarah, already making plans to fix the place up even though it was tidy inside from the cleaning it had gotten the day before. As Leo got closer to the cabin, she also noticed María's flour sack on the far edge of the porch. She shook her head at the way everyone had assumed Luther's cabin could be handed over to someone else so easily. *Just yesterday we gave it to María*, she thought. *Now here we are bringing in someone else's things.* She looked around for María but didn't see her anywhere.

"You just gonna stand there?" Henry asked her with a puzzled look. "Grab something off this wagon."

Leo smiled at him. "Look at you being all bossy and such."

He shrugged sheepishly. "Things are happening so fast, Leo." He jumped up into the back of wagon and handed her a chair that had been jammed against a bedstead. "Things are changing. Those little boys don't have a father now. That makes me sad. I don't even know the little fellas and I'm worried about 'em already."

Leo set the chair on the porch and got a suitcase and set it next to some other things there. "You can't replace the loss of a father in a child's heart," she said, "but we can all make a difference in their lives." Leo scooted a trunk to the end of the wagon. Together she and Henry carried it to the porch. "When you do things with your own kids, think about Essie's kids, too."

"I will," Henry said.

Luther and Uncle Jake were back out on the porch now, moving some of the furniture into the cabin. There was some grunting and direction giving, but no grumbling.

"Essie is family," Leo said as she helped Henry with the bedstead. "Her boys are family. We can make things better for all of them. I know how we are and I know how you and the others feel about that."

Henry nodded. Together they got everything else out of the wagon and stacked and piled it on the porch. Leo got up in the front of the wagon and headed the horse in the direction of the barn. Taking care of Essie and getting her settled was their main priority now. *Family comes first*, Leo thought.

"They're good little boys," Luther said to Leo as the two of them pointed toward a mother hen and her brood of chicks. The hen chased down a grasshopper, causing the chicks to scramble out of the way for a moment. Essie's three boys were a little more relaxed as Leo continued to show them things and talk to them.

"See if they're hungry," Leo said to Luther.

He held out his hands for the two younger ones to take. "Let's go see what we can find to eat," Luther said.

Leo was certain it wouldn't take long before all the children would be playing together. For now, Leo was sure Essie's immediate needs were being met by a number of Trask family members. As she squinted in the direction of Luther's old cabin, Leo could see Henry and Uncle Jake standing on the porch taking a break. It would be good for Jake to have his daughter close to him again.

Leo walked back over to Essie's cabin to see if she could help with anything else. Too many people in one place only tended to get in each other's way. Leo also wanted to find María. It wasn't fair that yesterday she had her own cabin and now she had nothing.

Leo looked for María everywhere and finally returned to the barn to see if María's horse was still there. With a deep sigh of relief, she saw it in one of the stalls eating hay. It made sense to Leo that she offer her own cabin for María to stay in. There was plenty of room and Leo even thought she would enjoy María's company. She looked up as she heard Henry and Uncle Jake talking on their way past the barn.

"Have either of you seen María?" she asked.

"She's in the garden chopping out some weeds," Uncle Jake said. "It sure needs it, too."

"We've been thinking, Leo," Henry said. "Essie and Sarah could use a bigger cabin already."

"Maybe add on to that one like we did Henry's last spring," Jake said.

"Let's give them a chance to get settled first," Leo said.

"I want to move there with them," Jake said. "Once we add the other room."

"Luther's not going to want to live alone," Leo reminded them.

Henry shook his head and laughed. "He can stay with us if he likes."

Leo watched as Henry got on his horse to get back out there and finish the work he'd started earlier in the day. She needed to be out there as well helping mend the fence in the back pasture, but first she wanted to find María.

Chapter Twenty-Seven

Leo could hear the sound of a hoe chopping weeds in the dirt. They needed rain again already. When María saw her, she stopped working and leaned against the hoe.

"We try and take turns tending to the garden," Leo said. María had done an excellent job ridding the garden of weeds and loosening the dirt around all the plants.

"A garden needs attention," María said. "Very much like people do." She wiped her brow with a bandanna that she seemed to pull out of nowhere. Seeing the bandage on her wrist, Leo asked how her burn was.

"Better," María said. "Thank you."

"I wanted to talk to you about the cabin," Leo said.

"I understand about the cabin."

Leo felt dismissed, but had more to say. "It wasn't fair of us to offer it to you and then—"

"I understand," María said. Her expression was unreadable and her tone of voice no different than it had ever been.

Is she upset? Leo wondered. *I'm sure I would be if I were in her position.*

With a slight shrug, Leo said, "I also wanted to thank you for what happened this morning."

"There's no need to thank me. I'm sorry the little ones here were eventually upset by what I said and by what happened."

"I don't think they were upset."

"They are," María said. "Henry's children fear being together that way and seeing Luther with a rifle. He makes them feel protected and they see him as strong . . . someone who will try to keep them safe from harm. But when their mother becomes afraid, the children can't forget as easily."

"So you're saying some of the children are still upset by what happened this morning?"

"Yes."

Leo sighed. "I see. Thank you for telling me."

"And the new children," María said. "The ones who arrived today. They are hurting inside. Everything that has happened has not been properly explained to them." María tucked the bandanna into the waistband of her long skirt, then she took the hoe and resumed working in the garden. Leo once again felt dismissed by her.

"María," Leo said. "Are you angry with me?"

"No."

"Then look at me, please."

She stopped hoeing again; her dark, penetrating eyes met Leo's, but her expression was still unreadable.

"I understand about the cabin," María said. "I've known all along it was meant for someone else."

"That doesn't make it right."

"You can't take on everyone's worries and troubles, Leona. It's time to take on your own."

Leo didn't know what to say to that. She refused to stand there and be lectured to about anything—especially something she didn't even understand!

"I just wanted you to know that you're welcome to stay with me at my cabin," Leo said.

"That's not really what you want."

Leo was stunned for a moment. "Why would you say that?"

María began slowly wielding the hoe again, loosening more dirt. "Henry said I could stay with him and his wife Dell."

"Oh," Leo said. It surprised her how truly disappointed she felt.

"You fight so hard, Leona. You must learn to trust yourself and those things you do want. You'll never find happiness without that."

"It must be nice to know everything," Leo snapped, sounding childish.

Before Leo could apologize, María said, "I don't know everything, but I do know when to at least be honest with myself."

"Why is it you think I don't want you to stay with me? I wouldn't have offered my home to you unless I meant it."

María smiled as she continued working with the hoe. "You don't want it bad enough, Leona." She glanced up at her briefly and added, "At least not bad enough yet."

Leo met up with Henry in one of the back pastures where he was finishing up the hole for their newest outhouse. The dirt was piled high and Leo was pleased at the progress he was making.

"I'll go finish those posts I was working on earlier," Leo said. "But while I have you here, I want you to be thinking about some new things we can give Uncle Jake to do. He's looking tired to me."

"How about we let him dig the next hole we need here?" Henry suggested as he wiped the sweat from his brow.

"How's that gonna make Uncle Jake be less tired?" Leo asked with a laugh.

"It would make *me* less tired," Henry clarified with a grin.

"Keep thinking," Leo said. "We'll talk about it more later."

Leo finished replacing the posts she'd been working on and then rode over to where Henry and Luther were working on the frame for the outhouse. Once she got there, Leo decided to ask Henry about what María had told her earlier.

"María says she'll be staying with you and Dell."

Henry laughed. "Dell won't let her outta sight once she's there either. With the kids around and that Indian scare, Dell wants María right there with her so she'll know what's going on all the time. Dell is a believer."

"I see," Leo said. Even though that made sense, Leo was disappointed that María now had another place to stay. "Well, I've got room at my place if yours gets too crowded."

Before long Leo and her two brothers had the frame up. An hour later, the Trask clan had a brand-new outhouse there in the pasture.

Leo sent Henry on home to be with his family and offered to ride the perimeter one final time. Earlier, she and her two brothers had a good talk about Uncle Jake and Essie's situation. One of the things Leo liked the most about her brothers was their compassion and their sense of family. That was just one of the many things they had all gotten from their mother.

It had been Henry who suggested they give Uncle Jake the responsibility of riding the perimeter.

"He likes being in the saddle," Henry said, "and that would leave us more time to do other things."

"How good can he see?" Luther asked. "We can't just give him something important like that if we're worried about how well he can do it."

"We can send María out with him," Henry suggested. "She'll let him know if anything needs tending to, and he won't have to see anything."

After the laughter died down, Luther said, "If that's the case, why don't we just put María on a horse and stick *her* out here?"

"Why put the horse through all that?" Henry said. "María can check the perimeter while she's sitting in a cabin!"

More laughter erupted as they put up boards and hammered away.

"This isn't helping," Leo said. "Uncle Jake needs to feel useful, but he still needs to take it easy."

"I've been doing most of the work in the smokehouse," Luther said. "There's more of us to feed now. Curing and smoking meat could be a much bigger job in the future."

"We'll also need a bigger garden," Leo noted. "As well as taking care of it better. So let's keep thinking about this. We need to change some things around and take another look at what we've got and what we need."

Thinking back on that conversation as she rode her horse along the back wall of Eagle Canyon, Leo knew her thoughts should be focused on Essie, Uncle Jake, and Essie's three little boys; however, all she could really think about right then was how María would be staying at Henry and Dell's place from now on. Leo didn't want her to be there . . . she wanted María to stay with her instead. But Leo had no idea how to express how strongly she felt about that. As it stood now, Leo was barely able to admit such a thing to herself.

It was dark in her cabin when she finally got home. Leo threw a few sticks of wood in her fireplace. She was tired; it had been a long day. Leo rolled up her shirt sleeves and filled the basin with water. She washed her hands and face, then began brushing her long dark hair.

Henry had invited everyone over to his cabin again for the evening since he and Dell liked having company. Leo was just glad Essie, Sarah and Essie's three children would have something else to do besides think about losing a husband, a brother, and a father. Being able to see María again was the only reason Leo would even consider spending time with so many people now. She preferred being alone, but knowing that María would once again be the center of attention at Henry's place wasn't something Leo wanted to see right then. She was still uncomfortable with the amount of time she spent thinking about María, but on the other hand, Leo was also glad she had stopped wondering about what María's relationship with Cordy had been like. She had wanted to ask her about it several times, but Leo could never bring herself to actually do it. Leo thought that in a way, she really didn't want to know what they had meant to each other, but in another way she had to know everything. *Why torture yourself like that?* she wondered. *Stop thinking about such things. María is here now,* Leo reminded herself. *Whatever she had with Cordy obviously wasn't enough to keep Cordy in one place.*

Leo finished brushing her hair and wanted to clean her boots and her gun before she went to bed. In the morning she and Henry would do a check outside of Eagle Canyon. With the recent Indian encounter she and María had experienced, they needed to see what exactly was out there and then keep up with it in a way that didn't draw any undue attention to themselves.

Leo heard someone on her porch, then a light knock on the door. She went to open it and found Luther standing there.

"Come in."

Luther had a plate of food covered with a small white cloth. He set it on the table for her. "María sent me over with this," he said. "She made tortillas for everyone tonight. They sure are good."

Leo wondered why María didn't bring the plate over herself, but didn't say anything.

"How are Essie and the kids?"

"I heard Essie laugh earlier," Luther said. "Uncle Jake is good about that. He can say some of the stupidest things sometimes."

They both laughed.

"How are Essie's boys doing?"

"They aren't as shy anymore. When I left, all the kids were playing together. They'll be fine."

"Did you and Henry talk more about Uncle Jake?"

"Yes, we did. I gave Henry more ideas. Don't go thinking you can push Uncle Jake to the side, Leo. He'll kick our butts all over this place for even suggesting it."

Leo pointed to the chairs at her table. They both sat down.

"Tell me what's going on at Henry's place tonight." She uncovered the plate to find smoked ham, boiled potatoes, two flour tortillas and a fork.

"Dell asked María to tell the Indian story again," Luther said, "then they made her explain how she knew Jake and Essie were coming in the wagon. They probably have María telling their fortunes again by now," he said with a laugh.

Leo took a bite of the ham, then realized how hungry she was. "Tell me what you're thinking about, Luther. Something's on your mind."

He shrugged. "María, I guess."

"What about María?"

"I thought I really liked her," he said. "She told me she was too old for me."

Leo smiled. "She's also married."

"Yeah, I know. She mentioned that, too." Luther drummed his fingers on the table. "Then I started talking to that Sarah person. That friend of Essie's."

"She seems to be very nice."

Luther sat up a little straighter in his chair. "I started stumbling all over my words, Leo. It got so bad I couldn't talk anymore." He shrugged. "Maybe I'm just confused. Yesterday all I could think about was María. Now I'm worried that Sarah thinks I'm a—"

"Luther," Leo said. "Do you remember the other night when we were at Henry and Dell's place? Remember what María said to you?" She popped a piece of stewed potato in her mouth. "María said you would meet someone soon . . . and you would be happy."

He nodded nervously. "I remember." Luther's fingers began drumming faster on the table. "So what can I do now, Leo? My mouth doesn't work when I'm around Sarah."

Leo smiled. "This might be something your brother can help you with. Henry was the same way, from what I've heard from Dell."

Luther nodded. "Or maybe I should ask María. She seems to know everything."

Leo finished chewing another piece of ham. "Ask your brother first."

Chapter Twenty-Eight

Leo was up and dressed early. She banked the coals in the fireplace and then slipped on her jacket. There was a nip in the air, and soon they would have to focus more seriously on preparing for winter. She heard someone on her porch again. Leo answered the knock on her door and let Uncle Jake in. He handed her a plate with another white cloth covering it.

"María wanted me to bring this over for you," he said.

Leo shook her head and thought, *María wants to feed me, but doesn't want to see me. That can't be good.*

"We were all up late last night," he said.

"Did anything interesting happen?" Leo poured them both some coffee before sitting down at the table. Uncovering the plate, she found two warm tortillas and several thick slices of bacon.

"You should've been there," Jake said. "Henry told some stories on you kids from when you were little. He had Essie and Sarah actually laughing a few times there. He brought up things no one had thought about in years. Even María had a good time, and I haven't seen her laugh that much either."

As Leo began to eat, she realized how much she wanted to see María right then. Leo couldn't stop thinking about her. *She's already worked her way into my family's heart and she hasn't even been here a week yet,* she thought.

"Why weren't you there last night with the rest of us, Leo?"

She looked at him across the table, then took another tasty bite of her breakfast.

"I was tired."

"You and Luther stayed up talking for quite a while. You weren't too tired for that."

Trying to get an idea about what he was thinking, she looked at him more closely this time. Jake didn't sound angry, but the way he pushed her for an answer wasn't like him. "Are you mad about me not being there last night?"

Uncle Jake's silence answered her question.

"You know I'm not good at socializing," she said lamely.

"It was Essie's first night at Eagle Canyon, Leo. Out of all of them, you're the one she's always been the closest to."

"I doubt seriously that I was missed by anyone."

Leo hadn't thought about it being Essie's first night there with them. The whole evening she had been focused on María and how uncomfortable it would have been to see so many people around her. *There's a word for it, Leo,* she thought. *You knew how jealous you would get if you were to see María in such a situation with so many other people. You would prefer to have her to yourself . . . not share her with someone else.*

"You're right," she said. "I should've been there. I'll apologize to Essie the next time I see her."

Uncle Jake reached over and took a piece of bacon off her plate. "So why weren't you there?"

"I said I was tired."

214

"We were all tired last night. We're tired every night, but we've always managed to make time for each other."

"What do you want me to say?"

Jake grew quiet again and slowly chewed on the bacon slice. Under his scrutiny, Leo was no longer hungry. She nudged the plate away and got up from the table to finish getting dressed.

"Something's going on with you," he said.

Leo struggled to pull on her boots. "Whatever is going on with me is no one's concern, Jake."

"Ha! Then there *is* something!" He reached for another piece of bacon and wrapped the remaining tortilla around it.

Leo was getting angry now, but it served to help her get her boots on faster. She stood up and reached for her holster, then put on her hat.

"I'm not leaving until you tell me what's the matter," he said with his mouth full. He waved the bacon taco at her and exclaimed, "Dang, this is good!"

"Didn't you have breakfast already?" Leo asked as she pushed a wisp of her long dark hair up under her hat.

Jake nodded. "Yes, I did. But you're about to waste some good food here."

"Well," Leo said, "just make sure you close the door when you leave."

Jake scrambled out of his chair and snatched up the last of the bacon off the plate. Stuffing the rest of it into the tortilla, he followed her out the door.

"Leo," he called. "Tell me what's going on with you. Please."

She kept walking with her rifle tucked under her right arm. When Uncle Jake caught up with her, he touched her on the shoulder. They both stopped walking then. Leo waited. She didn't know what to say to him. Everyone usually took her solitude and moodiness in stride, but now she was beginning to wonder if even more of her feelings of frustration, confusion and sadness were being reflected. It was unnerving the way Jake was so relentless in his search for an answer from her now.

"Leo," he said in a low voice. "This isn't like you. Tell me what's—"

"I can't, Jake." To Leo's horror, she felt tears on the way. She cleared her throat and took a deep breath, swallowing hard to keep her emotions in check.

"It's me, Leo," he said quietly. "You can tell me anything."

Leo just stood there, afraid to move for fear the tears would start in earnest. How could she tell him how her heart seemed to ache for no apparent reason anymore? Or how lonely she felt in a room full of family members? How she lay awake at night remembering the touch of a woman's lips on hers? She no longer associated any of those explosive, intimate feelings with Cordy, however. Leo now thought of María in this way . . . María's lips touching her, wanting her, loving her. These were thoughts she couldn't share with anyone. They were thoughts that made her afraid.

"Leo," Jake said. He gently tugged on her arm and made her turn around. "Whatever it is that's causing this—"

He stopped and seemed to suddenly be at a loss for words. Jake let go of her arm and looked down at the ground. "Me and the boys are just worried about you, that's all. If it'll make you feel better, we'll go out and look for Cordy on our own. I can probably find her for you."

Cordy! she thought. Leo looked at him closely again as if trying to read his thoughts. *He thinks you're feeling this way because of Cordy?* Then as if someone had given her a thump on the head, she remembered if Cordy hadn't kissed her in the first place, her heart probably wouldn't be in the condition it was in right now. But Cordy hadn't been a concern for Leo in quite some time. Cordy might have been the initial reason she had launched into this dreary longing, but Cordy was not the reason for the state Leo now found herself in.

"Just tell me what we can do," Jake said.

Leo shook her head and then gave him a hug. Uncle Jake held her for a moment before squeezing Leo with a strong, firm grip.

"I'll be fine," she whispered. "I'm sorry I can't tell you more." She let go of him. "I don't know much more myself."

Jake stepped back to get a better look at her. He nodded after a moment, then said, "You've got plenty of people here wanting to help."

"I see that now. Thanks." She turned and headed toward the barn. To stay any longer would have made her cry.

Henry's horse was already saddled when Leo got to the barn, but she didn't see him anywhere. Like a soothing habit, she brushed her own horse and scratched him behind the ears. Just being close to him made Leo feel better. Not long after getting the saddle on her horse, María came into the barn, looking for the pail to milk the cow in.

"Good morning," Leo said. She felt jittery inside just seeing María again. "Thank you for sending breakfast over this morning. You don't have to do that." She led her horse away from the stall, toward the barn door where María was standing. "And for sending over supper last night," she added. "My family tends to think I can't fend for myself."

"Your brothers insisted that someone take you something to eat."

Leo had hoped the delivered meals had been María's idea, but should have known better. It disappointed her a little.

Finding the milk bucket hanging on a nail, María said, "You have been avoiding me. I make you think about things you would rather forget."

Leo's jaw dropped a few inches and the jitters moved to her stomach. She wanted to talk to this woman for hours at a time, but Leo couldn't bring herself to say even one word.

"There you are," Henry said as he came into the barn. "You ready?"

Leo got on her horse and looked down at María holding the bucket. Once again she realized she had so many things she wanted to say, but nothing would come out of her mouth. María had a slight smile as she turned and walked out of the barn. Leo knew then that whatever this "thing" was that had been going on between them—it wouldn't get better until Leo got her thoughts together. *You can't keep going around with your mouth hanging open and your heart doing flips all the time. Toughen up and get on with it. Everyone's watching you now.*

Leo and Henry rode together as they made several large circles around the outside of the canyon. Mostly they were looking for any new trails and even more importantly, any signs of Indians or other unwelcome visitors. They picked their way through thick brush. She and Henry made this trip about once a week so they'd be able to see if anything new appeared.

"Thought any more about new chores for Uncle Jake?" Leo asked.

"I like the smokehouse idea," Henry said. "He's good at that and could probably take on the hog slaughtering with Luther's help."

Leo nodded. Dell and Essie would probably be able to help as well. There was also María and Sarah now to lend a hand.

"I have a question for you," Leo said after a moment. "Do you think Essie will stay here?"

"She has no place else to go," Henry said. "It's a comfort to her now to be close to her father. She'll find her way among us, I think."

Leo wanted to ask him if he thought María would stay with them, but she didn't know how. Leo felt emotionally fragile whenever María's name came up. She tried to find a word to describe exactly what she was feeling, but the emotions were so new and powerful that Leo was afraid of them. She had never felt this way before. Her heart seemed to have a dull ache in it all the time, and Leo was certain María was the key to relieving whatever pain and loneliness she felt. There were times when Leo wished she had more worldly experience in such matters, or that she at least had someone to talk to about it other than her brothers or her uncle.

"We missed you last night," Henry said.

"Uncle Jake has already gone over that with me."

Henry smiled. "Well, we did miss you."

"I know. I know."

"Uncle Jake said you wouldn't talk to him this morning."

Leo sighed. *Here it comes again*, she thought.

"I didn't have anything to say." She urged her horse around a cluster of scrub oaks and continued to scan the area for anything new or out of the ordinary.

"So you're not gonna tell me either?"

"There's nothing to tell, Henry. I have some things to sort through, that's all."

"It's not about Cordy," he said. It was a statement, not a question. "That's what Uncle Jake and Luther think, you know. They think it's all about Cordy."

Leo couldn't look at him. "You're right. It's not about Cordy."

Henry offered a shy smile. "So you're still not gonna tell me."

Leo was surprised at his persistence. "There's nothing to tell," she said again. "So have I been that bad?" Leo already knew the answer.

"I can tell when you're unhappy, Leo. You've never been one to hide that kind of thing well."

That settles it, she thought. *I have to do something about this.*

She got down off her horse and led him through a narrow stretch of trees. *I can't have them worrying about me this way*, she thought. *Everyone has enough other things to worry about. They don't need this, too.*

"Did you find anything?" Uncle Jake asked when Henry and Leo returned later that afternoon.

"A campfire close to the north ridge," Henry said. "It was two or three days old."

"No sign of horses, though," Leo said.

"No sign of anything but the campfire," Henry added.

"How close to the north ridge was it?"

"At the bottom near the trees," Henry said. "If it's Indians, they might be passing through. If it's one of their hunting parties, we didn't see anything they left behind."

"Not much we can do about it, I guess," Uncle Jake said. "Other than keep our eyes open."

"I'm headed out to the back pasture to tell Luther," Henry said. "You two tell everyone here to keep a sharp lookout."

Leo unsaddled her horse and brushed him down. Uncle Jake gave him some grain in a bucket.

"How's Essie?" Leo asked.

"She's doin' about as good as can be expected. It's not easy watching someone you love die." He set the bucket of grain down in front of the horse. "Jonathan was in so much pain at the end, sometimes Essie would pray for him to die. I think that's the part she's having to face up to now. She's trying to be strong for them little ones. Sarah is a big help to her."

Leo couldn't imagine being in such a position. She decided to spend some time with Essie later.

"Dell is keeping Essie busy," Jake said. "That's the best thing for her now."

Leo looked around the horse at him. "Luther was telling me about Sarah. I think he likes her. How long will she be staying with us?"

"Can't say," Jake said, "but if we keep talking about Indians, it probably won't be long." His laughter made Leo laugh.

That evening everyone gravitated toward Henry and Dell's cabin again. After her earlier encounter with Uncle Jake, Leo had no choice but to go and be sociable. *I might even accidentally have some fun*, she thought with a reluctant smile..

The children were playing in front of Henry's cabin. Essie's boys had blended right in with the other children. Leo stopped to get hugs from her niece and nephews. Their dirty little faces made Leo laugh. She gave Essie's boys a special hug and tousled a few heads when she stood up again.

Inside Henry and Dell's cabin, Leo found a flurry of activity. To her amazement, María and Essie were making tortillas, while Dell and Sarah tended to the new baby. Leo had felt more comfortable outside with the children.

"It's good to see you, Leona," María said.

She had a way of looking at Leo that made her feel all warm inside. Leo wasn't sure words would even come out of her mouth if she tried to say something. Seeing María's involvement with the others made Leo want to join in the fun just to be close to her. *This is a mistake*, she thought suddenly. *I can't stay here like this.*

"Leona," Essie said. "It's been years since I've heard anyone call you that!"

Leo smiled. "It's been years since anyone's called me that." She leaned over and peeked at the baby. Little Milton looked like all the other Trask babies had at that age. With the tortilla-making and baby-feeding that was going on, Leo hoped no one would really miss her as she slipped out of the cabin. Henry, Luther and Uncle Jake were at the side of Henry's cabin roasting a hind-quarter of beef over an open fire. She made sure they saw her before she went to the barn. There among several of the horses, Leo could finally breathe again.

Part Four

Two Weeks Later

Chapter Twenty-Nine

Leo continued to keep to herself and worked hard all day. In the evenings she was exhausted, but still wasn't able to sleep well. Her waking moments were spent thinking about María, even though Leo avoided her during the day as best she could. It seemed easier when she did that, in the event there were moments when María wasn't in her thoughts. Unfortunately for Leo, those moments were indeed scarce. It remained important to her that no one see how much she was hurting inside. The loneliness seemed to have seeped into her bones and Leo didn't know what to do or how to find her way out of the situation she was in. As a last resort, she turned to the children for emotional comfort.

Leo invited all the children over to her cabin for the night and made a big pallet on the floor and sat down in the middle of it with them. She told stories about their father and uncles when they were little boys, and with Essie's children she had stories about their mother and their Uncle Frederick when they all lived together as children. From their expressions, Leo could tell none of Essie's sons had ever thought of their mother as a little girl. There was laughter and silliness well on into the night, and for Leo, it was a relief to not feel so alone for at least a few hours.

The next morning they all woke up early with the help of a crowing rooster. Leo made them jackcakes with sugar sprinkled on top while the children folded up the blankets and set them on the bed. After breakfast, they wanted Leo to read to them, and eventually they all went outside to play. Before long Leo was alone again. Even though the distraction was short-lived, it had been good for her.

After endless days of mending fences and herding sheep to new pastures, Leo rode the perimeter each evening until it was almost dark. It helped free up Henry to spend time with his wife and children and gave Uncle Jake an opportunity to be with Essie and his grandsons. Many nights Leo put her horse away by the light of a lantern, and as she returned to her cabin each evening, she could usually hear laughter coming from the other homes. Leo assumed everyone continued to gather at Henry's place before eventually retiring for the evening. Already there were new traditions coming into place for the Trask family.

Leo had hoped to get to the point where she could once again mingle with everyone and not feel as though her emotions were pasted all over her face. Neither of her brothers mentioned anything personal to her now, and Dell was too involved in her own family's needs to worry about anyone else's problems. As far as her cousin Essie was concerned, Leo liked the way Essie and her family had blended in so easily with the rest of them. Essie's talents as a dressmaker were coming in handy for adding frills to all the cabins. It was nice to see that Essie and her sister-in-law Sarah were finding a place for themselves within the small settlement.

One evening several days later, Leo unsaddled her horse in the barn and gave him water and grain. She brushed him down and could feel the tension melt away from her body with each brush-stroke she gave him. After a while, Leo put the brush away and let the horse out into the corral with the others. Holding her lantern high, Leo went back through the barn on her way home.

"I've been so worried about you," came María's voice near the barn door. Standing in the darkness, she was even more of an enticing mystery than Leo remembered.

"Worried about me?" Leo said. "Why?"

"I don't know. Something's not right."

Leo lowered the lantern, bringing a more direct light between them. María looked tired and drawn. A distant roar of laughter came from Henry and Dell's cabin. Leo wondered why María wasn't there with everyone else.

"I thought you might be hurt or something," María said.

"Hurt? No, I'm not hurt. I'm fine." Leo couldn't take her eyes away from this woman. It suddenly occurred to Leo what she was feeling—what all this inner turmoil was about. *It's love*, Leo thought. *I'm in love with her! Nothing else makes sense.* María was the part that had been missing from her life for so long. María was exactly what she had been looking for. Admitting her feelings lifted the burden. Loving someone else was the easy part for Leo, but admitting it and then dealing with it was totally foreign to her.

"Leona," María said softly.

Adoring the way María said her name, a shiver raced through Leo's body. "Yes?"

"Why do you treat me this way?"

Puzzled, Leo blinked in confusion. "Treat you what way?"

"I never see you. I can never talk to you anymore. I know how often you avoid me."

Again, María had managed to state the obvious. Everything María said was true.

"I didn't realize you even noticed," Leo said quietly.

"There's a lot you don't realize yet," María said. "It hurts me, Leona. I don't understand why you can't see that."

Maybe because I'm hurting so badly myself, I can't function anymore, she thought.

"The things you do affect everyone, Leona. Your family needs you," she said, then she added in a near whisper, "but most of all, I need you."

Leo felt her heart begin to swell and a thin layer of fog lift from her muddled head.

"How do you need me?" Leo asked, holding her breath as she waited for an answer.

"I need you like I've never needed anyone else before. I can say it, Leona. Unlike you, I'm not afraid of what I feel."

"I have reasons to be afraid," Leo said. "This is all very new to me."

"There's never a good reason to be afraid to love."

Leo heard someone in the distance calling María's name. It was Luther.

"They're already looking for you," Leo said with a weak smile.

"Come back with me and let's spend time with the others." María held out her hand. "Please."

Luther called María's name again; he was much closer to them now. In the light of the lantern, Leo could see María reaching out to her. It took all of Leo's strength to not go to her then.

"There you are, María," Luther said from the edge of the barn. "You have to come and tell us what you know about Sarah."

Leo's eyes never left María's. She cleared her throat to test her voice again. "What about Sarah?" Leo asked him.

"Leo!" Luther said. "Come on over to Henry's place. We're all there. María, you have to tell me what you see happening for Sarah. She's the one you mentioned to me before. I just know she is! Sarah has to be the one."

After a moment, María said, "Please, Leona. Come and join us at Henry's cabin."

❧

Henry and Dell's cabin was warm and full of chatter when they arrived. Everyone was gathered around the table and moved chairs to make room for Leo. Dell found a clean plate for her and pointed toward the stove where the food was being kept.

"Sit here this time, María," Luther said as he pulled out a chair for her.

Leo saw dirty dishes stacked on a small table by the fireplace; everyone else had apparently had supper already. She didn't see any of the children, so it had to be later than she realized if they were asleep already.

"María knows a lot of things," Leo heard Luther say. She glanced over at María, who was sitting between Luther and Uncle Jake at the table. Leo's earlier conversation with her in the barn was still playing itself over in her head. If Luther hadn't come looking for María when he did, Leo wondered if they would have shared a kiss. *So it's possible she wants the same thing I do*, Leo thought. It wasn't often she even allowed herself to indulge into that line of thinking. Once again Leo could feel that dark cloud of sadness slowly beginning to lift. Her heart felt lighter and her thoughts were more positive as she took a seat at the table and watched as her family playfully interrogated María in order to coax new information from her.

"What about Uncle Jake?" Henry asked María. "Do you have any impressions of him?"

María studied Jake for a moment. Her smile was so endearing that Leo felt a nice warmth spread through her.

"I sense a young person in him," María said. "Jake is kind and loves his family. He regrets many things in his past and wants to make up for the bad decisions he made long ago."

All eyes were on Uncle Jake now; the room was very quiet. He looked uncomfortable having such deeply personal things revealed about him.

"I also see him as a man who will do whatever it takes to make the lives of his family meaningful," María said. "Jake still has much to do and will give his grandsons the kind of attention he thinks he failed to give his own children. Jake is a man who will always have a young outlook and a kind heart."

Everyone in the room remained quiet, then Essie got up and gave her father a hug.

"I wonder if she knows about that skeeter bite on my backside," Jake said as Essie kissed him on the cheek before returning to her seat.

The laughter eased some of the tension at the table.

"For Essie," María said, "I see many new things ahead."

Everyone turned to look at Essie now. "I just want my boys to be safe," she said.

As Leo looked at her cousin, she noticed how the sadness was no longer as evident in her eyes. Essie brought something new and refreshing to Eagle Canyon, and Leo hoped she would learn to love it there as much as the rest of them did.

"Tell us what you see, María," Dell said. "What lies ahead for Essie?"

María once again became the focus of everyone in the room. All heads were turned in her direction.

"For Essie," María said, "the fear of being alone . . . the fear of raising her children without their father . . . both of those fears will gradually go away."

Essie's expression changed as María seemed to pique her interest. She tilted her head to the side as if that would help her listen better. After a moment she said to her father, "Yes, Papa. If María knows about my fears, then she probably does know about that mosquito bite on your backside."

Once again, the low chuckles that went around the table helped everyone relax a little. As Leo slowly continued to eat warm boiled potatoes and smoked ham, she could see the weariness in Essie's expression begin to slip away. María's words had not been specific, but somehow more comforting than anything else. Essie's pain was deep and certainly life-altering, but María had given her hope its intensity would not last forever.

"What about Sarah?" Luther asked. "What do you see happening for Sarah?"

The young woman blushed under the attention now being given to her. Leo smiled at Luther's determination to get as much information about Sarah as he could.

"Sarah has a shyness about her that is often mistaken for something else," María said. "There is sadness caused by her brother's passing. She also loves her brother's children and has been a comfort to them."

Essie reached over and squeezed Sarah's hand. "She's been a comfort to me as well."

With a hint of impatience, Luther said, "What else?"

Leo watched as María took her time looking at Sarah, as if trying to see inside of her or read the young woman's thoughts. It was the first time Leo noticed such a direct attempt at sizing up an individual. Things usually seemed to come to María so easily.

"Sarah will find love," María said after a moment, "and she will have many new decisions to make."

"Love?" Sarah said as if the word was foreign to her. "Oh, goodness."

"New decisions?" Luther asked. "What decisions?"

"Luther," María said. "I'm sorry I don't have answers. I'm only telling what I feel . . . what I sense about someone. It could mean nothing."

"Got any feelings about rain tomorrow, María?" Uncle Jake asked. "We could sure use it."

Leo could see the relief on María's face at the sudden change in subject. Leo also noticed that the question about the weather set Luther off into a full-fledged pout.

"I'm sometimes able to sense a change in the weather," María said. "There will be rain soon."

"Well, I'm tired," Uncle Jake said. "Me and my skeeter bite are goin' home to bed."

"Me, too," Essie said. "I'll walk with you." To Dell she said, "I'll come and get my boys in the morning. Thanks for letting them stay here tonight."

After Uncle Jake and Essie left, Henry was the next one to go to bed. Leo, however, couldn't bring herself to go home yet. Being there with María was the only thing she could think about right then.

"Just like our house-mouse days, Leo," Luther said as he put scraps in the slop bucket for the hogs.

Leo smiled at him and dried the plate Dell handed to her. Luther was showing off a little for Sarah, who was helping him stack the dirty dishes, but Leo liked seeing him happy and finally interested in someone. With Sarah there to keep him busy, it would hopefully mean Luther was no longer smitten with María.

"House-mouse?" Sarah said. "Is that like an ordinary mouse?"

Leo, Dell and Luther laughed.

"An ordinary mouse in the house?" Sarah asked, seeming to enjoy the sound those particular words made together. She brought more dirty dishes over to the washtub for Dell.

"There's nothing ordinary about a house-mouse," Dell said. "I have Leo to thank for so many things."

Luther nodded. "So do I."

María came in from another room where one of the children had been crying. She closed the door and immediately met Leo's gaze. Leo was thrilled being in the same room with her again, but suddenly having María's attention made Leo's heart skip a beat.

"Someone had a bad dream," María said.

Dell handed Leo another plate to dry. "Thank you, María," Dell said. "You're so good with the children. The baby should be waking up soon."

Leo put the dried dishes away on the shelf next to where the spices were kept. She watched as María wiped the table down with a damp cloth. Her black hair framed her face and made her look so young. The graceful way she moved each time she leaned over was enough to keep Leo mesmerized for a few moments.

"That's everything," Luther said. "I'll walk Sarah home." He put on his hat and opened the door for her.

"Good night," Sarah said to the others.

As if on cue, the baby began to cry in another room and María went to get him. Leo stayed long enough to see a hungry little Milton when María came back with him. Leo pushed all the chairs closer to the table in an attempt to prolong her stay, but Dell and María were visibly tired and no doubt wanted nothing more than to feed the baby and get themselves settled for the night.

"I'll see you both tomorrow," Leo said, and left the cabin without really wanting to. Once out into the cool, night air, Leo could smell the smoke from a fireplace and heard the low snort of a horse in the corral. As she followed the path that would take her home, she could see Luther and Sarah in front of Essie's cabin. The moon made a romantic silhouette as they shared a kiss. Leo stopped to watch them until Sarah finally pulled away from Luther and went inside. Leo felt several new emotions roaring through her body as she watched her younger brother walk back to his cabin with a new glide in his stride. *Could that have been our little Luther's first kiss?* she wondered. Leo was both happy for him and at the same time envious of him. *How easy it is for men and women*, she thought. *They find each other in such simple ways.*

Leo was also conscious of how seeing that kiss had sparked something new inside of her. She felt sad at the thought of possibly never experiencing such a thing again, and she felt a sense of longing over wanting to share something that intimate with María. Whatever feelings Cordy's kiss had inspired in Leo those many months ago were nothing compared to merely being in the same room with María now. Cordy had set the wheels in motion so that Leo would wake up and realize what it meant to feel desire for someone. María, however, had given Leo a potent dose of something so electrifying that Leo was having trouble concentrating and functioning whenever María was near. Cordy's kiss had been the spark, but María Montoya and her incredibly sensuous nature was a raging inferno.

231

Leo made her way to her cabin by the light of the moon as it peeked through the clouds once again. Her thoughts were with María and their earlier conversation in the barn that evening. As Leo prepared herself for bed, the other vision that kept rattling around in her head was of María leaning over the table earlier as she brought the damp rag carefully over its surface.

Leo got into bed and wondered what the morning would bring.

Chapter Thirty

The sound of children playing woke Leo up the next morning. She dressed for the day and answered the knock on her door a while later.

"Breakfast is here," Luther announced. He came in with a plate containing ham and jackcakes.

"You're smilin' mighty big this morning," she said with a grin.

"Sarah likes me," Luther said. "I can't think about anything else. I'm too excited to sleep or eat. My insides get all jumpy whenever I'm close to her." His eyes seemed to sparkle as he spoke. The one thing about her younger brother that reminded Leo the most about her father was how expressive his eyes became when he told a story. It made Leo happy seeing him this way.

"All I want to do is follow her around and listen to her talk, Leo. Hear her laugh and make her smile!"

Leo found it interesting how different she and her younger

brother were. Luther had embraced things with Sarah—the walks in the evening, constant dialog and easy laughter, while she herself had avoided almost all contact with María.

"This has to be love, Leo," he said. "I remember when Earl first told me how he felt about Hattie. He said I'd know what it was like some day. It makes so much sense to me now. Love can make a person do things they never thought possible before." He sat down at the table and took the napkin off the plate of food for her. "I know why Earl and Eb had to leave Eagle Canyon the way they did. I don't think I'm mad at them anymore."

In the beginning when the twins decided to leave Eagle Canyon and make new lives for themselves and their brides, Leo didn't like the idea at all, but eventually she accepted their decision to leave. Earl's new wife was from El Paso where her father owned a large cattle ranch. It was an offer for legitimate employment and a chance to some day have such a spread of his own. Earl begged the rest of them to come with him, but Eb and his new wife were the only ones willing to go. At the time, young Luther had struggled with his own decision about whether or not to leave his home. Leo didn't encourage any of them to seek new lives away from the family, but let each of them make their own decision. Once Luther decided to stay at Eagle Canyon, he had taken the twins' departure the hardest, and seemed to finally be coming to terms with his anger at them for leaving.

"So now you're in love like Earl was," Leo said.

Luther shrugged. "All I know is—if Earl felt this way about Hattie—the way I feel right now about Sarah, then there's nothing that will stand in my way, Leo. I'll do whatever it takes to have her and keep her."

"Even if it means leaving Eagle Canyon?"

Luther met Leo's steady gaze across the table and nodded. "Even if it means leaving Eagle Canyon."

❧❧

Leo and Uncle Jake rode the fence line in the back pasture later that morning. Fences were in constant need of repair due to cows rubbing on the posts or poking their heads through to try and get to the grass just barely out of reach on the other side. The Trasks kept different areas fenced off so the grass in adjoining pastures would continue to grow. A unanimous decision to not raise more sheep had only recently been addressed again with the same old arguments.

"They eat the grass all the way down to the roots," Leo said.

"And they stink," Uncle Jake added.

By late afternoon, Leo felt satisfied that all fences had been adequately repaired and the herd would stay put for a while longer. She was tired and looking forward to winding down for the day.

"It's time to get busy in the garden again," Jake said. "I'll get Luther started on working the ground for that tomorrow."

They both looked up at the sound of a rider coming toward them. It was María riding her horse bareback.

"What's the matter?" Leo called, alarmed.

"Something's not right," María said. She stopped her horse and had a worried, drawn look on her beautiful face. "At first I thought something had happened to you, but now I see you are safe."

"Is everyone else all right?" Jake asked. She had his attention as well.

María closed her eyes and became very still. She shook her head and then opened her eyes again. "Someone's hurt, Leona. I can sense it."

"Who?" Leo asked.

"I don't know," María said as she turned her horse around. "It's not one of us. Someone's hurt outside Eagle Canyon."

Leo and Uncle Jake followed her to the front entrance. Once they got there, Jake opened the gate and followed them out. The three of them picked their way through the brush for about twenty minutes before María stopped and slid from her horse. Jake was to the left of Leo.

235

"What's that over there?" he asked as he squinted. The brush was too thick to really go any farther on horseback. Leo and Jake got off their horses and followed María.

"Over here!" María yelled.

"It's Cordy," Leo heard Jake shout after a moment.

Leo had been searching in another area and hurried toward the sound of their voices.

"She's been shot," María said, "but she's alive. Help me get her on my horse."

In one graceful motion, María was sitting on the horse and reaching down for Cordy. Leo and Jake struggled to hoist Cordy's limp body up to her. Then with a firm grip on the horse's mane and an arm around Cordy, María took off riding back to the gate.

"You follow them," Leo said. "I'll look for Cordy's horse and be right along."

Finding Cordy's horse was no easy task, but she heard him snort and eventually located him in the thick brush. By the time Leo returned to the gate, she could see the chaos up ahead in the cabin area. She closed and secured the gate, then led Cordy's horse to the barn. There was blood on the saddle and the horse's withers, but it was Cordy's blood and not the horse's. After some water and grain, Leo turned it loose in the corral with the others. Noticing María's horse in front of Essie's cabin, Leo ran over there to see how Cordy was doing.

"She's lost a lot of blood," Uncle Jake said in a detached, solemn tone. "No telling how long she's been out there."

"But she's alive," Leo reminded him with a sigh.

"She took a bullet in the shoulder, looks like," Jake said.

Seeing that there were plenty of people to help already, Leo found a rope and slipped it around the neck of María's horse. She led it back to the barn and then put it in the corral with the others. Leo then got on her own horse and rode back to the front gate again. *Did Cordy get shot somewhere else and then try to find her way to Eagle Canyon?* she wondered. *Or was Cordy on her way here and got shot before she reached us?* Leo wanted to check the area where they had found her to see if she could find any signs of other riders. *We would've heard a shot this close,* she thought once she got to the right place again. Several feet away from a pool of drying blood, Leo noticed Cordy's saddlebag. She got off her horse and picked it up. As she expected, it was crammed full of money.

By the time Leo finished her riding chores for the day, she was too tired to do anything but tend to her horse and find her way to Essie's cabin to see how Cordy was doing. Leo was uneasy about the location where they had found Cordy. If others were out there looking for her, it was possible they could find Eagle Canyon. Riding the perimeter and continuing their checks on the outside were even more important now.

Leo knocked on the door to Essie's cabin; Sarah answered it and let her in. Cordy was lying on one of the children's beds in the corner asleep. Leo noticed Cordy's shirt was off and her shoulder was wrapped in a large white bandage.

"How is she?" Leo quietly asked her cousin.

"She'll be fine if there's no infection," Essie said. "She's drifting in and out of it now."

"Let her know I found her saddlebag," Leo said. "I have it if she asks about it." Leo glanced over at the corner of the room again. This time she saw María kneeling beside Cordy's bed. A streak of jealousy ran through Leo's heart that was so fierce it nearly made her gasp. Seeing them together felt like a blow to Leo's entire being. María's obvious concern and love for Cordy was too much to take in and deal with right then.

"How do you know this woman?" Essie asked her.

Leo forced herself to look away from Cordy's bed. "She's a friend of the family's," Leo said. "Your father knew her first, actually."

Then Leo heard what she thought was Spanish being spoken. It was Cordy's voice initially, then Leo heard María answer her in Spanish.

"She's awake," Essie said. "That's a good sign!"

As their low voices continued in the corner of the room, Leo could feel a queasiness in her stomach. The light was gone from her eyes, and her heart felt empty and cold.

"Whose idea was it to bring her here?" Leo finally asked. Her voice was husky and filled with emotion. "To your cabin?" She could hear more Spanish being spoken, and it made the jealousy bubble up into her throat. The way Cordy and María were speaking to each other made it sound so intimate and personal. *They've been lovers,* she reminded herself. *And now they're together again.*

While Essie was explaining something about being familiar with caring for sick people, all Leo could do was think about Cordy and María together. It was an imaginary visual that she couldn't shake. *And here Cordy is again,* Leo thought. *She comes back and everything changes.*

Cordy seemed to be fully awake now, and the conversation in Spanish continued on to the point where Leo couldn't stand to hear another word of it.

"Does she speak English at all?" Essie asked her, confused.

"Yes," Leo said. "She speaks English." She had to get out of there. "I'm going home," Leo said. "Cordy's in good hands here. Thanks for all you've done." She was suddenly tired, disappointed, and felt as though her heart was breaking.

She left Essie's cabin and walked home—too tired and depressed to even cry right then. She got to her place and lit the lantern. *It's getting dark already,* she thought. *Everything's happening so fast! One minute things are fine and the next minute it's all falling down around me.*

Leo washed her face and hands, and felt sad at the way Cordy's arrival had changed everything so quickly. *I'm glad Cordy will be all right,* Leo thought, *but having her here now can't possibly be good. María and Essie will patch her up again, and then María will want to leave with her. That's the way I'll lose María. I knew it would happen somehow. I just hoped it wouldn't be so soon.*

Leo built a small fire to get the chill out of the room. She sat down at the table and stared at the flames. As if in slow motion, she remembered the first time she saw María at the well in San Benito. María had been shy then, but also determined to get to know Leo. The memories continued as she peered into the glowing coals in the fireplace. After a while, Leo finally got up and took off her boots. She tossed another stick of wood on the coals, then got undressed and slipped into her nightgown. Leo couldn't stop remembering the cadence of Spanish that was stuck in her head. She could only imagine what María and Cordy had been saying to each other then. With her mind still racing, Leo knew she wouldn't be able to sleep no matter how tired she was. She tried blaming all this uncertainty on Cordy, but in her heart she knew that wasn't fair either. Leo was glad Cordy would be all right. *She's gone off and gotten herself shot,* Leo thought. *Cordy could have died out there if María hadn't found her.*

Eventually Leo allowed herself to think about María again and how much she loved being around her. *She almost kissed me in the barn last night.* And with that thought, tears filled Leo's eyes and scampered down her cheeks. *And now you've lost her.* She took a deep, painful breath. A sob caught in her throat. *You've lost her before you even had her.*

Leo jumped at the sound of footsteps on her porch. She dabbed her eyes on the sleeve of her gown before answering the light knock on her door. She didn't want to see anyone now, but with her lantern lit, there was no way to hide the fact that she was awake. She slowly opened the door to find María standing there.

"Leona," she said.

On impulse, Leo pulled her into the cabin and closed the door. María reached up and took Leo's face in her hands and kissed her deeply. Leo could feel a swirling dizziness take over her body as María's lips touched hers. Leo had never wanted anything the way she wanted this woman. María's mouth was soft and eager, while Leo's knees became weak as her body churned with want and desire. María took her lips away and looked into Leo's eyes.

"You've been crying," she whispered, then gently brushed the tears away with her fingers.

Leo didn't want to talk. She couldn't have spoken anyway. She kissed María again, and María's arms tightened around her. Leo never wanted the kiss to stop . . . she wanted to hold her this way forever.

María covered Leo's face with scores of tiny kisses and then finally rested her head against Leo's chest.

"I'm so tired," María whispered after a moment. "I'm so very, very tired."

Leo took María by the hand and led her toward the bed.

"Get undressed," Leo said. "I'll find you something to wear."

"That won't be necessary."

Leo went to pour fresh water in the basin for her and found the nightgown her mother used to wear. Sometimes Leo wore it when the nights were chilly. She turned out the light from the lantern, then stoked the fire, which gave the cabin a nice warm glow. Leaving the fire, Leo sat down at the table with her back to María and the bed. The fluttering in her stomach from María being in the same room with her made Leo feel almost lightheaded with excitement. Even though the memory of their kiss kept her trembling with desire, Leo wasn't sure what would happen next.

She could hear the rustling of clothing, then the sound of water from the basin being used. Leo continued to stare at the glowing coals in the fireplace, and imagined herself sitting there all night in that same exact position—almost paralyzed from nervousness and anticipation. Once she realized there were no more water sounds coming from the basin, she closed her eyes and took a deep breath. *Is she asleep already?* Leo wondered. In a way she almost hoped so, then in another way she hoped not. *If she is,* Leo thought, *I can sleep here.* She looked down at the table where her hands were folded. *You should be tired enough to be able to sleep anywhere right now.*

"Leona," María whispered from behind her, close to Leo's ear.

Leo opened her eyes and felt the scampering of goose bumps down her arms. Her breathing was shallow and her heart was beating as though she had been running for hours. María's arms slid around her from behind, pulling Leo close. María gently moved Leo's long hair before kissing the side of her neck. Leo could hear her own ragged breath as pure desire scorched its way through her body. She had never felt so alive.

María pulled her up from the chair and slowly turned her around. Leo's eyes were closed again as fresh tears rolled down her cheeks.

"Please, look at me," María whispered.

Leo took another deep breath and did as she was told. She saw María's eyes, dark and searching, and noticed they were also brimming with tears. Her shoulders were bare, then Leo realized María was naked.

"Are you afraid?" María asked.

Leo felt such joy at that moment she couldn't speak, but she managed to smile and shake her head. She had no idea what would happen next, but whatever was involved, she wanted to be a part of it.

María leaned forward and kissed the corner of Leo's mouth, then slipped the nightgown over her head. Once they were both naked, María touched Leo's cheek with the back of her hand as her eyes continued exploring Leo's face. She let her fingers make a slow trail over Leo's cheek and then down along her throat. She moved her hand to Leo's right breast, before leaning over to take a nipple into her mouth.

Heat and desire seared their way through Leo's body. She closed her eyes again and heard a moan escape from her throat. Leo put her hands in María's dark mass of curls just as María's tongue circled first one then the other taut nipple. After a moment, she raised her head and kissed Leo with such passion it left them both breathless.

"You're the one," María whispered between slow, deep kisses. "I knew you were the one I've been waiting for."

Like a tiny miracle, Leo felt the exact same way as she sensed the heat radiating from María's body. Touching María and being touched by her was all that mattered any longer. With nipples aching to be sucked again, Leo put her arms around her and felt María's warm, soft skin against her own for the very first time. There was a sense of completeness for her as their bodies touched. Leo knew in her heart she would remember this moment for the rest of her life.

"Come to bed with me, Leona," María said. She took Leo by the hand and led her to the bed. "Don't be afraid."

Leo got in bed beside her. "I'm not afraid," she said, surprised at the truth behind the words.

María smiled and gently touched the side of her face again. "I'm not as tired as I thought," she said. Her hand moved up into Leo's hair. "Let me show you how much I want this."

Ready to surrender her heart and her body to this woman, Leo was once again at a loss for words. María urged her down on the bed and searched Leo's face as if memorizing each tiny detail. For the first time ever, Leo felt cherished by someone. She could see it in María's eyes . . . the way she looked at her and studied her. Leo could also feel it in the caress of those thin, curious fingers each time she touched her.

"Let me show you how much I want you," María whispered as she slowly leaned down to kiss her on the lips. "Let me show you how much I love you," she said. Her soft lips moved to Leo's chin and then made their way to her throat again.

Leo's shallow breathing became ragged and halting as María continued to kiss her body. As if Leo's hands had a mind of their own, she reached for María's breast and heard a delightful moan fill the air. Leo wasn't sure which one of them made the sound, but it was something she wanted to hear over and over again as the night went on. It was a sound she could spend the rest of her life hearing if given the chance.

❧

Leo couldn't get enough of her. She loved the way María's body fit against hers and the way their kisses made Leo tingle with anticipation. María raised herself up with her arms and let their nipples barely touch. Dragging her long soft hair across Leo's skin became the focus for them both for several enticing moments. Leo felt as though she was being kissed by more than María's lips and mouth. Leo loved the way María used her body to bring them both alive. Like the smooth gentle placing of velvet against her skin, Leo wondered how she had lived so long without experiencing the touch of another woman. She would never be the same after this. Her life and her heart were now changed forever.

Leo could feel more tears of happiness on the way as María nuzzled her neck and shoulder. María's touches sent a wave of wonderful chills washing over sensitive flesh. Leo was consumed with sensation and overwhelmed with love.

"Open your legs," María whispered. "Wrap them around me."

Leo did as she was told and immediately felt a direct, pulsating pleasure spread through her body at their newly enhanced closeness.

"Can you feel me?"

"Yes," Leo whispered. "Yes, yes . . . "

Then as if the mere physical connection between them wasn't enough, María began to move against her in a slow, rocking motion. Immediately swept away with warmth and passion, Leo became alive all over again. Her body began to move on its own in a primitive, erotic dance. Leo put her hands around María's back and pulled her body closer. The connection was intense and powerful. Their movements slowly became more demanding as the tension and pleasure began to build, until a frantic release exploded from the very center of her being. Leo's body shook with such pleasure she thought her heart would pound its way out of her chest.

Leo could only utter bits and pieces of syllables and sounds as María continued to move against her. When it was over, Leo lay beneath her exhausted, but so emphatically happy that the tears were automatic. The tenderness of María's touch as she searched Leo's face and eyes was almost overwhelming. Leo hugged María tightly and was afraid to let go of her. Once again she didn't know what to say to her, so she expressed her emotions by kissing María in a deep, breath-taking exchange of tears and soft laughter.

"You are a very passionate woman, Leona."

Leo hugged her again, then rolled María over on her back. "Whatever that was, I want more of it." The words had just popped out of her mouth. It was uncharacteristic of her to be so vocal about her feelings and desires.

María laughed delightedly and tucked Leo's hair behind her ear.

"Teach me everything," Leo said. She felt reborn and almost invincible. Being with María this way had truly opened her eyes to how lonely she had been all this time. "I want you to feel the way I do this very moment."

"How I feel . . . " María whispered, her voice brimming with emotion. She reached up and brushed more tears from Leo's cheek. "If you only knew how happy you've just made me."

There was such a huge sense of relief that left Leo's body. She wanted to be all things for her, to include being a friend and a lover. "Show me how to touch you," Leo said. "Show me how to love you. Teach me everything."

"Everything?" María repeated with the hint of a smile as she kissed Leo on the lips.

"Yes, everything," Leo whispered. "Teach me tonight and every night from now on." She kissed her again and whispered, "Every night until I take my last dying breath."

Chapter Thirty-One

Cordy woke up to a throbbing shoulder and grumbling in her stomach. The cabin was dark and cold, and she had no idea how late it was or even how long she had been there. The cabin sounds were strange to her—no crickets chirping, no hooting owls and no raccoons or skunks rustling in a near-by bush. All she heard was light snoring coming from the other side of the room.

As she tried to get comfortable on the bed, her body seemed to be reminding her that things were not as they should be. The pain in her shoulder was nonstop, but the other dilemma that would be facing her soon was her need to get outside or find an outhouse somewhere.

"María," she whispered into the darkness. *"Donde está?"*

She didn't get an answer, and since María didn't snore, Cordy knew there were others besides María also sleeping in the cabin. At some point earlier, she vaguely remembered waking up and hearing women and children talking; however, Cordy hadn't recognized any of their voices. She felt alone and helpless now; both feelings were new and unsettling for her.

The next thing Cordy knew, a crowing rooster woke her up and it was light enough to see inside the cabin now. The arrival of morning made her feel less uneasy and vulnerable. Across the room Cordy could see a bed with three little shaggy heads poking out from under the covers. There was another bed with at least one blond-headed adult in it. Cordy tried to sit up, but the stabbing pain in her shoulder brought tears to her eyes. She also had pain in her back. *Did I get shot more than once?* she wondered suddenly. *Why is my back hurting so badly?*

With nothing more than pure determination and grit, she managed to throw the quilt off. Cordy was glad to see her trousers were still on, but had no idea where her boots were. She looked down at the bandage wrapped around her shoulder and entire chest and ribs, leaving only her right arm free from the binding. She wondered where her shirt was. Her immediate concern now became getting dressed and finding the closest outhouse. Hopefully she could accomplish that without waking up anyone.

After getting out from under the quilt, she rested for a few minutes. Cordy was counting on her boots and shirt being somewhere close to the bed. She didn't want to waste too much precious strength and energy on having to look for clothes. She finally convinced herself that sitting up was the key to success at the moment. Once she accomplished that, the remainder of her plan was possible.

Then from the other side of the room, Cordy heard a female voice say, "It's cold in here."

"I know," another woman quietly agreed. "Whose turn is it to start the fire?"

After hearing a giggle and then the creaking of a bed, Cordy could see someone getting up, but she still didn't recognize either of their voices. *Maybe María's still sleeping,* she thought. From her peripheral vision Cordy saw someone scurry over to the fireplace where the coals had been banked for the night. The woman wore a long white nightgown and had dark hair that hung loosely at her shoulders. She put a few sticks on the coals, then pulled a coat over her nightgown. With the two women more than likely up for the day now, Cordy realized it was too late to try and get out of bed on her own without being seen. Unable to wait any longer, she tried to sit up again. The effort made sweat pop out on her forehead.

"Good morning," the woman by the fireplace said. "You're finally awake." She came over to the bed and put an arm around Cordy's back to help her sit up. Cordy managed to slowly swing her feet to the side without passing out. She sat on the edge of the bed and already felt totally exhausted from her efforts. Her lower back hurt and she was stiff and sore all over.

"Good morning," Cordy said.

"How are you feeling?"

Cordy wanted to lie down again, but she couldn't. She had to get outside. "Where are my boots?" Her voice was so low and weak, Cordy wasn't sure the woman had heard her question. "I need them. I need . . . to go . . . " Suddenly, she felt dizzy and nauseous, and gripped the edge of the bed.

The other woman was out of bed now and brought Cordy's boots to her. They were both beautiful women, but Cordy was too ill to fully appreciate them right then. It did occur to her that the woman who was keeping her steady on the side of the bed reminded her of Leo. *But she's much kinder than Leo would be in this situation*, Cordy thought. Had she not been so close to fainting, she might have laughed, but instead she asked where her shirt was.

The two women exchanged a look and then seemed to answer each other with a shrug.

"Where's María?" Cordy asked. *María will help me*, she thought. Then she wondered why María had left her alone with these strangers in the first place!

"She's at Henry's, I'm sure," the first woman said. "I'm Essie, Jake's daughter, and this is Sarah."

"Jake's daughter?" Cordy said. If her shoulder hadn't hurt so badly and her bladder hadn't been about to pop, she would have enjoyed the introductions. There had been many nights when Jake had talked about his children over a campfire. Cordy felt as though she knew Essie and Frederick already. *No wonder she looks so much like Leo*, Cordy thought.

Essie helped her put on the boots, while Sarah searched for Cordy's shirt.

"There's dried blood all over it," Sarah said apologetically.

"And a bullet hole," Essie added with a frown. "We can find something else for you to wear later. Do you think you can stand up?"

"Yes," Cordy said. She was determined to do it no matter how hard or painful it proved to be. At that particular moment, the alternative was not an option. She had to get to an outhouse soon.

Essie moved to Cordy's right side and then helped her stand up while Sarah draped the shirt over Cordy's shoulders and helped her get her right arm in the sleeve. With the bandage covering the entire upper portion of her torso and having her left arm immobile and snug against her chest, Cordy's greatest fear now became the posiblity of not being able to take care of some of her most personal needs. More sweat formed on her brow and upper lip as Sarah fastened as many of the buttons on the shirt as she could. Nothing was exposed other than Cordy's tan neck. Essie and Cordy stood there beside the bed until Cordy finally felt well enough to try and walk.

"Lean against me," Essie said.

Cordy did as she was told, and by the time they were out on the porch, she could hear the rumble of thunder off in the distance. Together they maneuvered the steps on the porch, and once Cordy was standing in the yard she took a deep breath and rested against Essie for a moment.

"I can make it now," she said.

"Are you sure?"

"Yes. Thank you."

As Cordy shuffled along on her own toward the outhouse, she could see various members of the Trask family venturing out of their cabins. All she wanted right then was an empty bladder and to see María again. María would take care of her.

After insisting on not getting any help from Essie, Cordy spent a good thirty minutes taking care of business and getting her trousers up enough to walk back to the cabin. Luther met her along the way and helped her get to the front porch where they sat down while Cordy rested.

"Where's María?" she asked him.

Luther scuffed the toe of his boot into the dirt. As she waited for an answer, Cordy caught the scent of fried bacon in the air and was grateful that her stomach didn't growl again.

"She's been staying at Henry's place and helping Dell with the children."

The cabin door opened and Luther jumped up and turned around to see who was there. He snatched off his hat and smiled.

"Sarah," he said with a nod. "Mornin'."

Surprised at his sudden movement, Cordy looked at him and watched as Luther nervously fingered the brim of his hat. *He looks like Milton*, she thought. It had been quite a while since she'd thought about Milton and her Pa. Those were painful times for her, and Cordy didn't dwell on it much anymore.

"Good morning, Luther," Sarah said as she came down the steps, her long skirt swooshing as she walked. "Can we help you inside?" she asked Cordy.

Having rested awhile, she nodded and thought she would be able to make it up the steps and back inside the cabin now. The thunder was getting closer and sounded more angry. Cordy let Luther help her up the steps; they slowly made their way into the cabin just as it started to rain.

"Good morning, Luther," Essie said once they were inside. She was dressed and tending to the bacon in a skillet on the stove. "Have you had breakfast?"

"Not yet."

"Might as well stay 'til the rain lets up." Then to Cordy, Essie said, "You must be hungry."

"Luther's here!" one of the little boys in the bed yelled excitedly. All three of them scrambled up.

Cordy eased back down on her bed in the corner and at least didn't have to worry about soiling her clothes any longer. She lay there listening to the rain, the children's laughter as they played with Luther, and the chatter of female voices. *So much noise,* she thought. *I'm not used to hearing so much noise this early . . . or being around so many people at one time!*

Cordy didn't know how long she would have to be there at Eagle Canyon, but the prospects were not looking good right then. *I can barely dress myself,* she thought. *How long will it be before I can saddle a horse or load a pistol on my own?*

"Here's something to eat," Essie said. She sat on the edge of the bed and had bite-size pieces of thick bacon already cut up for her on the plate. Next to the bacon was a hot, fluffy biscuit. "I'm sure you're in a lot of pain and can't find a comfortable position in that bed. If there's anything I can do to help, please let me know."

"Thank you," Cordy said. She chewed on a piece of bacon and couldn't remember anything tasting so good. Having a beautiful woman sitting so close to her almost made Cordy forget about such things as not being able to move her left arm, the stiff muscles in her legs and the pain in her back. Essie was indeed pretty enough to make Cordy wish for a slow recovery. *Well, almost,* she thought.

Chapter Thirty-Two

Leo woke up the next morning to the sound of thunder in the distance and with María's arm around her waist as their bodies relaxed in a nice, comfortable spooning position. Memories of their night together made Leo smile and feel warm and peaceful inside. With the arrival of rain, they had an excuse to stay in bed a bit longer. Leo wanted to wake up like this every morning—with María beside her after a night of passion.

She turned over and kissed the corner of María's mouth. María smiled in her sleep and slowly stretched herself more awake. As the quilt slid away and exposed their bodies to the morning chill, Leo could see María's breasts as she continued to stretch and nestle against Leo's soft, warm skin.

"How did you sleep, Leona?" she asked in her early-morning voice. María touched the end of Leo's nose with the tip of her finger before moving a wisp of hair away from her eyes. María's finger then slowly traveled from Leo's temple, down along her jaw line, easily inching its way to her bottom lip as she outlined Leo's mouth with a delicate caress.

Leo stopped breathing and tilted her head back, the thumping of her heart beginning all over again. She parted her lips and touched her tongue to María's finger, taking it in her mouth gently . . . easily.

Feeling an urgency for more, Leo wanted to recapture the magic they had created the night before.

Leo's body responded as María leaned forward and kissed her, lightly at first, and then hungrily as the kiss grew deeper. It was like falling into a swirling cloud of desire and emotion. Leo felt the tumbling begin at the very center of her being . . . the need to be wanted and possessed by this woman. Time had no meaning for her now; nothing beyond this moment mattered any longer. Leo opened her lips and offered her tongue. As if being kissed for the first time, the softness was as new and precious as she imagined it would always be for her.

María's hands moved through Leo's hair and continued along the back of her neck, pulling her closer with slow, breathtaking abandon. They broke away from each other long enough for Leo to explore her throat and the soft hollow of María's neck. María said Leo's name in a whisper, and Leo found her mouth again, needing no further encouragement. Making love to this woman had suddenly become the new priority in Leo's life. She would make María happy any way she could, and she was willing to do whatever it took to make sure that happened.

Leo made breakfast for them, and she could tell that María found it incredibly sweet.

"No one but my mother has ever cooked for me," María said with a warm smile.

"I don't cook that often," Leo said. "It's usually too much trouble for one person."

"You like having others bring you food."

Leo laughed. "That's their choice. I just don't discourage them."

Leo didn't want their time together to end that morning. It certainly made her appreciate the rain more as it continued to beat against the roof. There wouldn't be as much activity at Eagle Canyon that day, at least through most of the morning, but as María pointed out, there were still chores to be done.

"The chickens will be looking for me and the cows need to be milked," María said as she came up behind Leo and put her arms around her waist. She kissed the back of Leo's neck, sending a delightful chill racing through her body.

While thick slices of ham sizzled in the skillet, Leo and María shared slow, lingering kisses by the stove. Leo loved the way María touched her hair and would occasionally suck gently on her tongue while they kissed. María could be possessive and giving, and suggestive and subtle all at the same time. She was an attentive lover, and eager to please as well as teach all she knew.

Leo tugged at María's bottom lip with her teeth, and closed her mind to everything but loving her. She couldn't imagine being anywhere else at that moment. Her life had been so shallow and empty before learning what it meant to be really loved by someone other than her family.

"I was afraid you wouldn't allow this," María whispered as she nuzzled Leo's neck again.

"I adore this."

The pop and sizzle of the ham cooking brought them back to the present. With a shy smile Leo suggested they eat breakfast from opposite sides of the table. Touching her was too tempting, but at least this way Leo could see her and remind herself that it was all very real.

They had to make an appearance and attempt some semblance of normalcy before the morning was over. Even though staying in bed and making love all day was a tempting thought, it wasn't something they could do.

"I must see how Cordelia is before I start my day," María said.

Cordy, Leo thought. *How could I have forgotten about Cordy?!*

After a moment, Leo said, "I was wondering about tonight." She pulled on her boots and felt nervous for the first time since their initial kiss the evening before. "You'll stay with me tonight, won't you?"

"Of course I will."

Leo felt the relief and worry gradually leave her body. They got dressed and shared a lingering kiss by the door. Leo didn't want to let go of her.

"While you're doing your work today," María said, "think about being with me again tonight."

Leo was surprised as another shiver raced through her. María kissed her again and then left the cabin. Leo watched her step lightly around little puddles on the way to Essie's cabin.

"What happened to you?" Jake asked Leo a while later when she got to the barn. Jake and Luther were repositioning barrels at the side of the barn to capture the rainwater streaming off the roof.

She looked down at her clothes, but didn't see anything unusual other than a little mud on her boots. "Nothing. Why?"

He raised his eyebrows and playfully cut his eyes over in Luther's direction.

"She's smiling," Uncle Jake said to Luther. "When's the last time you saw your sister smile?"

"Not since that day the bull ran Henry up a tree," Luther said with a hearty laugh.

Leo shook her head, but she couldn't stop herself from laughing along with them. She barely noticed the gloomy, rainy day any longer. There was only sunshine in her heart now.

Leo handled the good-natured teasing from her brothers pretty well. The reason for her new and improved mood was never directly mentioned by anyone, but the general consensus seemed to be that as long as Leo was happy, the reason didn't matter. However, the way Leo and María felt about each other was hard for them to keep a secret. They stopped trying after the first ten minutes in the company of Leo's family. A special look across the barn yard or a crowded cabin was something neither wanted to hide. They weren't openly attentive to each other, but a hand on a shoulder or straightening the collar of a jacket when they were around others was a common occurrence.

While adjusting to all these new emotions, Leo was quick to notice several changes going on within herself. She no longer felt such intense jealousy over María's past relationship with Cordy. That became evident a few days later when Cordy was feeling well enough to have visitors. Leo found Essie and Cordy sitting on the porch of Essie's cabin.

"Cordy," Leo said with a nod. It had been a long day where Leo had been working with Uncle Jake on getting the smokehouse ready for another hog slaughter. "How are the boys, Essie?" Leo sat down on the porch next to Cordy. Essie was beside them with her long skirt billowing out and covering almost all the steps below where she was sitting.

"The boys are fine," Essie said. "They love it here."

"You seem to be feeling better, Cordy," Leo said. "Your color's better at least. I thought you were dead for sure when María found you."

"I am feeling better," Cordy said. Her shoulder was still bandaged up. "I've been sleeping a lot, but I still get tired easily."

"Healing will take some time," Essie said. "I need to see how the wound is doing, but Cordy here won't let me."

"If you need some help with that," Leo told her cousin, "we'll get María after it."

Essie and Leo shared a laugh. Cordy, however, didn't appear to think it was too funny.

"I have your saddlebag," Leo told her. "You must've dropped it before you fell off your horse. I keep forgetting to bring it over to you."

255

Alarmed, Cordy looked at her, then glanced around her to peer at Essie.

"Thanks."

Essie stood up and straightened her skirt. "I need to start supper. Will you join us, Leo?"

"No, thanks. I'll have something later with María."

After Essie went inside, Leo asked Cordy if she felt strong enough to take a walk. Cordy nodded and slowly got to her feet. Leo could see the dressing from the open collar of her shirt. Moving slowly, Leo wasn't sure if she should offer to help her or not.

"At least my back is feeling better," Cordy said. She laughed lightly. "I'm not used to sleeping in a bed either. I think that's part of the reason it was bothering me so much."

"You probably hurt your back falling off the horse," Leo pointed out.

Cordy pursed her lips, but didn't say anything. They began slowly walking toward the barn; Leo let Cordy set the pace.

"I need to ask you something," Leo said after a moment. "How did you get shot?"

"The bank in Dos Diablos," Cordy said. "I was in and out of there just fine. Got the money and jumped on my horse." She stopped walking and shook her head before continuing on. "The posse followed me for a long ways." With a slight shrug of her good shoulder, she added, "I wanted to have some fun with them."

Leo couldn't believe what she was hearing. Whenever she and members of her family were out on a run, all any of them cared about was getting back home alive. If they made it back safely with a little more money than they left with, then it was considered a successful run.

"So the posse followed you," Leo said. "Then what happened?"

"I got to the foothills and thought I could lose them there," Cordy said, "then I heard shooting coming from another direction. I took a bullet in the shoulder before I saw two Indians hiding in the rocks. They were shooting at me *and* the posse. I was able to get on my horse and I headed this way. How close did I get before I fell off my horse?"

"Close enough for María to find you."

Dos Diablos, Leo thought. *She robbed the same bank we robbed the last time! Then she rode toward Eagle Canyon, bringing a posse and Indians this way!* It was all Leo could do to hold her temper. Cordy had put them all in danger.

"I knew I was hit bad," Cordy said. "I wasn't sure I could find this place on my own, but I didn't have anywhere else to go."

"You could have died, Cordy."

"I know," she said quietly. They started walking again. "It's like I didn't really care about that anymore . . . about dying and all."

Her statement made some of Leo's anger slip away.

"I've got a bag full of money and a head full of memories, Leo. But other than that, I've got nothing. No home and no real friends other than you, your family and María. It says a lot about a person when their only source of pleasure these days comes from wanting someone to chase them on a horse. I'm starting to question a lot of things about myself."

They stopped walking again, but didn't look at each other.

"I know what you're thinking," Cordy said after a moment.

"Only María knows what any of us are thinking," Leo said dryly.

Cordy chuckled. "That's for sure. Isn't she something?"

Once again, Leo felt all warm inside just saying María's name, but it seemed strange to be discussing her with Cordy this way. She no longer felt jealous of Cordy. Leo was more worried about her than jealous of her.

"She's incredible," Leo agreed.

"I know how she feels about you," Cordy said.

Leo didn't want to discuss any of this with her. Changing the subject, she said, "We're not talking about me right now. We're talking about how you put yourself in danger and then tried to bring a posse to Eagle Canyon."

They started walking toward the barn again.

"If you want to get yourself killed, that's one thing, Cordy, but I won't let you drag all that here for the rest of us to help you fix. Anyone could've followed you here."

"Get off your high horse, Leo. No one but you and your brothers can find this place anyway!"

"You got too close for my liking."

"I had no place else to go, Leo."

"Then you need to think about what that means."

There was silence before Cordy finally asked, "What *does* it mean?"

"It means we're the only family you've got. At least that's what it means to me."

Cordy hung her head and eventually nodded. "Yeah, you're right. That's what it means to me, too."

Chapter Thirty-Three

Cordy mistakenly thought she would have the final say-so in how her recovery would go, but she was learning quickly that her opinion wasn't the one that mattered.

"It's fine," she argued as she tried to sit up on the bed one morning. "You don't need to do anything."

"I disagree," Essie said. "We don't know much right now. All we *do* know is you don't have a fever, so that's good."

"See?" Cordy said adamantly. "I told you I was fine!"

"I'm taking the bandage off," Essie said. "That's already been decided."

"Decided by *who*?"

"By me," Essie informed her.

Cordy could see her attempts at persuasion were not working. Whining had almost become her only option.

"Do you think you can keep your shoulder wrapped up this way forever?"

"Why not?" Cordy countered. "It's not hurting me now."

"Well, then," Essie said, "since it's not hurting you, let's take a look and see how things are going in there."

The thought of anyone touching her shoulder frightened her, and Cordy didn't frighten easily. She was finally able to sleep at night as long as she remained in one position. The throbbing that had been there constantly before was finally beginning to subside. Her fear of tampering with the bandage and possibly opening the wound to fresh pain caused panic to rise up in her throat.

"I'll be careful," Essie promised. She pulled two chairs up close to the bed. In the seat of one chair she had clean strips of cloth, a small container of salve, a knife and a basin of water. Essie sat down in the other chair and waited. Finally, she said, "Even though I'll try my best to be careful, this will probably still hurt you a bit."

With a nod, Cordy resigned herself to the fact that the old dressing needed to come off and a new one had to be put on. *She's right,* Cordy thought. *So let's just do this and get it over with.*

Essie helped her sit up on the side of the bed then slowly began unwrapping the bandage from the back. The amount of cloth that Essie peeled away surprised Cordy. Essie held the loose bandage in one hand and then reached for the knife with the other.

"What are you gonna do with that?" Cordy asked in a trembling voice. Her eyes were the size of walnuts.

With a weary smile, Essie said, "I'm going to cut the bandage." She made a small slit in the material with the knife, then tore the rest of it away. "I think you should lie down now," Essie said. "The bandage has been supporting your arm. If you're lying down it'll take the pressure off your shoulder when the rest of it comes off."

Cordy eased back down on the bed. *Why did this have to happen to me?* she wondered. *Why would my luck change this way?*

"Who shot you?" Essie asked as she fiddled with the dressing.

"Indians."

Essie stopped what she was doing and looked at her. With dark brown eyes the color of Leo's, it seemed as though Essie was trying to determine whether or not to believe her.

"Where are you from?"

"Where?" Cordy repeated. "No place really."

"There's nowhere you think of as home?"

Cordy found the question quite interesting. *Where is home?* she wondered. *The small farm where we buried my mother? Palo Duro where me and Pa spent our summers? María's shack where we would make love until I got too restless to stay another minute longer?*

"I've never been in one place long enough to think of it as home," Cordy finally admitted. "What about you? Where's home for you?"

Essie tore another piece of cloth away. "Wilson Creek. My husband's buried there and my three boys were born there."

Cordy didn't know what to say. After she and Pa had buried her mother, Cordy often thought she would go back to the farm just to see it again, but she never did. During many of her travels with her father, Cordy knew he went to great lengths to keep them away from that part of the state. She imagined the pain of losing his wife had remained with him up until the very end of his own life.

"We had a small farm and a nice crop of corn every year," Essie said. "When Jonathan got sick, I didn't know what the boys and I would do without him."

"I've been to Wilson Creek," Cordy said. She remembered it as a small town with a nice General Store where she had replenished supplies once. *But there wasn't a bank*, she thought.

Essie took one of the strips of cloth and let it soak in the basin. She had removed most of the bandage now, which exposed Cordy's right breast. Essie didn't seem to notice, but it made Cordy uncomfortable. She then realized that if the entire dressing were to be removed, both breasts would then be uncovered.

"Maybe I can do this myself," Cordy said.

The look Essie gave her made Cordy realize how silly such a statement was.

"The easy part's almost over," Essie said. "Tell me how you met my father."

"Jake? That old scoundrel?"

Essie smiled. She folded the rest of the bandage back until it wouldn't go any further. Cordy felt her skin pull a little.

"He used to bring us money when Jonathan first got sick," Essie said. "Lots of money." She took the strip of material soaking in the basin and dabbed at the bandage that was stuck to Cordy's skin. The wet strip was cold against her tender flesh.

"How much of that money did you help him get?" Essie asked. Cordy squirmed as she tugged on the bandage.

It's stuck to dried blood or something, Cordy thought. *Or maybe raw skin around the bullet hole . . . and that cold water! Ugh!*

"How much of that money did you help him get?" Essie asked her again, only a bit louder this time.

Cordy groaned as a portion of the bandage was pulled away a millimeter at a time. In a painful, halting whisper, she said, "You need to ask your father that."

Essie continued to gently tug on the cloth that was stuck to the wound. "I'm asking you."

Cordy's jaw began to hurt from gritting her teeth so hard. "Wait, wait," she said finally, almost out of breath. "You have to stop."

"I'm sorry. I know it hurts."

"Can you just pull it off real fast and get it over with?"

"Is that what you want me to do?"

"No. I want you to leave it alone until my arm rots off, but I can't see you letting that happen."

Essie's laughter made Cordy relax enough to take a deep breath. At least for the moment she wasn't hurting anywhere.

Essie dunked another small rag into the basin and shook her head. Cordy liked seeing her smile. Essie had a very *nice* smile.

"Let's see if this fits," Essie said. She held the shirt in front of her for inspection and then held it up to Cordy to see how it looked.

"This is for me?" Cordy asked incredulously. The shirt was gray and was made from the softest fabric Cordy had ever felt before. It had wooden buttons, long sleeves and a high collar that stood up on its own, giving the garment more of a tunic look.

"It used to be Jonathan's favorite shirt. I made a few adjustments and left it big on purpose," Essie said. "It'll be easier for you to get into that way."

It must be hard for her to see someone else wearing something that had belonged to her husband, Cordy thought, but saw only a flicker of sadness in Essie's eyes.

Cordy loved the way Essie unbuttoned the shirt she was wearing—the shirt with the patched bullet hole and faded bloodstain. The old shirt didn't fit well with Cordy's left arm tucked close to her body and the left sleeve empty. As she stood there letting Essie help her get undressed, she couldn't stop thinking about how much Essie resembled Leo. *A softer, kinder Leo,* she thought. Cordy had often wondered what it would have been like to get to know Leo better. The kiss she had stolen from her after the Dos Diablos holdup had been a spontaneous attempt to shock her. Cordy knew she had accomplished that, but she occasionally wondered what it would've been like to stay at Eagle Canyon afterward. *We probably would've ended up shooting each other,* she thought.

Once Essie got Cordy's shirt unbuttoned, she helped her put on the new one. It was too long on her, but it served its purpose with her injured shoulder and the fresh bandage.

"Thank you," Cordy said as she gently touched the fabric again.

"I gave his other things away, but I couldn't part with this," Essie said with a smile. "It looks good on you."

Cordy's health continued to improve and to her surprise she adjusted quite well to living in a cabin, sleeping in a bed and just overall domestic life in general. There were times when she missed being out under a blanket of stars and hearing chirping crickets lull her to sleep, but the comforts of a cabin and the protection from the elements during the cool fall nights had been easier to adapt to than she ever imagined. As her shoulder continued to heal, Cordy could feel other things about her changing as well. Getting shot had calmed her spirit and tamed that wild, restless streak that had plagued her for so long. She liked Eagle Canyon and the people there. *Maybe you do have a home after all*, she thought.

Cordy also wanted to repay all the kindness everyone had shown her during her recuperation. Their concern was genuine and she appreciated all the help and encouragement the others had given her. She got up early every morning to tend to the chickens and let the horses out into the back pasture. Her shoulder felt better, but Cordy was still very protective of the left side of her body. The wound was healing, and Essie made sure the dressing got as much attention as Cordy would allow.

"You should be using this arm more," Essie said one evening after changing the bandage for her again.

Cordy sat on the edge of the bed, while Essie was in a chair beside her. Even though having the dressing changed wasn't a pleasant experience, Cordy found herself looking forward to it every other day just so she could be close to Essie again.

"The more you use it, the faster it'll be back to normal."

Cordy nodded, but couldn't see herself doing anything with that arm as long as pain was involved. It also didn't seem possible that she would ever be "back to normal" again either. Nothing was easy for her any longer, and for the first time since her Pa had disappeared those many years ago, Cordy had to depend on someone else for help with something. Even though all of that was foreign to her, she was adjusting to others wanting to do things for her. It was Essie's natural instincts as a mother and a caregiver that made the biggest difference in how Cordy saw things now. She had never been around anyone like Essie before. In the past, Cordy had been able to get anything she wanted with stolen money and sweet words, but that was no longer the case. The things she wanted now were not for sale.

"There," Essie said as she put the finishing touches on the dressing. She was careful not to hurt Cordy, while at the same time Cordy loved the way Essie touched her whether it hurt or not.

"So try and use it more," Essie said.

"I will."

"I mean it."

Cordy smiled. "I *will*."

Essie helped her put her shirt back on. Cordy didn't even attempt to try and fasten the buttons. She liked the way Essie took her time putting her back together again anyway. There was a certain look in Essie's eyes when they were finished with changing the dressing each time, and every time she saw that look, Cordy wished she had María's insight into what was ahead for someone.

"What are you thinking right now?" Cordy asked quietly. Essie was so close to her that she could almost hear her breathing.

Essie finished buttoning the shirt and smiled at her. "I was thinking how nice it is to help someone get better."

Her husband, Cordy thought. *She was thinking about her husband again.*

"Life is a precious thing," Essie said. "Most people don't cherish it enough. Once a life is gone—it's gone forever."

Each time Cordy thought there was some sort of a connection between them, she was reminded Essie still ached from the loss of her husband. Cordy often wondered if someone would ever love her that way . . . would ever miss her if she was gone . . . or hurt from the pain of losing her. *That's what I want*, she thought. *That's all I've ever wanted. I need someone to love me enough to ask me to stay with them . . . someone who would miss me if I weren't around.* This recovery period had given Cordy a lot of time to think and reevaluate her life. She knew there were only a few options open to her, and she wasn't comfortable with any of them. Cordy was afraid of the future and was tired of being lonely.

One Week Later

Chapter Thirty-Four

"I can tell you're feeling better, Cordelia," María said the following week as she laid down a bandanna with warm tortillas in it.

"How can you tell?" Essie asked from the stove where she was attempting to fry salt pork and potatoes for breakfast. The cabin was warming up slowly from her efforts.

"She's complaining more," María said with a smile. She and Essie enjoyed a nice laugh together. Cordy cut her eyes over at them and shook her head.

"That's not funny," she said in Spanish. After some frustrating effort, she finally got her right boot on by herself. The left one wouldn't be as easy, but Cordy was determined to get dressed every morning on her own now.

"*Pobrecita,*" María said. "You make things so hard on yourself. Why do you—"

"I'm doing fine. Don't you worry about me."

Her shoulder was healing nicely and was no longer bleeding. The dressing had been clean the last time Essie checked it. Cordy had a new sling for her arm, which made it easier for her to use it. Working through the pain and stiffness had become her next priority as far as getting better went.

The cabin door opened and Sarah came in from milking the cow. She set the pail of milk on the table and plopped down hard in a chair.

"Luther just asked me to marry him," she said. Sarah put her hand up to her mouth as if trying to keep more words from falling out.

All three of the other women stopped what they were doing and looked at her. With her blond hair caught loosely in a bun on the back of her head and her eyes wide with shock, Sarah was even more pale than usual.

"He did?" Essie said. "He *did*?"

"What did you tell him?" María asked excitedly.

"I said yes."

"Oh!"

From there Cordy heard an escalation of squeals and clapping as the other three women all began talking at once. Cordy's left boot finally went on, so she stood up and went outside. Once on the porch, she could see Luther and Jake near the barn where Jake was slapping Luther on the back. Across the yard, Cordy noticed Dell on her way to Essie's cabin with baby Milton in her arms and a string of children following behind her.

"Did you hear?" Dell asked as soon as she reached Essie's porch.

"I heard," Cordy said. She stood there watching Luther, who kept dancing around in a circle by the barn. He threw his hat up in the air and dusted it off as soon as it hit the ground, only to pick it up and throw it in the air again.

María and Leo, Cordy thought. *And now Sarah and Luther. What is it about this Eagle Canyon place that makes people so happy?* She felt disgruntled and irritated, as if everyone was flaunting their good fortune in front of her. *When did you become so cynical?* she wondered. *There's nothing wrong with being happy.*

Once Luther stopped throwing his hat and doing a jig, he ran into the barn. Not long after that, he rode out on a horse. *Probably going out to find Leo and Henry,* Cordy thought.

She readjusted the sling and made sure her left arm was as comfortable as it could be under the circumstances, then she walked over to the barn where she found Jake and some of the children. He had the kids lined up on benches with saddles perched on them. Two of the children were his grandsons, while the third one was Henry's four-year-old daughter.

"And this lady here is one of the best riders I've ever seen," Jake said as he motioned toward Cordy.

She smiled at being referred to as a lady. It was a term that had never been used to describe her before.

"Them saddles are kind of big, don't you think?" Cordy said.

"They'll do for now," Jake said with a laugh. He showed the children how to get comfortable in the saddle and how important it was to make sure it was cinched up properly.

"I suppose you heard the news?" he said to Cordy.

"I heard."

"That boy's crazy in love."

"Well, Sarah looks more scared than anything else, if you ask me."

Jake grinned. "Can't blame her. Maybe Luther will quit pesterin' me and his brother about this. Gettin' all married will be the best thing for him now."

Cordy nodded. *Even the boy with the pig found himself somebody to love,* she thought.

Cordy shook her head and went to feed the chickens. Lately, being in such close quarters with Essie had been harder on Cordy than she thought it would be. Now that she was well enough to only need a sling for her arm, there would no longer be a need for Essie to change the dressing for her. Cordy had spent the last few weeks looking forward to Essie's attention and all the fussing she usually did over her. Cordy found herself at a crossroads now. When she was well enough to saddle her own horse and load a pistol by herself, then it would be time for her to move on again.

Maybe go back to Palo Duro Canyon, she thought. *Or maybe I'll see if I can find the old farm Pa and I left behind just to see what it looks like now.*

She threw some cracked corn out for the chickens and wondered what it would be like to have a set routine every day. *Could you herd sheep or cattle and slop hogs like most people do their whole lives?* she wondered. *Why not? Isn't it better than running from a bullet and bleeding to death over a saddlebag full of money?*

"You really are getting around better," Essie said a few days later. "You should still be trying to use your arm more."

"I am," Cordy said. Even though it hurt to move it, she was indeed working through the pain a little more each day.

"It should be a lot different around here once Sarah and Luther get married," Essie said. "Papa should be moving in with us soon."

"Jake's moving in here?" Cordy glanced around the cabin and tried to picture him there on a more permanent basis. *Where would he sleep?* she wondered. Essie's three boys liked being in the same bed because it was warmer at night that way. Cordy suddenly felt as though she had worn out her welcome. *Maybe it's time to move on anyway,* she thought. *But I can't really go anywhere if I can't ride yet! Well, if nothing else, I guess I could sleep in the barn.*

She went outside on the porch and sat down on the steps. Cordy slipped her arm out of the sling and tried to straighten it out. The pain was excruciating, but she kept at it for what seemed like forever.

"You don't look so good," Henry said.

Cordy jumped. She hadn't seen him walk up.

"Sorry," he apologized. "Didn't mean to scare you."

"Guess I was thinkin' too hard."

"Leo and I were wondering if we could talk to you about something."

Cordy couldn't imagine what they would want with her, but she didn't have anything else to do. She shrugged and followed him over to Leo's cabin.

Leo poured them all some coffee and then sat down at the table.

"We want out of the bank robbing business," Leo said, coming right to the point.

To Cordy, Leo looked younger than she remembered. The intensity was gone from her eyes and there was a sense of peace about her that made Cordy stop and really look at her for a moment. *She's happy*, Cordy thought suddenly. *Being with María really makes her happy.*

"Uncle Jake's getting older," Henry said, "and I have to admit that bullet you took scared me."

"Yeah, it scared me, too," Leo agreed. "So the Trask family has robbed its last bank."

Cordy nodded. She also had to admit the thought of robbing a bank no longer was appealing to her either.

"But we've been thinking about something else," Leo said. "We want to raise horses here at Eagle Canyon, and we'd like for you to help us do it."

"Uncle Jake says no one knows horses the way you do," Henry added.

With a cool smile, Cordy slowly said, "Jake would be right about that."

Henry and Leo both chuckled at her confidence.

"But I'm not sure I want to stay here at Eagle Canyon," Cordy said. "I'm lookin' to move on as soon as my arm's better."

"Oh," Henry said.

After a moment, Leo asked, "Is there anything we can do to change your mind?"

"I don't think so."

Leo drummed her long, thin fingers on the table, then asked, "Does your decision to leave have anything to do with María?"

Cordy met Leo's steady gaze and then shook her head. "No. It's got nothing to do with María." She noticed the sigh of relief that came from Leo. *But it might have something to do with Essie,* Cordy thought. The more time they spent together, the harder it was to be around her. Cordy was drawn to Essie in a way she had never experienced before. For Cordy, the attraction was strong, and under different circumstances she would have attempted to do more than encourage just a friendship between them. But Essie was different from the other women Cordy had known. She was at a loss as to how to deal with her growing feelings for her. Cordy had always found it easier to pick up and go when a woman started demanding too much from her, but with Essie the exact opposite seemed to be happening. Cordy didn't know how to handle Essie's kindness and willingness to want to help her. She asked for nothing in return and seemed to actually enjoy helping her. Cordy thought it best to leave Eagle Canyon before she did something totally unacceptable. Being with Essie every day was getting harder instead of easier.

"Maybe I should handle this, Henry," Leo said.

He nodded and got up to leave. They both watched him go out the door, then Cordy and Leo slowly looked back at each other.

"Maybe it's not easy for you to see María here this way."

"María?" Cordy said. "María and I are getting along fine."

It wasn't so much that she resented Leo being with María now. Cordy was just disappointed that María didn't miss her more.

"Does Essie know you're thinking about eventually leaving?" Leo asked.

"Essie and I don't talk much."

"Well, I know Jake would miss you if you left."

Cordy shrugged. "He might."

Leo began drumming her fingers on the table again. "Before you make a decision about leaving," she said, "just hear me out. Good horses can bring in lots of money, Cordy. Cows, chickens and hogs can feed us, but with good horses to sell, we'll have all the money we'll ever want and not have to worry about another posse chasing us. It would be hard, honest work."

"I'm sure it would be."

Even though Cordy had lost her desire to play cat-and-mouse with a posse, she hadn't given much thought to what she wanted to do with the rest of her life.

"Think about what I've said."

"I will."

Cordy tried to imagine what it would be like to do a real day's work . . . have a set routine and know where she'd be sleeping every night. No more looking over her shoulder to see who was following her. No more watching for wanted posters. No more dreading the spring rains or looking for a place to water her horse during the dry season. *Maybe Eagle Canyon is big enough for all of us,* she thought.

"So what else would you need from me besides my horse sense?" Cordy asked.

"A promise not to rob any more banks, first of all," Leo said.

They laughed together for a moment.

"And some money to help us buy more horses as soon as you're better."

Cordy had been listening to her, but tried not to get her hopes up yet. All this could fall through just as easily as it had been brought up.

"If I stay," Cordy said, "I'll need my own place. Nothing big or fancy. Just my own cabin."

Leo smiled and Cordy's heart skipped a beat. *She looks like Essie when she smiles,* Cordy thought.

"We can get started on that tomorrow if you like."

Cordy laughed. "I said *if* I stay. I haven't made up my mind yet."

"Well, think about it. I know we can make this work, Cordy. We all want you to stay. I can speak for everyone about that."

Chapter Thirty-Five

Leo tended to the fire before getting undressed. María's smile in the glow from the coals made Leo's heart race. She moved her hands along the flatness of her lover's belly to the firm swell of her breasts. María's nipples were dark and hard, and she made the most delightful sound as Leo took one into her warm, wet mouth.

The fire in the fireplace grew, and the blue flames slowly licked upward along the side of the wood. They moved to the bed and continued to touch each other. María's hands were on Leo's shoulders and into the softness of her hair.

"You're beautiful," María said huskily and raised up to kiss her. They both became lost in feverish desire, readjusting their position in the bed until their deep, hungry kisses made Leo's very center begin to throb. With each second that passed, there was an onrush of yearning and eagerness to touch each other.

"I need to feel you," María whispered against Leo's mouth. Her warm breath played at Leo's throat just before she outlined an

274

earlobe with her tongue. With sensuous tenderness, she kissed Leo's bare shoulder. Leo absolutely loved the way this woman touched her.

Even after several nights of making love this way, for Leo it still felt like a dream. It was new and exciting, and there were times when she felt overwhelmed with love and desire.

"You have the most perfect mouth," Leo said as she reached up and filled her hands with María's hair. Leo would never get enough of touching her . . . never.

María kissed her again, then moved to lie beside her. As their lips continued exploring newly exposed flesh, Leo eased her hand down along María's hip and thigh. Their tongues touched, bringing a whirlwind of heat soaring through Leo's body. She moved her hand again with only one destination this time. Leo gently opened María with her fingers and slowly dipped into wet, velvety softness. She pulled her lips away from María's and teased one of her nipples with the tip of her tongue. Sucking it into her mouth, Leo flicked her tongue over the nipple until María began to squirm. Matching the movement of Leo's fingers with the thrusting of her hips, they danced their way to orgasmic bliss with ease and determination.

María grabbed Leo's head and pushed her other breast into her mouth, all the while lacing her fingers in Leo's hair. Leo had been ready from the beginning. María's urgency had now become their urgency.

The moan started deep in María's throat and didn't stop until her legs finally tightened around Leo's hand. Leo stayed in María's arms and kept her fingers in the warm, moist center of her. María's breathing eventually returned to normal and she opened her thighs again in weak, limp exhaustion.

"Leona," she whispered. Her voice trailed off as she kissed Leo's forehead. She put her arms around her and found Leo's mouth again, kissing her longingly, as if her strength were gradually coming back to her by way of Leo's lips.

"I love you," María whispered.

Leo rubbed her cheek against María's. "I love you, too."

She moved her fingers in and out slowly as they melted together in an embrace. María's body began to quiver, then she kissed Leo with such passion they both eventually trembled from the afterglow of orgasm.

Leo was proud of herself for being able to work through the initial uneasiness of having Cordy there at Eagle Canyon. Cordy was getting around better, and had recently taken on even more responsibilities. She hadn't given them a definite answer about whether or not she would be staying, but the longer Cordy was there, the more encouraged Leo and Henry became.

One evening a few weeks later, everyone gathered over at Henry's cabin. The children were tying up their Uncle Luther in the yard, while Henry and Jake discussed planting winter wheat in one of the pastures. The women were inside preparing a feast where María and Dell already had a stack of tortillas made. There wasn't anything Leo and Cordy could help them with, so they went to the corral to check on the horses.

"Essie wants me to stay," Cordy said. Her arm was still in a sling, but Leo noticed earlier that she was using it more. "She's an interesting woman."

"She's been through a lot," Leo said as they watched a colt kick up its hind legs as it ran around the corral. "But then so have you."

"I never had to watch someone I love die."

"I have," Leo said. "It's something you never forget. It changes you inside."

"Well, I hope I never have to do it. I guess what I'm trying to say is, I want to stay here, Leo. I want to help you and your family raise horses."

Leo smiled. "We'll start building your cabin tomorrow." She could hardly wait to tell Henry and Jake the news.

Cordy laughed. "What will we do for fun around here if we're not robbing banks anymore?" There was silence for a moment, then Cordy said quietly, "It's all I know, Leo. Farming and ranching aren't the things I'm good at."

"Horses, Cordy. We'll breed horses. It's time we all work harder and take what's given to us."

Cordy smiled. "There was a time in my life when horses were my best friends. My only friends!"

They both laughed.

"You've got real friends now," Leo said. "You've had them for a long time."

Cordy turned toward her and looked down at her boots. "I'll give it my best, Leo. I never thought I'd be good at sleeping inside and knowing what I'd be doing each day either, so maybe I'll be better at it than I think."

"Well, we can't keep on robbing banks and thumbing our noses at a posse," Leo said. "We've been lucky so far. Raising horses is something you were born to do."

Dell called everyone to supper and Leo and Cordy headed back over to Henry's cabin. Along the way, Leo let Cordy go on ahead. Leo stopped to help Luther get untied and she noticed the children giggling just inside the cabin door. When they saw their Aunt Leo stop to untie him, Henry's two oldest kids ran back over to help her get their Uncle Luther back on his feet.

"They're getting better," Leo said as she nodded toward the children standing beside her.

Luther laughed and dusted himself off. As they walked toward Henry's cabin, Leo saw María waiting for her at the door. Leo smiled and felt a warm rush of desire spread through her.

"You did a good thing," María said.

"What? Untying my little brother?"

María smiled and gently touched Leo's cheek with the back of her hand. "You helped take some of Cordelia's fear away. No one's ever been able to do that before."

Leo moved her head and kissed María's fingers as they caressed her cheek. "How in the world do you know such things?"

María smiled again and said, "I just know."

About the Author

Peggy J. Herring lives on seven acres of mesquite in south Texas with her cockatiel, hermit crabs and two wooden cats. When she isn't writing, Peggy enjoys fishing and traveling. She is the author of *Once More With Feeling, Love's Harvest, Hot Check, A Moment's Indiscretion, Those Who Wait* and *To Have and to Hold* from Naiad Press and *Calm Before the Storm, The Comfort of Strangers* and *Beyond All Reason* from Bella Books. In addition, Peggy has contributed short stories to several Naiad anthologies, to include, *The First Time Ever, Dancing In the Dark, Lady Be Good, The Touch of Your Hand,* and *The Very Thought of You.* Peggy is currently working on a new romance titled *White Lace and Promises* to be released by Bella Books in 2004.

Publications from
BELLA BOOKS, INC.
The best in contemporary lesbian fiction

P.O. Box 10543, Tallahassee, FL 32302
Phone: 800-729-4992
www.bellabooks.com

DISTANT THUNDER by Peggy J. Herring. 277 pp. Bankrobbing drifter Cordy awakens strange new feelings in Leo in this romantic tale set in the old West.   ISBN 1-931513-28-7 $12.95

COP OUT by Claire McNab. 216 pp. 4th Detective Inspector Carol Ashton Mystery.   ISBN 1-931513-29-5 $12.95

BLOOD LINK by Claire McNab. 159 pp. 15th Detective Inspector Carol Ashton Mystery. Is Carol unwittingly playing into a deadly plan?   ISBN 1-931513-27-9 $12.95

TALK OF THE TOWN by Saxon Bennett. 239 pp. With enough beer, barbecue and B.S., anything is possible!   ISBN 1-931513-18-X $12.95

MAYBE NEXT TIME by Karin Kallmaker. 256 pp. Sabrina Starling always believed in maybe next time . . . until now.   ISBN 1-931513-26-0 $12.95

WHEN GOOD GIRLS GO BAD: A Motor City Thriller by Therese Szymanski. 230 pp. Brett, Randi, and Allie join forces to stop a serial killer.   ISBN 1-931513-11-2   12.95

A DAY TOO LONG: A Helen Black Mystery by Pat Welch. 328 pp. This time Helen's fate is in her own hands.   ISBN 1-931513-22-8 $12.95

THE RED LINE OF YARMALD by Diana Rivers. 256 pp. The Hadra's only hope lies in a magical red line . . . Climactic sequel to *Clouds of War*.   ISBN 1-931513-23-6 $12.95

OUTSIDE THE FLOCK by Jackie Calhoun. 224 pp. Jo embraces her new love and life.   ISBN 1-931513-13-9 $12.95

LEGACY OF LOVE by Marianne K. Martin. 224 pp. Read the whole Sage Bristo story. ISBN 1-931513-15-5 $12.95

STREET RULES: A Detective Franco Mystery by Baxter Clare. 304 pp. Gritty, fast-paced mystery with compelling Detective L.A. Franco ISBN 1-931513-14-7 $12.95

RECOGNITION FACTOR: 4th Denise Cleever Thriller by Claire McNab. 176 pp. Denise Cleever tracks a notorious terrorist to America. ISBN 1-931513-24-4 $12.95

NORA AND LIZ by Nancy Garden. 296 pp. Lesbian romance by the author of *Annie on My Mind*. ISBN 1931513-20-1 $12.95

MIDAS TOUCH by Frankie J. Jones. 208 pp. Sandra had everything but love. ISBN 1-931513-21-X $12.95

BEYOND ALL REASON by Peggy J. Herring. 240 pp. A romance hotter than Texas. ISBN 1-9513-25-2 $12.95

ACCIDENTAL MURDER: 14th Detective Inspector Carol Ashton Mystery by Claire McNab. 208 pp.Carol Ashton tracks an elusive killer. ISBN 1-931513-16-3 $12.95

SEEDS OF FIRE:Tunnel of Light Trilogy, Book 2 by Karin Kallmaker writing as Laura Adams. 274 pp. Intriguing sequel to *Sleight of Hand*. ISBN 1-931513-19-8 $12.95

DRIFTING AT THE BOTTOM OF THE WORLD by Auden Bailey. 288 pp. Beautifully written first novel set in Antarctica. ISBN 1-931513-17-1 $12.95

CLOUDS OF WAR by Diana Rivers. 288 pp. Women unite to defend Zelindar! ISBN 1-931513-12-0 $12.95

DEATHS OF JOCASTA: 2nd Micky Knight Mystery by J.M. Redmann. 408 pp. Sexy and intriguing Lambda Literary Award-nominated mystery. ISBN 1-931513-10-4 $12.95

LOVE IN THE BALANCE by Marianne K. Martin. 256 pp. The classic lesbian love story, back in print! ISBN 1-931513-08-2 $12.95

THE COMFORT OF STRANGERS by Peggy J. Herring. 272 pp. Lela's work was her passion . . . until now. ISBN 1-931513-09-0 $12.95

CHICKEN by Paula Martinac. 208 pp. Lynn finds that the only thing harder than being in a lesbian relationship is ending one. ISBN 1-931513-07-4 $11.95

OFF SEASON by Jackie Calhoun. 208 pp. Pam threatens Jenny and Rita's fledgling relationship. ISBN 0-9677753-0-2 $11.95

WHEN EVIL CHANGES FACE: A Motor City Thriller by Therese Szymanski. 240 pp. Brett Higgins is back in another heart-pounding thriller. ISBN 0-9677753-3-7 $11.95

BOLD COAST LOVE by Diana Tremain Braund. 208 pp. Jackie Claymont fights for her reputation and the right to love the woman she chooses. ISBN 0-9677753-2-9 $11.95

THE WILD ONE by Lyn Denison. 176 pp. Rachel never expected that Quinn's wild yearnings would change her life forever. ISBN 0-9677753-4-5 $12.95

SWEET FIRE by Saxon Bennett. 224 pp. Welcome to Heroy—the town with the most lesbians per capita than any other place on the planet! ISBN 0-9677753-5-3 $11.95